THE DECADE OF DESTRUCTION

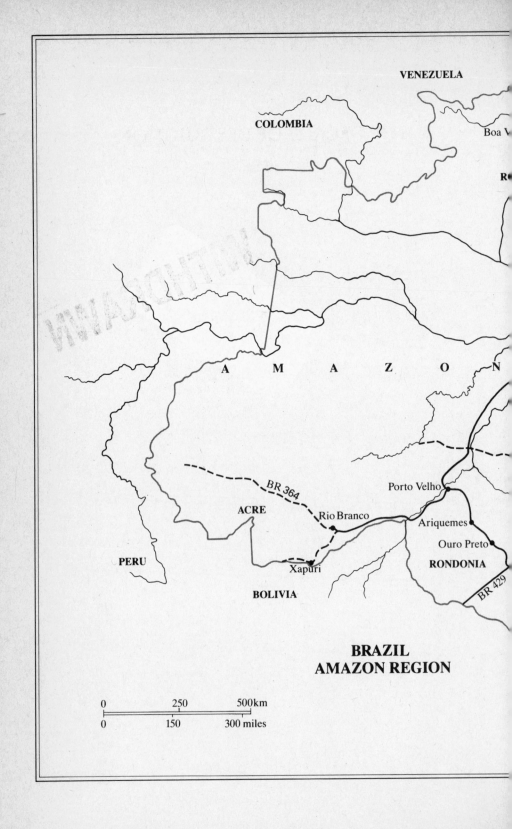

VENEZUELA

COLOMBIA

Boa V

R

A   M   A   Z   O   N

BR 364

Porto Velho

ACRE

Rio Branco

Ariquemes

Ouro Preto

PERU

RONDONIA

Xapuri

BR 429

BOLIVIA

BRAZIL
AMAZON REGION

0	250	500km
0	150	300 miles

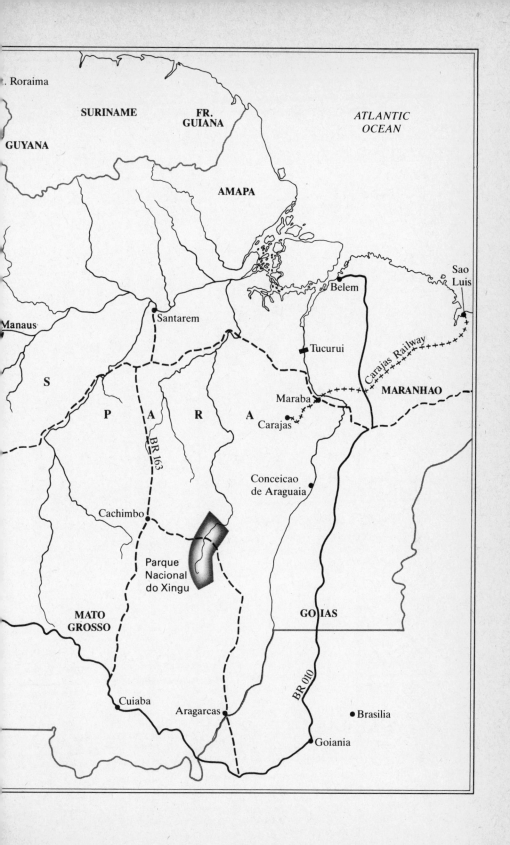

THE DECADE OF DESTRUCTION

The Crusade to Save the Amazon Rain Forest

Adrian Cowell

ANCHOR BOOKS
DOUBLEDAY
NEW YORK LONDON TORONTO SYDNEY AUCKLAND

An Anchor Book
PUBLISHED BY DOUBLEDAY
a division of Bantam Doubleday Dell Publishing Group, Inc.
666 Fifth Avenue, New York, New York 10103

ANCHOR BOOKS, DOUBLEDAY, and the portrayal of an anchor
are trademarks of Doubleday, a division of Bantam Doubleday
Dell Publishing Group, Inc.

The Decade of Destruction was originally published in hardcover
by Henry Holt and Company, Inc., in 1990.
The Anchor Books edition is published by arrangement with
Henry Holt and Company, Inc.

Library of Congress Cataloging-in-Publication Data
Cowell, Adrian.
  The decade of destruction: the crusade to save the
Amazon rain forest / Adrian Cowell. — 1st Anchor
Books ed.
    p. cm.
  Reprint. Originally published: New York: H. Holt,
© 1990.
  1. Man—Influence on nature—Amazon River Region.
2. Deforestation—Amazon River Region.   3. Rain forest
ecology—Amazon River Region.   4. Forest conservation—
Amazon River Region.   5. Environmental policy—
Amazon River Region.   6. Amazon River Region—
Social conditions.   I. Title.
[GF532.A4C69   1991]   91-16998
333.75'137—dc20   CIP

ISBN 0-385-42032-3

FOR XINGU

CONTENTS

INTRODUCTION

The first time that I travelled in Amazonia, our objective was to make a film about a mountain. And looking back it now seems predictable that the film should not have been about the beauty or intrinsic interest of the mountain, but about how it inspired Conan Doyle's romantic, visionary novel – *The Lost World*. The year was 1957. I was 23, my companions on the journey, John Moore and Stanley Jeeves, a little older. We were part of a student expedition which had been given a cine camera and a few hundred pounds by David Attenborough of the BBC, and as we trudged across the bleak savannahs on the frontier of Brazil, the Indians with us uttered a long-drawn, high-pitched cry that echoed about the hills, 'Roraaaaaiiima'. This was taken up by the others with 'Haaaaaiiiiaaas' and similar shrieks so that as we marched towards the great mountain on our horizon, it drew us on and into the romantic mists of our quest.

At the time of its discovery in the nineteenth century, the enormous tableland of Roraima, with its vast cliffs 2000 feet in height, had captured the imagination of both explorers and scientists. Expanding on Darwin's theory of evolution, zoologists had wondered whether a plateau cut off by cliffs from the rest of the world since prehistoric times could conceal separate evolution or arrested zoological development. And Sir Arthur Conan Doyle had summed up much of this speculation in his novel. In it, Professor Challenger discovers apemen, pterodactyls and dinosaurs on the summit.

On the morning that we climbed the mountain, a strange cloud formation lay in the rift valley that cuts Roraima in two, and a freak of wind held the clouds in a long line of vapour flicking them, hypnotically, in and out like a lizard's tongue. Then an ominous curtain of mist dropped down as we entered the belt of tree skeletons that circles the last of the foothills. It swirled about the trees and amongst the hundreds of spiders that had spun webs from plant to plant. Clammy mosses clung to every surface, greasy fungi sprang from every tree. Groping through the fog as we climbed the ledge, we once walked into a great jet of water spouting from the rockface, and another time passed under a waterfall that must have fallen from such a height that it only reached us as scattered drops of rain. Finally, when we reached the summit, mist smothered our camp, concealing everything. During the long and nervous night that followed, suspense blossomed within us like yeast in all too willing dough.

And so it was that when we explored the tableland, we discovered that the two streams that drained the immense saucer of black rock from opposite directions plunged into rock fissures close together in the centre. There they disappeared in a series of deep caves till they emerged – presumably – in the waterspouts we had seen hundreds of feet lower down the cliff face. As one of our party, Stanley Jeeves, had spent half his life exploring the potholes of England, he knew that if the rocks of the summit were so eroded by wind and rain, then the passage of vast quantities of water since the beginning of time must have hollowed out caverns in the centre of the mountain. We had seen the streams go in and come out, and it was apparent that several of the gorges on the surface were in fact caverns with roofs that had fallen in. It was by no means illogical to assume that part of the mountain was a maze of passages, wells and cathedral-like caves. A new and enticingly unexplored Lost World.

A Brazilian geologist had once told us that the diamonds which have been washed down the rivers of Guiana, Venezuela and Brazil over the centuries all stemmed from a kimberlite core somewhere in the Roraima range. Was it so impossible that this cave cross-section of the mountain could have trapped some heavy gems as the water cascaded past?

Sitting in the theatric mists of that wonderfully eerie world, we were completely unable to halt reason in its slide to fantasy – unable not to join the long and, as I was to discover, calamitous tradition of Amazonian adventurers who have tried to tear secrets and fortunes from the forest. We had neither the equipment nor the necessary food supplies. But the vision was before us.

Next morning, while we were making a preliminary survey, Stanley, our climbing expert, slipped on a belay. He fell 30 feet onto the rocks below, fracturing his foot. We rescued him, and next day, because of the difficult footing, he had to crawl most of the 3000 feet down to the foothills. And that is how I came to spend a week on the northern watershed of the Amazon basin, waiting for horses and ruefully gazing out over the great expanse of primaeval forest that stretches for 2000 kilometres across the heart of South America. At my first encounter with Amazonia, we had followed a dream and stumbled. For the first of many times, I sat on a hard rock under a cold drizzle, and, like so many before me, contemplated reality. Today, after more than 30 years, I am astonished how often that pattern of romantic enthusiasm, sudden disaster and sorrowing meditation has repeated itself – both for myself and for nearly everyone else who approaches Amazonia. For the last ten years we have been filming a documentary series (for Central Independent Television) along the Amazonian frontier. And as we record what is certainly the greatest – in the literal meaning of the word – holocaust that man has ever known; as year by year the earth's largest mass of vegetation turns itself into the greatest cloud of smoke the atmosphere has ever received; as farms fail, projects go bankrupt, migrants die of malaria; as the ashen smog from the blazing trees fills hospitals, grounds airlines and shields the forest from the watching satellites; what astonishes me is that so few people seem to gain from it. In terms of simple fire-power, we are recording the greatest incineration that man has achieved. But what takes one's breath away is its pointlessness.

And so I have begun to return to that first disaster on Roraima and to wonder whether the key to understanding what is happening should be looked for not in Amazonia, but in our visionary perception of it. When you look back, the history of the earth's greatest forest is a surprisingly eccentric record of men who have sought disaster in almost every conceivable way: from Sir Walter Raleigh – beheaded; to Daniel Ludwig – sold out at massive loss; from Bishop Sardinha – eaten; to the President of the World Bank – 'The Bank misread the human, institutional and physical realities of the jungle, and the frontier got out of hand'. Relics of their unlikely visions can be found scattered around the jungles very much like tourist litter: abandoned gold mines, ruins of missions, overgrown plantations, decaying towns, the opulent little-used Opera House in Manaus, and the rotting Perimetral Norte Highway. It sometimes seems as if most intruders in the forest – from the first conquistador searching for his non-existent El Dorado to the modern migrant trying to recreate a European-type farm in the tropics – have been walking backwards, visionaries unconscious of their surroundings, with eyes riveted on some dream or ambition from their past.

A revealing but sad example from the 1920s was the English explorer Colonel Percy Harrison Fawcett who 'saw', during a London seance, the blue-eyed, red-haired people of the lost continent of Atlantis flee into Amazonia. For no reason that seems very convincing, he then decided that their living cities were to be found between the River Xingu and the River das Mortes – where it is now known that they could not have been. Elsewhere this romantic myth might have remained a harmless fiction. But, in Amazonia, it carried Fawcett, his expedition and several subsequent parties to their deaths. Likewise, in the 1980s, Pharaonic visions of economic miracles have led planners, governments and banks to one financial disaster after another, and to the devastation of thousands of square kilometres of forest. Obviously such differing tragedies are incomparable in nature and scale. But could they result from a common attitude which makes it hard for us to look at the forest except as a blank on the map where what is elsewhere impossible could there be possible; which turns the forest into a backcloth onto which we project our visions and ambitions?

It was a coincidence that as we sat on Roraima, at the end of 1957, gazing across the forest while mournfully ingesting Complan – according to the label 'a food complete in calories, essential proteins, minerals and vitamins for those unable to eat in a normal way' – the whole process of Amazonian destruction was just beginning. It was also pure accident that I was to go on filming in the region during what became one of the fastest processes of development the world has ever seen. But, whether by accident or some unknown design, for 30 years, I worked with some of the key people in the forest and was involved in some of the central crises that took place.

This book is an attempt to convey what that process was like. It describes a number of journeys that occurred at crucial stages in the development of Amazonia. It tries to open windows at different periods and from different angles on events and people that are otherwise difficult to understand. 'How can a man burn down a forest when he knows the land's so poor that he will have to abandon it?' I am often asked. 'How can speculators buy land, when they know it will produce nothing?' The answer lies in an individual's, and usually, a society's vision of the forest which, in some cases, can be as manic as a lemming migration. And these visions are hard to credit separated from their setting, from the man and his voice.

The main focus of the book, however, is not on the negative facet of destruction, but on the reverse side of the coin. For it is precisely when the invader trips over the forest that he first begins to look around; and it is after the forest has destroyed his image of it, that he tries to understand the nature of what he is dealing with. In fact, it seems to be a trait of Amazonian history that when the invaders survive their first disasters, they then turn around and try to fight off the next horde of invaders, not just in terms of warfare, but also with ideas and visions derived from their confrontation with the forest. And it is these ideas which provide hope for the future of Amazonia and the people who live within it.

What I have only begun to appreciate since the massive destruction of the 1980s is that on each journey I was also watching people grope for a partial solution to the apparently insoluble problem of the relationship between our dynamic and industrial society and the primaeval, and increasingly defenceless, forest. In most of the films we were making, we were trying to understand Amazonia through the eyes of someone struggling to cope with it. And I now believe that as we filmed explorers, Indians, rubber tappers, colonists and hunters trying to produce ad hoc remedies for their problems, we were also watching a hesitant process of evolution which has developed today into such movements as the rubber tapper, or *seringueiro*, campaign for 'extractive reserves'.

For this reason, though this book starts 20 years before the 1980s, its theme derives entirely from this Decade of Destruction. It is looking back from the holocaust that makes some journeys revealing and others too insignificant to include, and it is looking forward for a solution that invests a tentative step, somewhere in the forest, with a meaning much greater than any of us perceived at the time.

For despite the devastation, there is hope. In 1980, when we started filming 'The Decade of Destruction', we could barely find any grass-roots, pressure groups campaigning in the Amazon against deforestation. Now, at the end of the decade, every Amazonian state has its environmental campaign, and there is growing Brazilian national support for alternatives proposed – not by visionaries from without the forest, but by people who live and derive their solutions from within it.

As this manuscript goes off for printing, in April 1990, Jose Lutzenberger – an environmentalist who we have filmed with throughout the decade – has just been appointed Brazil's Secretary of the Environment. He talks with enthusiasm and dramatic gestures about his plans to stop deforestation and provide alternatives to it. But as I look out the window at the banks and development institutions all around us in Brasilia, I cannot help feeling that his success, or even political survival, must be looked upon as improbable. The weight of money and interest on the other side and the lack of a real power base on his, make the contest wholly unequal. And yet, if I then reflect on the enormous changes that have brought Lutzenberger, and Brazil, to this point, I begin to sense that we are riding on some sort of a wave and that one or even a dozen political failures may prove to be irrelevant. What seems more important is the nature and direction of the wave itself. And that is why this book starts by groping back towards its origins, trying to remember where it came from.

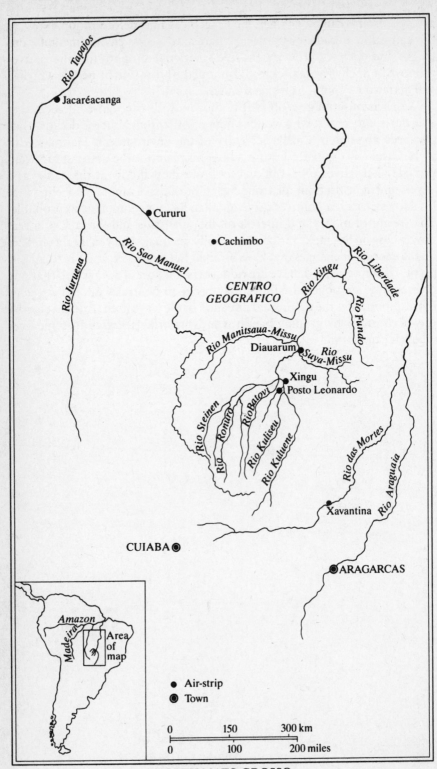

NORTH MATO GROSSO

one

THE HEART *of the* FOREST

XINGU
1958

In 1958, the forest of Amazonia was virtually intact. Books and magazines referred to it as the 'Green Hell' and no-one I was to meet during my first vist ever suggested that the forest could one day be threatened or demolished. And yet, during that journey, the first steps towards destruction had already been set in motion.

In 1956, Juscelino Kubitschek was elected President of Brazil, and in the five remarkable years of his Presidency, he transformed the entire pattern of Brazil's economy. To begin with, he raised customs duties to reduce the importation of foreign goods, and then provided tax and other incentives to induce foreign companies to set up factories in Brazil. This would soon make Sao Paulo one of the fastest growing cities in the world, and Brazil the industrial giant of South America.

Kubitschek also changed the country's traditional stance, moving its capital from Rio de Janeiro on the coast – looking across the ocean to Europe – to the great destiny of his country in its undeveloped interior. He placed his new capital, Brasilia, 1000 kilometres inland, on the lip of the Amazon basin, and from there started to build two arterial roads into the forest – the Belem-Brasilia highway moving north, and the Brasilia-Porto Velho moving west. These were to be the axis of the development of Amazonia, Sao Paulo its power house.

Despite these beginnings, in 1958 the pattern of all Amazonian life still lay along its rivers – as it had since the Portuguese first started to trade up the thousand tributaries of the Amazon. Before President Kubitschek's two roads, the only land penetration had been that of the Roncador-Xingu expedition launched in 1943 by President Getulio Vargas – who in part anticipated his successor. The expedition was managed by the Fundacao

Brasil Central – the Central Brazil Foundation – and had spent 15 years building a chain of airstrips across the forest to Manaus. In the future, this chain was to become the route of the BR080 development road, and airstrips like Aragarcas, Xavantina and Jacareacanga grew into towns that became 'the poles of development' for the central part of Southern Amazonia.

At the time we reached Xingu in 1958, the two leading explorers of the Roncador-Xingu expedition, Orlando and Claudio Villas Boas, were finishing their last airstrips at Cachimbo and Cururu. For over a decade, their expedition had been the spearhead of Amazonian development, and our party flew in to meet them on the headwaters of the Rio Xingu – a region they usually referred to simply as Xingu. Their main base was at the Post of Capitao Vasconcelos. But as they soon renamed it after their dead brother, Leonardo, this book refers to it throughout as Posto Leonardo.

ONE

Posto Leonardo was my first outpost of civilisation – a great wound in the jungle where man had blasted out a hole to live in. From the main hut the view was of a long line of vegetation that cut off the horizon, and the clearing was littered with black and rotting tree trunks lying where axe and fire had laid them. The whole compound had the gaunt outlines of a bomb site.

In the main hut, my hammock was tied between the wall and a central beam, and as I swung to and fro in the approaching heat of a Brazilian noon, I whiled away that morning in June 1958 by looking at the grooves my hammock ropes were wearing in their log supports. Only a few weeks had passed since my arrival and already a distinct curved line was running round the logs and cutting into the wood. Perhaps – if this exile continued – my weight and the boredom of this life would one day pull these ropes right through the last inch of wood. It was a new and welcome idea in the tedium of forest life. Perhaps the roof would fall down before the logs. Perhaps the logs were already riddled with termites. Perhaps ... like driftwood on a jungle river, thought tumbled and floated with the current of our day as we waited and listened for the one thing that could bring change to Posto Leonardo. We were three men hoping to leave on an expedition into the forest – it was the Centro Geografico expedition of the Brazilian government – and yet supplies were barely adequate for our base camp. For a fortnight the menu had been rice and beans and though, occasionally, one of the two was omitted, this variation had its limitations. There could be rice. There could be beans. There could be both. It was the only element of chance in the monotony of forest life.

And then, quite suddenly, all our lethargy vanished. A sound so faint that it could barely be heard seemed to materialise in the eastern part of the sky. I listened. It gradually swelled into a powerful roar coming down over the forest.

'The Dakota!' Juan shouted ecstatically into the roof. 'The Dakota!' he shouted again, and the three of us rushed out of our log-and-thatch hut and hurried up towards the airstrip. In front, Orlando Villas Boas brushed aside the foliage. Orlando's small stocky figure was completely naked, except for a pair of bottle-green shorts roughly assembled from camouflaged parachute silk.

'I told you,' he said over his shoulder. 'If you are patient, aeroplanes come.'

Behind him, Juan and I followed together. Juan was a short fussy man just under forty. I was a gangling obvious foreigner with an incipient beard.

When the Dakota eventually landed, we were standing – three urgent and dusty men – at the fuselage doorway. Suddenly the door swung aside, and the pilot appeared.

'Cargo,' he said flinching from the heat. 'I have cargo for Posto Leonardo.' And the three of us breathed a sigh of relief.

It lasted until Orlando walked over to the freight compartment and looked inside. His shoulders drooped, his legs sagged at the knees and all the weariness of our forest life came back into his voice.

'Food,' he said bitterly, 'but no gasoline.'

'It's always the same,' Juan said to the pilot. 'When you bring gasoline there is no food. So we have to send boats down river to fish. Now there is food and we have no gasoline. It has been happening,' his eyes flickered nervously, 'for a long time.'

Indeed, it had been going on for six months, ever since Juan and Orlando had started to await the supplies for their expedition in January 1958. Every week they had hoped to leave the week after. It was such an inexplicable and recurrent tragedy that in my eyes the plane had assumed the character of a gift-bearing but irresponsible Greek god.

A short time later the plane vanished into the sky and we were left standing motionless on the airstrip. I could see Juan looking at the vegetation, and it was almost as if we could feel the enormous pressure of the forest pounding in on the outskirts of our clearing, so that we were conscious of the hundreds of miles of unexplored wilderness straining around our vacuum in the trees. It was an ominous sensation that even penetrated into the hut. When we returned, it was as dank and shadowed as an animal's lair. There were no windows, the floor was of trodden mud, and the place was filled with the sombre gloom of deep Amazonian jungle.

'Aeroplanes are like pigeons,' Orlando said encouragingly. 'If you trust them, they come back.'

Juan made no reply. 'Things go round and round in my head,' he said. 'They go round and round so I can hardly talk,' he subsided into his hammock.

As if driven by the same inexorable law, Orlando and I climbed into our hammocks as well. It was a moment of true despair. The expedition would set out one day in the future – we were confident of that – but whether it would be seven days or seven months from now, there could be no way of telling. This was Amazonia. That was the rhythm of the forest.

The sun climbed higher into the sky, the jungle began to creak and rustle under the midday heat, and one of the post's tame woodpeckers flew onto my hammock and fell asleep close to my nose. For a student foreigner, there could have been few better introductions. Posto Leonardo was my first dead end in the forest.

Six months had passed since we had sat on Roraima at the end of 1957 looking across the Amazon basin. In that time our student party had descended by river barge down the Rios Branco and Negro to Manaus, and then by paddle steamer – which looked like a Mississippi river boat – down the River Amazon to Belem. From there we had travelled by Landrover along the coast of Brazil to Rio de Janeiro and Sao Paulo. And from there to Brasilia and then on to Xavantina from where we went by plane to Posto Leonardo in Xingu.

From time to time over the next few years, whenever I was staying at Posto Leonardo, Dr Acary Passos de Oliveira would fly in or out. He is an energetic man with a forceful voice who even in a hammock gives the impression of urgent and imminent flight.

'I was put in charge,' Acary would begin, 'when Getulio decided to build a Presidential house in the heart of Brazil, at the Isle of Bananal. Then when we were all staying at the house, and he decided to start his "March to the West," he made me second in command under Colonel Vanique. Vanique was head of Getulio's bodyguard. It was largely to get him out of the way that we were to spend so many years in the jungle.'

In fact, Getulio Vargas's initially fairly vague mission of 'The March to the West' had been refined under Acary and Orlando into the more immediate aim of building a line of emergency airstrips across the stretch of forest from Goiania to Manaus. After World War II, an air route had been started from Miami to Rio de Janeiro and this had involved flying across thousands of miles of uncharted forest. It was easy for planes to get lost, and in 1952 an American Stratocruiser crashed killing all its passengers. Orlando had led the party which found its remains.

It was to avoid this sort of disaster that the Roncador-Xingu expedition had started their line of airstrips across the forest so that the Air Force could set up radio-beacons for an air corridor above. In an emergency, planes in trouble could make a crash landing on these strips. In 1958, these bases stretched 2000 kilometres right across Southern Amazonia from Goiania to Manaus and the expedition that Orlando was preparing at the time of our visit was intended to bring all this to some sort of visible conclusion. For years the Fundacao Brasil Central had been struggling towards 'the ultimate defeat of the jungle.' But because it was an indeterminate area with no obvious point, like the South Pole, for the flag raising of symbolic success, it had been hard for outsiders to appreciate what they were doing. Some offficials in the department, therefore, had conceived the plan of constructing an airstrip at the exact geographical centre of Brazil. If an expedition could construct an airstrip on which President Kubitschek could land, it would symbolise his government's victory over the powers of nature. Brazil would have conquered the greatest forest on earth.

That was the stage at which our party of Oxford and Cambridge university students visited Posto Leonardo. Two weeks later when they left, I stayed behind. 'You can come on the Centro expedition,' Orlando had said generously, 'so long as you export your bones. Since Colonel Fawcett, our government has become tired of Englishmen getting killed all over the forest.'

It had seemed an opportunity not to be missed. The last stage of an historic expedition. The symbolic opening up of Southern Amazonia.

But as I lay in my hammock throughout that gloomy day of the aeroplane, I was increasingly aware of other views.

'The Centro Expedition!' Juan's voice was cynical. 'Risk lives to make an airstrip in the middle of nowhere. What progress is that? And this progress business. Speculators in the Chamber of Deputies talking of the triumphant stride of Brazil into the magnificent future of the West. No one will come here for land for 50 years, maybe a hundred. They just buy and sell it in land speculation offices so that rich people get richer. Claudio Villas Boas once took some Indians to the President with new wounds from *civilizado* bullets. And the President said that everyone knew that he, the President, was a friend of the Indian, and that he would send a memorandum about it to the House of Deputies. Indians dying, he sends a memorandum. The President. Ha.'

'It will be a fine expedition, Adriano, going to do something for which there is no point, and probably causing the death of Indians whose salvation is the only point worthwhile. Perhaps,' he became calmer, 'it will never go. Probably it won't go at all.'

Looking over at Orlando's hammock, I reflected that as this was no typical expedition, he was also no typical explorer. When I had first heard of Orlando Villas Boas I had thought of him using the imaginary portrait that serves most people for an explorer: a large man with boots, and probably a Roman nose. He was, in fact, small – five feet and six inches – bare-footed, bare-backed, with a potbelly lipping over his bottle-green pants. He might have been an attendant in a Turkish bath or a musician in a Paris salon. The only remarkable feature was a most powerful bearded face with many lines of hardship across it. It could have been a pirate's face, or the face of a hermit who had spent years in the desert.

Even more curious were the apparently contradictory aims of Orlando's policy. He and his brother were salaried officials of the Central Brazilian Foundation whose purpose was to develop the forest in the name of national progress. Yet recently he had been seconded to the Indian Protection Service whose officers were pledged to help the Indians. Every year they attempted to contact 'unpacified' tribes under the principle of their famous founder, Marshall Rondon. 'Die if necessary, but never shoot back.' The whole spirit of the organisation was to protect the tribesmen against the onslaught of civilization. It certainly seemed as if the explorers had entered the forest in the vanguard of a development campaign and had then changed aims and ideals to work directly against the progress that had originally been their goal. If this was so, then the purpose of the Centro Expedition was precisely contradictory to the objective of Orlando's life.

This was hardly reassuring for a young, expedition-seeking, ex-student. Not only was Orlando's expedition very much delayed, but its leader had apparently forgotten what had brought him here in the first place.

By the end of that afternoon, my head was gyrating like a psychedelic top. Everyone at some stage in life feels on the doorstep of lunacy, and that particular afternoon, surrounded by the powerful presence of the forest, the moment seemed to have arrived for me. And so, in desperation, I decided to abandon my fruitless questioning and instead to try and experience the forest life. Only after I had immersed myself for months would I again attempt to rationalise what I or anyone else was doing. It was not a particularly inspiring plan – an ex-university student now aged 24, qualifications nil, experience non-existent, motive the lack of any alternative action. But for one stranger marooned in Amazonia, it was to be the key to sanity. For like so many other intruders in the forest, only when I had forgotten why I had come, did I begin to look round to see what was already there.

TWO

Every day small parties of Indians came to Orlando's post from the eight friendly villages in the southern part of Xingu. Their settlements were at the end of trails in the forest like spokes on the Leonardo hub and the journey varied from a few hours to several days. Sometimes canoes were used, and often parties of women and children came for the excursion. But usually it was men alone who walked up from the river bank or stalked quietly out of the trees. They had the lithe, catlike physique of hunters.

Soon after my decision, I began to wonder if these men could be persuaded to teach a *civilizado* to stalk and live in the jungle. '*Civilizado*' was the word used at Posto Leonardo to distinguish the whiteman from the Indian. And in as much as the word 'civilization' stems from the Latin 'civis' and literally means the system of the city, I was to find it increasingly useful as a distinguishing term from 'Indian' – the man who represents the system of the forest. Quite visibly I did not belong to their system.

Nevertheless I walked up to several groups of Indian hunters as they sat on logs in the clearing and steered the talk cautiously round to the subject of beginners and hunting.

'There are deer and tapir in the forest,' I hazarded. 'Yes,' was the reply. 'This land has many deer and tapir.' The Indian faces looked solemnly out across the marshland to the hunting country of the Kuluene forest beyond, and there – in every case – the conversation would end. Invariably, I would be compelled to announce outright that I wanted a guide who would teach me to hunt in the jungle. To this, many looked encouraging; but always, at the crucial stage, their eyes passed from the dark shape of the distant jungle to my own face. By contrast it must have looked exceptionally young and eager. Not even for a mammoth bribe – their expressions said – would an Indian take a beginner like this into the land of the snake and puma.

I was forced to lay my trap.

For several mornings, I made sure that I was seen walking in the marsh and lake country between the post and the Kuluene forest. By dint of sitting under trees till birds settled in them above, I managed to bring in three or four pigeons a day. These I plucked in open view, sitting on the bluff above the nearby River Tuatuari.

After a week had passed, a young man from the Kamayura tribe, an elder from the Waura, and the chief of the Mehinaku had all paused to examine my gun on their journeys to and from the post. It was a single-barrelled BSA 12-bore and was impressively bigger than the .20 bore and .24 bores that were occasionally given out by Orlando as special rewards. The Indians had been impressed. Such a big gun for such little birds. Perhaps the *civilizado* was up to something.

Finally, on a morning when I had only brought in two birds, I looked up from my plucking to see Kaluana of the Aweti tribe standing above me. He was not big for an Indian, nor thick and stocky like some of the tribal wrestlers, but he gave the impression of being amazingly supple and well-built. His age was probably twenty.

'It's a nice pigeon,' he observed encouragingly. He picked it up and absent-mindedly pulled the head away from the neck with a soft plop. There followed a meditative pause. 'Tomorrow,' he offered, 'tomorrow I will carry you over to the forest by the River Kuluene. There are bush turkey there, and deer and pigeon, too.' His face, grave and reflective, was turned sideways to mine and as I considered the unexpected altruism of this offer, I was disturbed by something unusual in his appearance. Then, suddenly, I noticed. The normal red, white, and black toucan feather ear-rings that project on a diagonal slant across the cheekbones of a Xinguano were no longer hanging from his ears.

'There are toucan in the forest,' I suggested casually.

Yes. It appeared there were many fine toucan by the Kuluene.

It was then agreed that Kaluana should call me 'when the chicken first sings', and at about four o'clock next morning he must have slipped his hand through the hut's log walls to shake the rope of my hammock. Whang! There was a cry of anguish from the night outside.

Some days before, a passing and generous Indian had brought a stork to join the two bush turkey, the two jungle fowl, the woodpecker, the parrot, the macaw, and the other animals which lived as we did in the Leonardo hut, pecking food from our plates, perching on our shoulders, and occasionally spattering thoughtlessly onto our hair. But the stork had not taken easily to the change. For the whole of two days it had not moved, standing a foot away from the edge of my hammock huddled up in itself at the end of long bare legs. A red patch of disapproval had developed at the end of its beak; occasionally it would sneeze and sneeze. The last straw – obviously – had been Kaluana's visit in the night. His furtive hand was a perfect target and the stork had attacked. I awoke to the bird's hissing and beating wings.

Outside, I found Kaluana sucking blood philosophically from the end of his knuckles. 'The stork is savage,' he muttered casually, and in a few minutes we were down by the river swimming our guns and clothes across. It was dark, without a moon, and we marched for two hours, depending on the Indian's knowledge of the country. When the dawn arrived, we were in the deep forest of the swamp territory by the Kuluene River. Kaluana weaved amongst the trees and tangles of scrub; I stumbled behind. Huge tree trunks soared into the sky above and mysterious alleyways and false paths led off through the brush and saplings on either side. It was the confusion of a nightmare, and I thought of the many occasions I had imagined with pleasure this moment of first entry into the forest of Xingu. I had always pictured a tall rampart of trees and then myself as the leader of a brave little group that would slip between the portals of two gnarled trunks into the jungle within. The Indians would point out orchids, creepers, and bushes. They would describe the trees and show me the different types of medicinal roots and leaves. And thus, from the general to the particular, a graphic picture would grow in my mind and I would feel master of the situation. Instead we had entered blindly in the night, and now there was such a mass of detail that it completely overwhelmed the *civilizado*'s untrained senses. The vegetation concealed the forest as effectively as a fog hides the buildings along a London road. I clung to Kaluana as my only clue in a baffling wilderness.

Another hour. Then we stopped beneath a tall tree.

'Toucan tree,' the Indian gleamed, and sitting down he made a shrieking noise by blowing through two leaves pressed tightly between his thumbs. He repeated this once or twice, and soon three birds arrived in the tree above.

'Cannon,' Kaluana hissed, pointing urgently at my 12-bore. Then, to elucidate the point, 'Slaughter toucan dead.'

From my ambush, the tummied waistcoats of the friendly creatures above seemed uncannily like those of three elderly bishops nodding at each other in a London club.

'Good to eat,' Kaluana insisted. Then with further inducement to my hovering indecision: 'Good for feathers too.'

I lifted the gun to my shoulder.

Boom! Kaluana's face registered the explosion.

Whoosh. Three disgruntled toucan took themselves off to another part of the forest. My first lesson in hunting had ended in failure.

But later in the day, Kaluana repeated his whistle – it seemed to make the birds curious – and I shot a toucan very high in a tall tree. It came whistling down all black and red and pompous, a sad little body to be plundered by the lithe Indian at my side. He wrapped the feathers in a leaf and gave them to me; naked, he had no pockets. And then came a bewildering hunt in which he snatched my gun and disappeared at great speed between the undergrowth, returning with a bush turkey he had killed. That was for the post. The toucan was for him. Our bargain was complete, and I had acquired an Indian who would teach me to hunt. It seemed that I had a redoubtable 'cannon' and like every beast of burden, would have to be trained to carry and manoeuvre it.

For a fortnight we went out on alternate days, each trip lasting without rest from four in the morning till two to four in the afternoon. Usually – with much protest from the 'pack animal' part of the team – there was no food and sometimes no water from the time of dinner at six o'clock the evening before, till our return 20 to 22 hours later. Then there would be a day's rest. But in the second afternoon, Kaluana would call me, furtively, out into the clearing where no one could hear. (Many Indian arrangements are conceived in a melodrama of conspiracy.) Companionably, the Aweti would go through my pockets to see if anything new was to be examined, and afterwards the details of the hunt would come out.

The days passed. I began to change my perception of the forest.

At first, that dark line of vegetation was approached with a certain awe. This was part of the greatest forest on earth; writers of that time called it the Green Hell or even the enemy of mankind. Outside, the swamp grass would be warm and cheerful, but inside, the jungle seemed to contain all the horrors of a witches' wood. Nervously I would slip between the writhing shapes of twisted trees and enter a dark world where light, filtering between the leaves, would make the glades strangely eerie and mysterious. The branches would rustle, small animals would creep away. My hands recoiled from the reaching tendrils of poison-bearing lianas, and the gun would swing nervously as snakes and pumas pounced from imaginary ambush. But soon the Indian's attitude began to overwhelm that of the *civilizado*. The forest became simply the environment of our lives. As a city dweller never looks at bricks, so the Indian never looks at a tree. There are saplings for making bows, and jatoba for making canoes, and certain branches where animals like to sit, but there are never trees noticeable for self-conscious reasons – beauty, terror, wonder. The forest is their livelihood, and the eye of a travel writer would, for them, be meaningless.

On the other hand, the Indian's viewpoint is obviously more accurate than that of an imaginative man from the towns. He knows, for example, that in the jungle things go up and down, that they do not go along. Self-centred beings, we *civilizados* tend to assume that all life proceeds on the same plane as our own, that of the horizontal, whereas in the forest most life struggles up towards the sun and at death drops away from it. It is the rhythm of living. Trees battle with each other to gain their porthole on the sky. Victory is the death of an arboreal giant. After standing rotten for many years, it comes crashing to the ground where the human level of earth is no more than a graveyard. It would also be more accurate to conceive of the jungle animals as living in skyscrapers rather than on a piece of bush-covered soil. Different types of food are to be found at different levels in the vegetation strata, and so the animals feed and hunt in a movement that is upwards and downwards: not only the birds, and flying insects, but also the anacondas and tiger cats. In the forest, the Indian thinks vertically.

In a similar way, if a city man describes a tapir or panther, he tries to portray it from what he has seen in the zoo. But not so the Indian of Xingu. When asked, he invariably imitates the animal's call. 'That mmmmmmmmm, mmmmmmmmm,' he would say for a jaguar. And soon I realised that in the forest where the range of vision could be limited to five yards, a hunt of hours would proceed without sight of the prey till that final moment when, camouflaged by branches and undergrowth, a bullet would be fired into something that was barely distinguishable as part of an animal. The jungle is a world of the ears. Because of this, the little I could remember from the zoo confused rather than helped, since imagination was determined to fit the sound to a suitable shape. Once I warned Kaluana that a jaguar was roaring in the bushes and was told that what I had heard was really the song of a frog. Later it seemed inconceivable that the creak of a breaking tree was, in fact, an edible fowl, and that the screaming laugh of a hyena was merely the cry of a small pheasant-like bird.

And so, little by little, Kaluana helped me construct a new and more real image of the forest. But always, at the last stage of every stalk, he would seize my gun, whisper, 'Stay here, Adriano', and finish off the kill for himself. The gun was for killing. I was its inevitable but deplorable method of transport.

After his fifth or sixth disappearance into the undergrowth at the keypoint in a lesson, I rebelled.

At his call on the next morning, I lay doggedly in my hammock. 'I can't come,' I whispered. 'I am ill, Kaluana.'

'What sort of illness?' he hissed suspiciously through the logs.

'It's difficult to explain. I am a foreigner. I don't know the Portuguese for it.'

'Hmm,' said Kaluana from the darkness outside, where the cock had crowed once. He went off on his own, and later that afternoon I set out from the post on my first solo hunt. I canoed to a likely part of the forest and made camp as night came down.

The moon was in the tree at the end of my hammock when I heard the faint whisper of the sound I was waiting for. I lifted my ears above the cords of the hammock and listened, without moving, for five minutes.

It was roughly the hour before dawn. The sound came very faintly again.

I leaned back and touched the cartridges in my shoes, which were tied by their laces to the hammock rope behind my head. On the ground, in what was the natural arc of a falling hand, I felt the barrel of my gun resting on a broken log. I had put it there on the previous night when, on reaching this bank of a darkening river, I had made these few square yards the one point in the great waste of forest that was significant for the presence of a being with brain and purpose. Now the object of my purpose was making its call.

A few puffs were enough to blow up the fire by my hammock, and a young carnival of flames lit up my gun. While I was testing the firing mechanism a centipede that had slept there during the night crawled out and dropped to the ground. Soon after, I began the hunt for my prey. The *civilizado* had led himself to believe that he had learned from the Indians. He slid into the forest feeling as lethal and catlike as a tiger.

There was just enough light from the moon and the false dawn to etch shapes into the dark of the forest night and to silhouette the faint depression of the Indian trail. It was surprisingly easy to follow. In the height of day, the jungle's trellis-work of leaves tends to splash confused puddles of light across the ground that camouflage rather than reveal a path. Now, what little light there was made a sharp difference in tone between the trodden track and the unbeaten surrounding ground. My feet followed it, feeling through the soles of my tennis shoes along the beaten line; if they strayed onto unbroken twigs or leaves, they automatically sought the path again.

I crept quietly, looking no further than my footsteps, and aware that strange things seemed to be peering at me from the darkness. I forced myself not to think about them. The constant effort of focusing and refocusing between lianas a few inches from my nose through a maze of tangled branches at varying distances to an object some hundred yards away brought nothing else than a stabbing headache. It was better to walk 'carelessly' like the Indian, with eyes specifically on the ground and generally everywhere, watching not for colour or shape, but registering in split-second attention any movement within an arc of 250 degrees. By not 'looking' in front, the Indian seemed to catch movement behind. And though at first I attributed this to sixth sense, I later realised it was an instant reaction to something to which all his senses were tuned. Movement. It is betrayal in the forest.

With such limited vision, my ears were the radar of the hunt. I tried to pause for a fraction of a second at the arc of every step to gain a moment of silence and listening above the crackle and noise of my own progress. When I had first seen an Indian listening with his mouth open, I had thought that concentration had relaxed the muscles in his face. Now, straining to hear, I too dropped my mouth down to avoid the faint rasp in the nose that is the sound of a passing breath.

There it was! Like the soft vibration of a distant outboard motor. It was the cry of my victim. Not a sharp sound tied to a specific point in the forest, but a vague purr on the air that had to be located with the slow turning of my head, careful to avoid the creak of a neck vertebra that would distort and confuse the trembling on my ear-drums.

The air quivered once again. It was the summons of male to mate. I left the Indian path and pursued the line of the call.

The forest in this part was close to the river, and I was able to walk quietly on the tracks of a tapir's path to water before diverting onto the sodden ground of a stream-bed. This led in the direction of the summons, and as I knew my beast would probably be sitting high in a tree above a shallow mere, I hoped that the watercourse with its chance of quiet movement would lead me to him. Silence was vital. This part of the forest was hunted often, and my adversary would be listening and watching. At the faintest suspicion his cry would cease and I should be quite helpless in the maze of jungle – a navigator lost without a guiding beam.

By good luck, a breeze was blowing into my face and I moved forward in spasms, waiting till each gust shook the leaves in a covering 'smokescreen' of sound. By now the call had swelled into a rich snore. He must be less than a hundred yards away.

In front was a tiny mere, silver in the moonlight that was combining with the first brightening of day. I waded in. Small trees put an umbrella of protection over my head; gaseous muds sent up bubbles of decay under my feet. I climbed onto a giant treetrunk that had fallen into the deep part of the pool and crept along it with three cartridges dry in my mouth. And then, once again, back into the fetid, stirring swamp.

By this time the snore was close above, a deep purring sound like an uncle snoozing after dinner. I knew that my victim would be sitting at least 30 yards up in one of Amazonia's giant trees and that I should have to be almost underneath before the range was short enough to fire. Even then, I should be forced to creep in the undergrowth to find both a clear tunnel for the shot and an angle that would expose the head or breast. Step by step I advanced, making such an effort to be quiet that my legs grew stiff and my joints began to creak. In their effort to hear, my ears almost seemed to curve forward as they strained at the tangled criss-cross of branches above.

Now I stood in the water, peering through a trellis-work of leaves. I quartered the tree in front and ruled out the camouflaged places where he could not possibly be. The moon was still up, but the first rays, as the sun pulled itself over the rampart of the earth, were beginning to strike at the tops of the trees.

And then I saw something. It was no more than the stir of a leaf, but a stir that occurred with every snore. I moved slowly behind my screen of foliage. I peered about for a clear tunnel through the branches till I saw the leaf again from another angle, and beyond the leaf a tail, and beyond the tail a great Roman Emperor of a bird. A Caesar's beak it had, crimson against a head of purple, and a breast that was brown and gold and bigger than a swan's. It was the *mutum castanho*, the largest of the bush turkeys. Flying, he would look as big as a goose. Walking, he makes as much noise on dry leaves as a marching man. The wing-span varies from four to six feet.

Slowly I eased the gun between the twigs and branches and started to tip the muzzle up cautiously towards the sky. Suddenly his cry sprang out sharp as a soccer whistle. It ended in a long drawn-out hiss. He had seen. One jump and the *mutum's* back was towards me. As the stock came to my shoulder, he bent his legs for the leap. One more hiss, and then I caught him smack in the tail and slightly to one side. Triumph!

Thirty to forty yards above the ground the perch had been, and so dinner hit the deck with a thud. And then, to my horror, dinner leaped to its feet and started racing off through the undergrowth. Complete humiliation!

With a most un-Indian howl, I tore after what should have been my first real solo kill and what now appeared to be just another failure. A shot in the rump at that range would no more than wound. I plunged and tore and writhed amongst the undergrowth. The *mutum* was ahead, running with a strange rolling gait. He was slower than I was, but then branches, lianas and thorns were not tearing the shirt and skin from his back. After 60 seconds I realised that he was drawing away, but suddenly another mere in front forced him to turn and run at right angles along the bank. Cutting across the triangle, I soared through the air and came down upon him. Smack. In a great welter of mud, water, dead leaves and feathers, we thrashed about until the hunt came to its end. I was as cut and torn as if a jaguar had been my quarry.

But five minutes later, a 15 to 20 lbs meal was swinging from a liana five feet above the ground, covered by a twisted network of twigs to act as camouflage against hawks. Proudly I slipped another cartridge into the breech and went looking for the mate. The bush turkey is the easiest prey in the forest and the bread and butter of a man armed with a gun. It was my first real lesson from the Indians, but probably the most important. For it was by utilising the forest for myself, feeling its texture through my daily usage, that reality slowly began to expel the illusions of the *civilizado*.

One day between hunts, the slow rhythm of waiting at Posto Leonardo was broken by the arrival of Claudio Villas Boas. He had spent the incredible period of three years in the forest cutting a trail from the airstrip of Cachimbo to the airstrip of Cururu. I watched him step from the aeroplane with his shirt drooping out of his trousers and with his sandals flopping about his feet. He walked at his own pace towards the post, a strange tubby shape with no more baggage than a flour sack slung over his shoulder. He looked like Dick Whittington after a rough night.

Some weeks before, Orlando had told me that Claudio had once walked for 28 days through unexplored country with no more food or baggage than a .22 rifle. But this was not the man the story had led me to expect. Where Orlando was a baked Indian brown, Claudio's pale complexion had the green tinge of a forest shadow. Where Orlando had a sharp bold face, Claudio was chubby, wore glasses, and had the mild demeanour of a country grocer.

At lunch that day he sat at the other end of the table.

'Your airstrip is too short, Orlando.'

'It is 800 metres.'

'That is 200 metres too short.'

Orlando demurred.

'It is. I know. Aren't I your brother?'

'Yes,' said Orlando pacifically. Claudio's arrival meant that he could now fly out to resolve the problem of supplies and arrange the departure of the expedition. He was in a good mood.

After lunch Claudio retired to his hammock and for the next week I hardly saw him leave it. 'How does he keep alive without eating?' I asked Juan, and was told that, camel-like, Claudio stored up on food and sleep and then needed no more for long periods. I was intrigued and watched with care. When he did eat, I noticed it was at night, from the left-overs in the pans, so that we seldom saw him. He would scrape away in the dark and munch quietly to himself. During the day I would see his small and bearded form confined to a hammock, listening as Indian men and women came to put their crawling babies on his tummy. They would then relate something or converse in a low and endless monotone. Between visits he would read short sections from a pile of books and pamphlets on the ground below him and stare thoughtfully at the roof for an hour or so before his hand reached out and the next passage continued. Once, I looked at the titles. There were several works by Jacques Maritain relating Aquinas to the problems of the modern world, Bertrand Russell's *History of Philosophy*, a polemical pamphlet by Stalin, a heavy book on the significance of Communist development in China, and some reflections by a Brazilian man of letters on events during his lifetime.

When people had told me that, of the brothers, Orlando was the man of action and Claudio the thinker and philosopher, I had pictured the backwoods sage of American literature, brimming with saws and quips to the discomfort of everyone around. But gradually, as the months at Posto Leonardo passed, I was to realise that nothing could have been further from the truth.

When Claudio expressed his views they burst forth in hour upon hour of rushing, cascading, pouring talk. He spoke very quickly, digressing through the philosophers. He used Rome and other historical examples. He argued, thundered, exhorted.

Until that time, I had unconsciously assumed that men who lived and worked in the Green Hell of Amazonia would be – to continue the cliché – men of action, people who acted from the need of the moment rather than from ideals or philosophy. But the more I was to travel in Amazonia, the more I would become convinced that the reverse is true. The greater the obstacle, the denser the forest, the more essential was a driving set of ideas to maintain the man in his struggle with the impossible. Over the next few months, I was to spend countless hours listening to Claudio discuss and rediscuss the Indian problem and his plans for Xingu.

'Since the beginning of this century more than a third of the tribes of Brazil have passed into extinction. When our government expedition first entered Xingu, scores of Indians died in epidemic after epidemic. But even if we succeed in protecting them from all this – from the disease and bullets of the frontiersmen – all that we will have done is to have kept enough Indians alive to have a problem about.'

Claudio would then point out that the most successful defence of the Indians in the history of Brazil had been that of the Jesuit Reductions – their early missions in the seventeenth and eighteenth centuries. Yet once the Jesuits had fallen from royal favour, the entire edifice had crumbled. The Indians had been nothing more than passive subjects of the Reductions, organised for their 'own good'. Since the Reductions had no roots in Indian character, they had naturally vanished when the Jesuits left.

Claudio's proposal was that Orlando and he should play a less dominating role.

'The only hope,' he would say, 'is to preserve the core of tribal society and help the Indians graft on to it the more useful tools of civilisation. If an Indian asks for a metal cooking pot, then the request arises from his own needs. The use of the metal pot is a natural evolution for the man and his group. It will produce change, but not the same disruption as if I ordered all Xinguanos to abandon earthenware tomorrow. In this way, they can grow towards our civilisation, but in a manner and at a pace suited to their own nature.'

Alternatively, Claudio would say that the Villas Boas role should be that of a filter for civilisation.

'The holes, to begin with, will be small, and the least destructive things will come through. The Indians now live as they always have done, but with the tools of our world. Axes. Pots. Rifles. The old men use the guns – their sons will learn how to repair them. Their grandsons will be school and university graduates who will study the theories and science behind it all.'

Claudio's ultimate dream was of an Indian society gradually adjusting to a working relationship with our civilisation. The question was whether the Indians wanted, or were even willing, to cooperate on the path to this goal. In extreme cases, Claudio said, their rejection was so profound that they seemed to prefer just to lie down and die. And it was this deliberate choice of group extinction, an act almost impossible to comprehend for someone brought up in our culture, that blocked my somewhat frenetic quest to understand the forest and its people. During the seven months of my first visit to Xingu, I stayed in a number of Indian villages for a period of days or weeks. And though many of their leaders spent hours talking to me, explaining their problems and way of life, I always felt an outsider watching a culture in which I played no part. So perhaps it should be no surprise that the path that led me furthest was the path of the hunter.

Hunting is the breath of life to an Indian. It passes unnoticed in the course of daily existence, but only ceases in time of war or sickness.

During the days that followed Claudio's arrival, I resumed my apprenticeship with my first teacher, Kaluana. For two or three days on end, we would go out with no more baggage than salt, two hammocks, and a box of matches, exploring new lakes and woods, and given over to forgetfulness in the sheer lust of the chase. The weeks passed and our friendship developed. But it was largely an alliance between two animals for the common purpose of food and protection. Over the months to come, I was to hunt with the Kayabi and the Juruna, with Rauni who in the 1970s and 1980s became a national figure as chief of the Txukahamei, and with Bebcuche, his gentle cousin who was to be shot dead by a rubber tapper on the Rio Verde. During these hunts we would sometimes pause to drink or bathe, and this was when, idle and relaxed, the Indians would often open their minds.

'Tell me,' Rauni once said, 'you and I are friends, Adriano. Tell me, do you work women in your country?' The Portuguese word he used was 'trabalhar' – to work or labour.

'Yes,' I replied. We were lying under the surface of a small stream, careful that no part of our bodies were exposed to the biting flies.

'Very much?' Rauni's face glowed with expectant interest.

'Yes. Sometimes very much. And you?'

'Much too. All the time.'

'With your wife?'

'No. With my wife and with other women.' Rauni spoke carelessly, obviously trying to give the impression of a tribal Don Juan. 'I say to them, "You come with me" and afterwards I say not to tell their husbands. Husbands kill if they know. Do they kill,' he said with a kind interest in my affairs, 'in your land?' I thought for a few minutes about our system and side-stepped.

'When you marry,' I asked, 'does your father tell you who to marry?'

'Wait there. I think.' He looked reflectively at the water. Rauni's tribe had been first contacted less than two years before and he spoke very simple pidgin Portuguese. 'I say to girl, I like you. Then if mother likes me . . .'

'What about father?'

'Father too. Then I and girl go away to forest, and then if girl like me, we are married. I kill many pig and deer and monkey and *mutum*, and mother and father eat too. Then woman has son, she stay in hut and I no kill *mutum* and monkey. Only others.' A reference to a sort of tabu system.

'How tall is the girl when she marries?'

'Small, when I first talk to mother.' His hand indicated eight or nine years old. 'Afterward, she this high when we marry.' He indicated twelve or thirteen. 'Nice,' he said confidentially, 'when girl like this.'

Rauni told me that he was going to take another wife as soon as he returned, and I asked if his first wife was dead.

'No,' he said sadly. 'Other Txukahamei talk with my wife, and afterwards she go away with him. He work woman. So I say to my brothers, "This man has no beautifulness," but they have fear. So I put on paint all over me and then when this man comes back to eat with his mother, I go with my war-club. His mother says, "Why you war-club this man? He is my son and a good man." And then one runs away, two runs away, three runs away.' (These, I presumed were the offender's brothers who should have fought for him.) 'Then I beat,' Rauni hit his own shoulder to show me. 'This man falls, but there is not much how you call it.'

'Blood?' I ventured.

'Yes. Blood. And afterwards he goes away to other Txukahamei.'

'And your wife, Rauni?'

'She goes away too,' he said grimly. 'If she comes back, I war-club.'

'So, you had no wife after that?'

'Yes. I have another. But she dies.'

'No sons?'

'He die, too.'

This sort of conversation I never had with Kaluana, and I think it was because Kaluana never offered explanations that I was forced to try and explain him to myself. With Rauni and the others, I could suspend thought by asking 'Why do you do this?', 'Why is your tribe like that?'. But faced with Kaluana's intensely functional conversation, I was forced to explain his actions by building a model of the Indian hunter in my mind.

The Aweti was certainly an impressive figure. The Indians of the Upper Xingu have a fine eye for proportion and unlike other Indians do not distort their bodies with discs forced into their lips, staves thrust through their noses, or blocks of wood tearing at the lobes of their ears. On Kaluana's shoulders and thighs there were deep scratch marks made with the shark-like teeth of a fish called the *pirara*; but these had been drawn symmetrical to the line and flow of his limbs. In his ears he wore six-inch bamboo pins tipped with a bunch of toucan feathers so that when he turned there was a flash of colour in the forest's drabness; these were as perfectly proportioned to his Indian head as pendant ear-rings to a Marie Antoinette coiffure. And every part of him was in perfect balance to his purpose as a hunter. At the faintest sound, Kaluana could check one leg in the air, an arm half-way through a movement, the whole body frozen in the act of transferring balance from one foot to another, and yet in such perfect poise that the position could be held for minutes on end. He moved like a wraith that, having no substance, can disturb no obstacle, but in his case the secret was a form so supple that it automatically shaped and reshaped itself without conscious thought as it weaved between the bushes. At the end of a day, when I would be cut and marked all over, he would emerge without a single scratch on his naked skin.

And this refinement to the needs of hunting extended even to his conversation. Vatucu, the old Waura who occasionally went out with me, would sometimes rest on a log. 'Do you know what that tree is for?' he would ask. Then he would tell me in minute detail how an Indian would come, clear the ground about, cut the bark, fell the tree, and shape the result into a canoe. Sometimes he would pick up a certain type of soil. 'This earth is for making pots,' he would say. Sometimes he would stop by the larvae of a wasp's nest and describe how they should be cooked. 'Pass over smoke. Then eat.' This sort of information, Kaluana never volunteered. Once I asked him to repeat a toucan whistle for me to learn, but he refused. Toucan whistles were for toucans. In all our time together, he never ventured any forest information unless he was actually engaged with that particular stick or animal or leaf and, during the whole of a day's hunt and camp at evening, probably no more than a score of sentences would pass between us. His talk was functional, like the rest of his being.

At three o'clock on one particular afternoon we arrived at a small stretch of river by the Kuluene. I unsheathed my machete and started to clear the saplings, whilst Kaluana took a branch and swept a small piece of ground till it was clean of leaves, centipedes, and scorpions. Two hammocks were then slung six feet apart on tree trunks that were neither rotten nor laced with the little tunnelled tracks of termites.

I was very tired that night and so I told Kaluana that I had important things to think about. This statement with its implication of weighty matters to be considered usually impressed him. He moved 30 yards down the bank and built himself another blaze for light. During the next two hours, periods of silence would be suddenly interrupted by a tremendous splashing as he hauled a 30 lb *pintado* or *pirara* ashore. It would grunt and groan across the dark spaces of the river as he beat it over the head. Three minutes of violent noise, then silence.

Meanwhile I sat in my hammock staring at the other river bank where several storks were fishing. Nearby, a big hawk-like bird swooped and honked like an express train, and the water around about surged with fighting fish. It was rush hour in the forest, when the daylight animals were going home to sleep and the nocturnal ones were setting out to hunt. The trees, the land, and the river seemed to vibrate with movement and excitement. The only point of human significance in the blankness of the dark and the cruelty of this savage world was the little blaze of Kaluana's fire.

Here I thought was the dimension in which the Indian should first be approached. Obviously, it was more logical to start in the complex society of the village where the man was born and his mind formed. But the harshest reality of his existence and the greatest part of his life was spent in the forest. Above all, it was his adaptation to this that made him so different from the *civilizado*. At this very moment, without preparation or forethought, Kaluana could set out on the 2000 kilometre journey to Venezuela or on the 1500 kilometre trek to the mouth of the Amazon, completely self-sufficient in the wilderness. I should be helpless when cartridges and fish hooks gave out. But Kaluana, who could make a bow or canoe, whose sense of direction needed no compass, and who knew how to catch tortoises, rats and snakes, would have been as much at home a year's march away as he was this night by the Kuluene.

I had also come to notice that the more I adapted to Kaluana's requirements of me, the more I seemed in tune with other aspects of Indian life. Over the months I had acclimatised to the heat and sometimes I would hunt for twelve hours without rest, bending and weaving in the undergrowth; my reactions, though still contemptible to an Indian, occasionally drew a word of approval from Kaluana. But if the forest had refined my senses, it had also reduced the questioning of my brain. For instance, not once during this time did I feel any pity for an animal before I shot it; on the other hand, I never killed an animal for any reason but food. The mind of a *civilizado* was moving towards the functional brain of a hunting forest animal.

The most interesting change, however, seemed to be the altering purpose of my existence. The *civilizado* from England had come to Xingu for the vaguest and least commendable of motives, but in his wish to go on an expedition, and in his interest in the Indian problem, there had been a purpose: a desire to understand. As the expedition delayed, this purpose swiftly disappeared. Previously, I had fidgeted at the delays in the journey. But gradually I found myself pleased with every delay that would allow me to rise at dawn, stalk, kill and eat as much as I could.

It was what some outsiders have called 'jungle sickness.' For instance, missionaries at the Summer Institute of Linguistics are instructed to work in pairs largely to avoid this sort of adaptation. And the curious thing was that as purpose dropped out of my life and conversation, so the tribesmen appeared to become more friendly; so I seemed to have greater understanding for them, and the less I had to make the mental effort, 'This is how an Indian reacts and I must accept it because he is different.' For the difference between the Indian and the *civilizado* is not, as it has so often been put, the 3000 years between the primitive and the modern. It is the chasm between the man who lives in the forest and the man who lives in our civilisation – the system of the city.

Gradually, I began to realise that the Indian did not need to plan ahead to kill or store great reserves of fish and flesh simply because the jungle always provided for the man who just got up from his hammock and wandered into the limitless storecupboard of the bush. Wealth was an impossibility to the Indian, because everything that he possessed could be owned by any other Indian who cared to make a bow, build a hut, grind the stone head of an axe or shoot a macaw for a coloured head-dress. For this reason, accumulation did not figure greatly in the tribal languages. Txukahamei and Xavante numerals did not go on after six, and the word 'six' was the same as the word for many, because, to an Indian, six dead pigs were not significantly different from 200 dead pigs. They were both too many.

The point behind all this was that for the Indian the forest was so large in relation to his own powers that he did not try to measure it. The jungle's time was unceasing, and he never attempted to count it. The forest's strength was insuperable, and he did not struggle against it. The Indian, in fact, had yielded to his environment. As he could not climb out of his forest dungeon, he had accepted it.

This acceptance I sensed was the beginning of Claudio's problem. Enter we, the *civilizados*. Like all good liberators we tear the 'cage' away and the Indian, whose life has been moulded by 3000 years of acceptance of that cage, is like a man let out after a life-time in prison. The light blinds him. Like the 'liberated' so often in history, the Indian is equipped for the exact reverse of 'freedom'. He is an uncivilised man, and contact with us means he has to adapt to the system of the city. Then we are amazed that he does not fight the challenge that comes with change. But previously when the Indian was faced with a challenge, he met it by killing his enemy. Yet we, the *civilizados* who are destroying him, say that killing is wrong and refuse to fight. With his world tumbling about him, without the means of understanding the challenges, let alone having the weapons to conquer them, the Indian despairs in his bewilderment. He begins to lie down and die—the epitome of Claudio's problem. Once the Indians ceased to fight for their own survival, there was very little he could do for them. 'When a tribe has ceased to dance, to believe in its vision of existence,' Claudio said, 'it's usually close to extinction.'

That night of reasoning in a hunting camp was my first attempt to understand what was happening in Xingu as the *civilizado* encroached upon it. I was shining my one shaft of illumination, my hunting with Kaluana, onto Xingu's complex multi-dimensional society. It was a very limited vision. But one that I will always link with that facet of the Indian character personified by Kaluana, the man who by his adaptation to the forest was least suited to adapt to civilisation. Was it pure coincidence that of the three Indians who most formed my vision of Xingu, he was to be the one to die of a *civilizado* epidemic? On my next visit to Xingu I was intensely saddened to learn that the Aweti village no longer existed as a separate tribal group, and that Kaluana had died of measles.

That particular night, Kaluana came back with four large fish and told me that others had got away with his hooks; we lay in our hammocks dozing and chewing strips of meat from the pile that lay between us.

At midnight, it was cold and we both climbed out of our hammocks to crouch beside the fire.

'Kaluana, today I saw a deer.'

'Where did it sit?'

'In the roots of the big tree by the lake where you shot two *jacubim*.'

'I have seen a deer there too.'

For the next five hours we lay sleeping and listening for the sounds in the forest. At dawn, as on scores of mornings before, we would slide into the mist to kill where those clues would lead us.

THREE

For weeks after Orlando's departure for Sao Paulo, the sound of an aeroplane would draw a crowd to the airstrip. And in the sixth week, when we had all abandoned hope, a strange man appeared in the Dakota doorway. His hair was cut, he had a new shirt and jeans, his feet were in shoes. Difficult as he was to recognise, there could be no doubt about his identity. The whoops and cries spread about the airfield. Orlando was back.

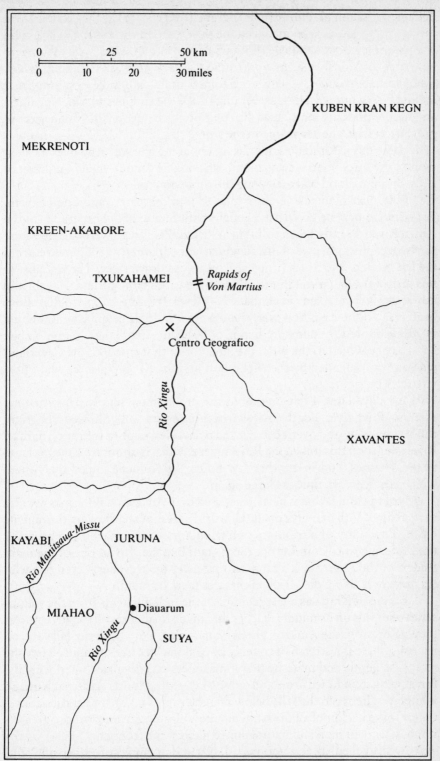

THE AREA OF THE CENTRO EXPEDITION

Huge 44 gallon gasoline drums thumped and clanged as they rolled down the pathway; Pioni, who managed the post, carried several cheap rifles and was wearing a new .22 single shot pistol. Another Indian staggered under a box of provisions; a Kamayura pulled a sack that was leaking beans; Kaluana had acquired – with accustomed skill – a bundle of clothes that looked heavy but was, in fact, very light. All the supplies for an expedition and all the presents for a great distribution to the people of Xingu were in procession from the aeroplane to the store.

'In three days,' Orlando said, 'the first boat must leave.' And over the next month, the three boats – two aluminium and one canoe – made a number of trips, dumping food and fuel along the route down river.

On the next plane came extra men to join the party, and one of them, Franklin Gomez the geologist, brought with him aerial photographs of the Xingu River recently taken by his firm PROSPEC. These were to help locate the Geographical Centre of Brazil, which was apparently 17 kilometres from the left bank of the River Xingu several weeks down river. The last post in this area was Diauarum. But the downriver tribes – the Juruna, Kayabi and the recently contacted Txukahamei – were friendly to the Villas Boas brothers. To the east, however, there were hundreds of miles of unknown territory hunted by nomadic bands of Xavante, Txukahamei and Kuben Kran Kegn. Whilst to the west, the huge forest that rose into the Cachimbo plateau was defended by the Mekrenoti and the Kreen-Akrore, who killed intruders on sight.

A few days later, I left on one of the preliminary supply trips carrying gasoline down river. For the first two or three hours, our hollowed tree-trunk canoe, unwieldy and overladen, yawed from side to side of the little Tuatuari River. But soon this joined the Rio Kuluene which is about ten times as large as the Thames, and in another few hours the Kuluene joined the Xingu, which is at least ten times as large again.

One of the things that is hard to get used to in Amazonia is the massive size of its rivers. With one fifth of all the world's fresh water flowing through its basin, a tributary of a tributary of a tributary of the Amazon can be larger than the biggest river in Europe. So a giant like the Xingu, one of the main feeders of the Amazon, is a monster that awes the traveller – even one who encounters it, as we did, 1000 kilometres from its mouth.

The fame of Xingu as a last redoubt of the Indians stems from the vicious series of rapids on its middle reaches that made further travel for adventurers moving up from the Amazon almost impossible. But above the falls of Von Martius, there is a stretch of roughly 200 kilometres free of rapids. Here the river is so gentle and majestic that it meanders on either side interlacing the forest with abandoned arms and oxbow lakes. And it was this stretch of 200 kilometres, between the falls below and the rapids on the tributaries above, that was the backbone of the kingdom the Villas Boas were trying to create – a new society of man and nature united against the frontier.

As we travelled, all the lagoons, islands and openings on either side of us made it difficult to realise that we were not floating on a land-locked lake.

Everywhere the river seemed to be surrounded by a confining wall of dark and mysterious vegetation. Each half-hour or so we would come to a twist in the bank, or an opening behind an island, to see the river running on once more into what looked like yet another dead end in the forest. And our course was even more tortuous than the stream itself. For with the dry season the water had dropped, leaving huge mile-long sandbanks that forced the river into channels of swift-flowing current. Upstream from these sandbanks, the helmsman steered as far away as he could; like icebergs, they sometimes reached out a quarter-mile underwater. Downstream, it was possible to pass two feet away, as the cliff of sand would drop sheer to the bottom, cut harsh by the sweep of the river. From side to side we went, backwards and forwards, sometimes heading south when I knew that our course must be north, often steering for what looked like a blind alley in preference to a great sheet of water leading into the distance.

When we stopped, game seemed to stand at the end of our guns. Fish, with enormous appetites, were waiting wherever we threw our hooks, and turtle's eggs were so plentiful that half an hour was enough to collect a few hundred. Once we saw 14 very tall jaribou storks sitting grouped in pairs. 'This sort of stork is always married,' Jose, the helmsman explained, 'and the women storks never let the men storks go away by themselves.' Large *capivaras* – rodents that look like water-rats and are bigger than pigs – crouched on the banks and watched us go by. And occasionally a turtle or giant otter would pop its head out of the water to blink cynically at our strange and hopeful passage.

After a few days we arrived at the Villas Boas advance base at Diauarum, and following one or two more supply trips, the whole expedition was assembled and heading down river. It was September, 1958. The party consisted of Orlando and Claudio; Franklin, the geologist; Sergio and Dilton, old expeditionary friends of Orlando; Raimundo and Clementi, experienced woodsmen from Claudio's Cururu trail; Jose, riverman, and Jorge, mechanic; five Indians, Pioni, Cerilo, Batacu, Rauni, Bebcuche; and one English, expedition-seeking, ex-student.

During the journey, Orlando told us that *seringueiros* (men who tap wild rubber in the forest) were setting out mandioca flour poisoned with arsenic on the lower Xingu outside his area, which they hoped would be found by raiding Indians. They had already succeeded in killing 40 of the Kuben Kran Kegn tribe.

At that time, most of the rivers of Southern Amazonia were occupied by *seringueiros* extracting rubber from the forest, except for the upper reaches of the Xingu where the falls of Von Martius had made the trade uneconomic. Since the start of the rubber boom in the mid-nineteenth century, *seringueiros* had pushed up the Xingu and its adjacent rivers, and tribes like the Juruna and Txukahamei had retreated behind the falls of Von Martius. From here, the Txukahamei still made nomadic journeys to plunder the *seringueiro* frontier. And from time to time, heavily armed expeditions of *seringueiros* or prospectors made raids back into Xingu.

Now Orlando had just heard that the Juruna tribe had killed two *seringueiros* on a sandbank down river.

It was an uneasy moment, therefore, when our boats approached the Juruna village on a bluff high above the water. They stood, 30 to 40 men, women and children, grouped around Bimbina, the chief, who was a great broad man wearing a garment like a furniture remover's leather apron. He held a wooden club that seemed to be a mark of his rank.

We all shook hands, all of us with all of the Juruna. And though no word was said, it was obvious that both Orlando and Bimbina were watching to see how the situation would develop. A few days before, two *civilizados* had been murdered. And though justice has no place in an Indian mind, revenge for murder is an essential part of tribal conduct. We might be expected to retaliate.

Up the bluff we walked and into a hut that was almost entirely filled by a great obstacle in the centre, with only just enough room for a man to pass. When the bamboo covers were drawn off, it proved to be two large canoes entirely filled with fermented Indian beer. I drank, happy to have something to cover my nervousness. It was a mandioca beverage prepared by the chewing and spitting of women, but of a slightly sour variation, something like the taste of rough cider. It was a pleasant drink, if you forgot the technology that produced it.

As we were sipping from our calabashes, the Juruna stood about dark and silent. I noticed, for the first time, that an Indian face when not deliberately expressing friendship does not have the softness of a European's in repose. The spirit behind it is different, not necessarily ill-meaning, but hard, born to the violent competition of life in the forest.

Soon after, Orlando broke the tension by leaving the hut for a conference with the chief and elders. 'They were frightened that I would be angry,' he explained when he came back. 'So I said that I was their friend and not the friend of the *seringueiro*. Then they told me.'

It appeared that two *civilizados*, bearded and carrying .44 Winchesters, had some days before paddled in a canoe out of the River Manitsaua-Missu into the Xingu. In itself this was interesting enough, for the Manitsaua-Missu had previously been used only by the Villas Boas. It was the ideal backdoor into Xingu from the west. Obviously, as news of the pacification work had spread, the old deterrent – fear of the Indians – had lost its power.

As the two *civilizados* had appeared at the mouth of the Manitsaua-Missu, they had been seen and had faced the danger by landing at the Juruna village, saying that they had come from the rubber areas across the watershed to the west and were hoping to descend the Xingu and Amazon to a town a long distance away (presumably Belem). They had been allowed to continue their journey.

A day and a half later, the two men had returned to say that, as the voyage was long, the Juruna must provide them with food. The women – all the men were away hunting – said there was no food in the village. The *seringueiros* had threatened that unless everything was ready next morning, several people would be shot. Then they had slept on one of the island sandbanks where the Juruna normally retreat when attacked by the Txukahamei tribe.

'During the night,' Orlando said, 'the Juruna men came back. If *seringueiros* threaten to kill Indians, Indians kill *seringueiros*. They went in canoes and . . .' He made two peculiarly expressive Brazilian gestures that flicked the thumb and fingers down onto the palm of the hand with a sharp cracking noise. 'Warclubs. They buried both. But Bimbina says one was dug up and eaten by a jaguar.' 'The *seringueiros* were sons of bitches, and Bimbina said he was frightened that I would be angry and kept the rifles to show me. I told them not to be frightened. Orlando isn't angry. He is their father.'

A few hours later I talked to Siriri, one of the men who did the actual clubbing. Though he knew little of his tribe's history, he had this to say:

'First we lived lower down the Xingu and worked for the *seringueiros*, but they killed many with rifles. So we came up here past the great rapids and lived till the *seringueiros* say they are friends and give us rifles. So we went down the river again and worked for the *seringueiros* till they killed more Juruna. Then we killed many *seringueiros* and came back here and killed Trumai and Kamayura Indians. Then the Txukahamei tribe came and killed almost all of us so that we are only twelve now.' (He meant twelve men, as women and children were not numbered in his count of the tribe.)

From what I could gather through Siriri's matter-of-fact description, the Juruna at that time were too weak to have any aggressive intentions. They would kill only in self-defence. But just as the Indian finds it difficult to distinguish between *civilizados*, so *seringueiros* must be hard put to differentiate between the various warlike and non-warlike tribes. Only two days before I had been talking to Bebcuche, one of the two Txukahamei on our expedition.

'Do you eat piranha in your tribe, Bebcuche?'

'Yes, we eat.'

'But how do you catch them? You can't shoot piranha with a bow.'

'No,' said Bebcuche. 'We kill with hook and line.'

'But before Orlando you had no hook and line. They don't grow in the forest like arrows and the poison for fishing.'

'In the forest,' Bebcuche insisted. 'Txukahamei find hooks and line. *Seringueiros* have them,' he explained. 'Over there where the sun goes to sleep, we kill all *seringueiros* in hut. Then we take clothes and rifle and knife.'

'You kill everyone.'

'We slaughter everyone. Man and woman too.'

'Why don't you keep the women.'

'Txukahamei only keep children. Much time before we have three girls from over there,' he pointed to the east. 'They all finished now, but axe and gun and line for fish still good.'

Killing *civilizados* had become an essential part of the economics of Txukahamei nomadic life. Birds were shot for meat and feathers, *seringueiros* for fishing line. That was my introduction to the ancient enmity between Indian and *seringueiro* – an enmity that was to be abandoned with surprising ease during the 1980s when Indians and *seringueiros* joined in the Amazonian Alliance of the Peoples of the Forest to defend themselve. against the onslaught of development.

Three days after our arrival at the Juruna village, the fast aluminium boat was sent back for supplies to the airstrip base at Diauarum, its crew being Jorge, Sergio and myself.

On the return journey, I was looking down the shore for game when, suddenly, I saw two canoes and a dozen paddlers lying close to the bank, with overhanging branches acting as a partial concealment.

We heeled over in a great surge of spray and swooped down to investigate.

Most of the people were obviously of the Kayabi tribe, which had lived on the Sao Manuel River until the Villas Boas had settled them in Xingu. But there was a strange Indian who proved to be a Bakairi, a tribe that lives on the headwaters of the Xingu. And there was also a *civilizado*, a great powerful man with a bearded and aggressive face, but eyes that were by contrast kind and sensible.

'Going far?' Sergio asked him.

'Oh, just up the river to get a plane at Xingu.' Casual! Considering that the journey he described meant one and a half weeks' paddling and that he must have spent roughly six weeks canoeing through hostile country to where we found him, it was casual indeed.

'Where have you come from?'

'Down the Manitsaua-Missu. From the Sao Manoel River. It has taken a long time.'

'Did you see Orlando at the Juruna?'

'No, we passed in the night.' Hmmm! So the Kayabi must have warned him about the Juruna.

'Are you a *seringueiro*?' Sergio continued the questions.

'Yes. I have been working over there for six months, but now I am finished. I am going home. Rondonopolis near Cuiaba.'

We continued back to the Juruna village. 'The son-of-a-bitch,' Orlando stormed. 'If he takes the Kayabi upriver without me, the Kamayura (who live near Posto Leonardo) will kill them. The Kayabi must come back.'

A boat was sent off with Sergio, Clementi and Pioni who could talk to his Kayabi fellow tribesmen. 'If the *seringueiro* has promised them presents for the journey,' Orlando ordered, 'he must give them immediately. He can go on. But not with the Kayabi.'

Sergio and Pioni took rifles and Clementi his revolver. When the party returned that night, it seemed that the situation was as bad as it could be. The *seringueiro* and his Bakairi friend had gone on without trouble, stripped of practically everything they had – guns, knives, clothes – in payment to the Kayabi for their service. The *seringueiro* would be safe, but he had left his mark. One of the Kayabi was down with flu.

'This is the worst thing that could have happened,' Claudio gloomed.

'It's just a bad bout of colds, isn't it?'

'I have had 15 years experience and I know that nothing delays an expedition as much as flu. People can't work. Indians die. And we have to stay in villages to fight the epidemic. The Kayabi will try to get back to their village, and with no medicine, they'll die there like flies.'

There was a discussion and eventually it was agreed that Claudio should stay behind when the expedition set out next day for the Centro. He would nurse the Kayabi at a camp near the Manitsaua-Missu River and try to keep them away from both the Juruna and their own village.

Later that evening when everyone else had retired to their hammocks, I helped Clementi roast the piranha to be eaten next day. They gleamed above the fire and the two of us sat and watched, occasionally turning the fish. Clementi talked about the *seringueiros*.

'These *camaradas* have a hard life, Adriano. They are poor. No clothes, no knife, no food, and they are told that if they work for a rubber *patrao* they can have these things in advance for the work they will do. They have no family, no house. They go.' Clementi waved dramatically.

'But then when they get there' – Clementi added suspense by stirring the fire – 'ah-ha, then they find that everything has to be bought at the *patrao*'s store and that there everything is dearer than on the Araguaia River. To live in the forest and to get rubber a man needs clothes, pans, a knife, a gun, mandioca flour, alcohol. On the Araguaia this costs ten contos but at the *patrao*'s store, ah-ha, it is 40 contos.'

'So this *camarada* goes away into the forest and works rubber. So! He works for six months and comes back with his rubber in a canoe. It is not enough to pay 40 contos. He goes again. But to go again he needs mandioca flour and new pans and knives. Thirty to 40 contos. He can work ten years and never pay. He works hard and doesn't eat well, because if he buys much food he will never pay his debt. And he can't go away without paying because the *patrao* owns all the boats and planes. Sometimes the *patrao* sends men to beat him to work harder, and sometimes he kills one and runs. So! Like this one today.'

Clementi was from the same background as the *seringueiros*, and his home was between the Rio das Mortes and the Araguaia where many of them came from. With but one twist in circumstance he could have been the *seringueiro* in the canoe that day.

Orlando rose early next morning and bustled up and down between the hammocks. 'Arise, bottom bruisers of Brazil, the expedition has almost gone.' Soon after, the mist cleared and our boats set off downstream.

Claudio stayed behind in the Juruna village. Feeling strangely sad, we watched his dumpy figure till it faded out of sight.

Two and a half days later, with the sun shining overhead and the water sparkling beneath our bows, our boats passed a small island on the Xingu River. The convoy had moved from one page of PROSPEC's aerial photography to another, and we knew that a line drawn due east from the Centro Geografico would cut the river in the middle of this photograph.

The boats were moored a kilometre downstream, and our work began.

The geologist, Franklin Gomez, had explained to us that the geographical centre of a country is discovered by the same method as the gravitational centre of any solid body.

'Cut Brazil out from the rest of the globe, and stick it on a pin at its geographical centre,' he said. 'If we do the job properly, Brazil should pivot like a top.' The calculations had been made by an organization in Rio; it was Franklin's duty to find this mathematical spot in our great unexplored wilderness.

Now that we were close to the site, Franklin worked out from the map and aerial photographs a point on the Xingu River directly east from the Centro Geografico. It was thus that, three mornings later, we all stood at a place on the left bank of the Xingu with the knowledge that we were exactly due east and 17 kilometres 70 metres from the geographical centre of Brazil.

Raimundo and Clementi swung their machetes. Behind them, Franklin balanced a compass on a tripod and directed two men until the line from his compass pointed exactly west through the poles that they held. Gradually, the first dent in the foliage became a track that was littered with stumps and logs but which was a clear and straight line for the compass. Then, when 100 metres had been cut from the river, the distance was measured and a mark made on a tree. Each day, between four and ten of these marks would be chalked up, depending on the density of the forest and each night, the cutting party would camp by the nearest stream. It was to go on for almost a month.

During this time the expedition was divided. There was always a team of seven men at the cutting head and those at the base camp varied from two to seven, depending on movements up and down the trail.

Two weeks later Claudio Villas Boas appeared, unexpectedly, at the base camp, walking up from the river bank and looking very tired and worn. The journey from the Juruna village which had taken the main party two days with motors, he and two Juruna had just achieved with paddles in two and a half. They had travelled all night.

Claudio's greeting was to seize and pluck the *mutum* I had just brought in. His chubby face was pale and very drawn.

'Things are bad, Adriano. The flu has spread to the Juruna.'

Feathers flew with each of his statements.

'There are four pneumonia cases. One is coughing blood and I am worried. They need all the pencillin and Vitamin C that I can take back.'

In half an hour the fowl was cooked and torn to pieces. Claudio and the two Juruna then set out on the return journey with medicines, an outboard motor, and Jorge the mechanic.

A few days later, Pioni, Jose and I were sent after them in the aluminium boat to help with the Juruna epidemic.

It was a long and stormy journey. The wind was high and nearly tossed us out of the boat to the piranhas so that when we arrived in the village we were tired and dripping wet. I was conscious, however, that we had been travelling amongst the great things of nature – a powerful expanse of water, burning sands, limitless sky, and a land that had nobility in its emptiness and size. The squalor of Claudio's hovel of sickness could not have been a more depressing contrast. The hut was dismal and slung with filthy hammocks. An old stove made from a tin can cast a miserly light about the corners. The Kayabi lay in filthy hammocks in filthy clothes, sick and showing that they knew they were sick; all the animal vitality that usually made them such noble beings had utterly gone. Bows, firewood, pans, odd bits of food were scattered amongst the dirt on the floor.

Claudio came up to us looking very dirty and with clothes hanging limply about his body. He seized with delight upon the *jacubim* we had shot on the journey. 'Good. This will do for lunch tomorrow.' I counted the people in the hut. One, two, . . . fifteen. A *jacubim* is no bigger than a hen.

Some time later, when we were all in our hammocks, Claudio told us that things had not been easy, with most of the Juruna and Kayabi down with flu and no one to hunt or to canoe up to the Juruna plantations for food. He had moved the Kayabi from the River Manitsaua-Missu into one hut and the Juruna were in the other three close by. But despite the daily tour with injections and Vitamin C, he dared not relax his attention for a minute. Each of the pneumonia cases had passed the crisis. But at any time of night or day a fevered Indian might decide – against all warning – to cool his burning body in the river. Then it would start all over again.

For the next four days I hunted almost incessantly to supply the village with food. It would rain all night and then we would set out in the wetness of a miserable dawn. Paddle. Paddle. Paddle. Not heavy thrusts at the water, as we had a long way to go, but a rounded swing that just missed my knees where they projected over the shallow side of the canoe. My legs would be cramped in the narrow sloping bottom and behind would be Siriri, the Juruna. We had been hunting together on my first visit to the village, and I knew him well.

One particular morning when we landed, Siriri took an axe to cut honey out of a wild bees' nest and I went after game, padding through the trees which were noisy with rain. The effect was similar to hunting in a smokescreen. I couldn't hear the cry or movement of my prey; my quarry couldn't hear me. It was thus that I missed the biggest prize that I could have shot for the village, an animal for which I had once waited half a night slung in a hammock between two branches 40 feet above the ground – a tapir. As casually as two ships passing in a fog, I saw its huge shadow moving amongst the other shadows 20 yards away before it disappeared into the greyness. But later, Siriri struck a band of *mutum*. He got two and I six in an incredible chaos of shrieking birds and swift movement through the trees. Distributed around the village, they were a temporary solution to the problem of food.

In about five days, most of the Juruna got better, and the trouble then mainly lay with the Kayabi. They disliked the Juruna, resented not being allowed to go back to their own village, and having no understanding of the idea of contagion, could not appreciate why they had to stay. It was straining all Claudio's years of friendship to make them do what they considered both pointless and unpleasant.

At first his problem was to make feverish patients stay in their hammocks and keep warm, instead of hunting and fishing in the rain. But now that they had acquired the idea of their own sickness, nothing would induce them to help themselves. They picked ticks quietly from each other's hair and lay, two to their double hammocks, heads sticking out of a vent in the cloth each side, giving a quaint impression, in that Indian hut, of steam baths made for two. Several were convalescent, but it was still we who had to do the cooking. Jorge, the mechanic, spent three or four hours a day pounding Indian corn into a fine dust. When this was stewed with water, it made an insipid but digestible porridge. The Kayabi did not offer to help, and it would have been unwise to order them to do so.

Claudio told me that epidemics were unusually destructive in Xingu because the *civilizado* had to work against the will of the patient. Without supervision, the sick took no rest, ate no food, and spat out medicine as soon as the doctor's back was turned. Only injections – painful and involving a fussy process of sterilization and manipulation – were appreciated, as a magic that was both interesting and powerful. As it was, all of us could feel the resentment creeping across the hut's filthy floor, licking over boxes, sliding round hammocks, and curling about our part of the building. The Kayabi were sick, they were weary for their home, and though they must have comprehended in some way that we were working for their good, they displayed a child's disobedience to everything its nanny does.

It even began to affect Claudio. 'Out of your hammock,' he said to a man one morning. 'Because you were ill days ago is no reason why you can't take two paces to get your own food now. Oh, Kayabi, my son, do you expect me to feed you like your mother?'

And then turning to us: 'Oh my people. What a trial my people are.' His words might have sounded histrionic anywhere else. But not in that hut with its poison gas of resentment seeping across the chasm of non-comprehension between our two cultures. The Indian had previously been proud as the king of his forest. Now he owed his life to a stranger. It was a bitter thing to swallow.

Some days later the epidemic was almost over, and Claudio decided that he would set out next morning to mark out a landing line for our supply plane on a sandbank near to the Centro Geografico. And when the plane arrived, the news it brought was that there was another flu outbreak at Leonardo and that the labourers there were almost in despair. Amongst those already dead were an Aweti and the chief of the Kuikuro.

⚚

On October the 14th, two weary-looking men cut past the seventieth metre after the seventeenth kilometre. It was the Centro Geografico. They sighed with relief. There was nothing to see but trees.

Orlando said that a small group could not hope to cut a 1000 metre airstrip in such dense forest and so he decided to make a clearing 100 metres by 50 metres. That would leave a mark visible from the air for five years or more. Then the expedition would have to burn an airstrip in a large savannah discovered by our supply plane 50 kilometres to the north. This could be used as a base for a later full-scale clearance team.

In fact, when Franklin Gomez, the geologist, eventually returned to Rio, he checked the figures again and this 'recalculation' conveniently relocated the Centro Geografico exactly by the airstrip that had been burnt in the open savannah. Some months later, it was here that the President landed to have his photograph taken at the geographical centre of Brazil.

On the next day, I came up the trail, and at the Centro found Sergio and Jorge lying on the ground under a banana-leaf lean-to. An enormous jatoba tree had been left standing just to the right of centre of the clearing. To this, various odd pieces of tin from the camp were nailed, and nearby a stake had been driven into the ground and carved with the information that this was the geographical centre of Brazil.

We pooled the jungle fowl that I had shot and the jungle fowl they had shot for a joint dinner that night. Then Sergio emptied his revolver into the jatoba tree.

'What was that for, Sergio?'

'I don't know.'

Together, we took a few photographs to show the historic place – it looked as if a bomb had blown a large hole in the forest – and next morning we tramped back to the base camp.

'Progress. Progress. Progress.' Claudio said to no-one in particular. 'We have symbolised progress. Our President Kubitschek has built our capital, Brasilia, on the edge of the greatest forest on earth. We, his officers, have carried progress to the heart of the forest. Would we achieve something more real if only for once, if only for a short time, if only for one tribe, the Indians did not die? Maybe if that happened, you and I and all *civilizados* would have achieved progress.'

What I had suspected months ago was now obvious. The leaders of the great Roncador-Xingu expedition which had started the whole opening up of Southern Amazonia, the spearhead of the long thrust of development stretching back through the chain of airstrips to Brasilia and the industrial revolution in Sao Paulo, the men who would go down in history as the initiators of the whole modern process of development in Amazonia, no longer believed in their mission. Their cavalier relocation of the Geographical Centre did not imply great respect for its importance or of development as an aim. In fact, it was apparent that they had carried out the expedition largely for the resources it gave them to travel around the tribes in their northern area – to defend the Indians precisely against the development they had brought.

It was from this time that I began to notice that this sort of reversal of aims was a repeating pattern in Amazonian history. From the Jesuits who used cannon to defend their Indian states, to the modern rubber tappers who defend their rubber groves against developers, the *conquistadors* of the forest have usually turned to fight off the next wave of conquest. And this seems to be a characteristic of the frontier – a place where men with the ideas of civilisation are brought in contact with a reality not just strange to our society, but totally unformed by its influence. A frontier is a battle ground between conflicting visions of reality.

The expedition I had taken part in had 'discovered' the Geographical Centre of Brazil. I had been present at the symbolic conclusion of the first stage of the development of Amazonia. But everything we had done, most of the objectives of the Villas Boas brothers, now seem surprisingly similar to the environmental and pro-Indian campaigns of the 1980s. Even their dream, which was to turn Xingu into a National Park so that the whole forest – its flora, fauna and human inhabitants – would all be protected together, is reminiscent of a variety of later proposals. What was different then was that – except for a few isolated crusaders elsewhere in Amazonia – they were alone and fighting a losing battle. For in the mid 1950s, the Government of the State of Mato Grosso started to sell off the whole area of Xingu. By Brazilian Federal Law all land occupied by Indians is inalienably theirs. But within the territory of each state, the right to sell unoccupied land belongs to the State Government. And so the Government of Mato Grosso sold off vast blocks of the forest of Xingu, unseen, and without mentioning that it was occupied by Indians. The land was advertised in papers in Britain and Germany and, soon after I left, heavily armed parties of surveyors started to invade Xingu to do crude, unreliable surveys and mark out blocks of land with wooden marker posts. They occasionally clashed with the Indians and it was clearly the intention of the State Government to drive the tribes away from the region. The Villas Boas may have won my heart by their gallant, altruistic battle. But in 1958, their campaign had all the appearances of a lost cause.

And it is this which illustrates the great contrast between then and now. During Brazil's presidential campaign at the end of 1989, Lula, the candidate of the left, campaigned on a platform that included radical measures to protect both the Indians and Amazonia. And in March 1990, his successful rival, Collor, took office with an equally positive programme for the protection of Amazonia through satellite monitoring and for accelerating the demarcation of Indian reserves. None of this means that his minister, Jose Lutzenberger, or subsequent ministers, will necessarily succeed in executing these programmes. But the issue has – at last – moved from the unknown periphery of our society to the centre of its political stage.

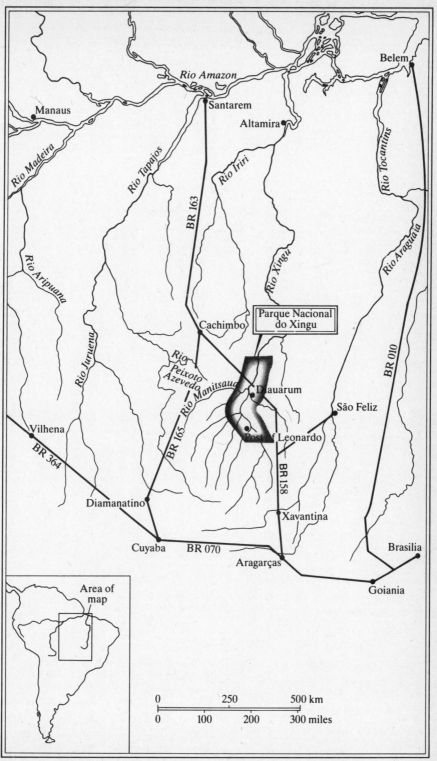

DEVELOPMENT ROADS IN SOUTHERN AMAZONIA

two

THE SPEARHEAD *of* DEVELOPMENT

XINGU NATIONAL PARK 1967–9

By 1967, ten years later, the situation of Xingu had greatly improved. For though the Government of the State of Mato Grosso sold off all the Indians' land, Janio Quadros had been elected President in 1961 on a reformist platform. He was a friend of the Villas Boas brothers and had once visited Xingu. Soon after his election, he decreed that an area of 40 kilometres on either side of the Rio Xingu down to the falls of Von Martius was to become a national park run by the Villas Boas brothers. And though Quadros resigned only a few months later, none of the subsequent governments tried to cancel the decree or to prevent the Villas Boas making the park a functioning reality.

A much greater threat was a policy decision by the military government that took over after the coup d'état of 1964. They made the occupation of Amazonia one of their strategic objectives. In 1966 they launched Operation Amazonia, which, amongst other things, used tax incentives, loans and subsidies to encourage industrial companies to turn large blocks of forest into ranches. One of the largest, over half a million hectares, was the Fazenda Suya-Missu on the eastern border of the Parque.

Another government priority was building roads across Amazonia, both for military purposes and to link it to the growing industrial markets in the south. First, they finished the westward Cuiaba-Porto Velho highway and improved the northward Belem-Brasilia highway, both started by Juscelino Kubitschek in the late 1950s. And then, in the centre of the V formed by these two trunk roads, they planned two other roads to cut through the completely untouched forests between the Rivers Xingu and Tapajos. They were to join at the airstrip of Cachimbo, which Claudio Villas Boas had built in 1956,

*and one of these roads was to follow the route of the Roncador-Xingu
expedition starting from Aragarcas and passing through Xavantina and
Xingu on its way to Cachimbo. As it would skirt Xingu, it would give the
Parque's land an immediate agricultural and speculative value. It was then
that the Villas Boas brothers expected the State Government of Mato
Grosso, and the many speculators who had bought title deeds to the land of
Xingu, to mount a campaign to destroy the Parque.*

ONE

It was a cold July morning in 1967, and we were in the main hut at Posto
Leonardo waiting for the first radio link-up of the day. Orlando was sitting
on his desk, waking up with a cigarette. He was looking at it with surprised
disgust, as if it had been dropped by a vulture.

The radio crackled. 'Posto Leonardo. Posto Leonardo. Are you being
attacked? Over.'

'Leonardo receiving. Leonardo receiving. Attacked by what? Over.'
Orlando had the microphone in his right hand and as he said 'Over' he blew
smoke at it.

'Posto Leonardo. Posto Leonardo. Request from the President of the
Central Brazil Foundation. Can you confirm you are not being attacked by
Indians? Over.'

'Posto Leonardo confirms to the President of the Foundation that it is not
being attacked by Indians. What codfish is this? Over.'

'The Kayapo have attacked the base of Cachimbo. Over.' (Kayapo is a
generic name covering the group of tribes that includes the Txukahamei.)

'Leonardo calling. Leonardo calling. Not Kayapo. Repeat not Kayapo.
They are here. Over.'

'The Kayapo are besieging the base of Cachimbo. Over.'

'Repeat not Kayapo. Repeat not Kayapo. Perhaps Kreen-Akrore. Over.'

'Calling Leonardo. Calling Leonardo. Who? Over.'

'Kreen-Akrore. K-R-E-E-N-A-K-R-O-R-E.'

A few minutes later the Air Force station in Brasilia came sputtering
through on the loudspeaker. They needed Indian scouts. Could they pick up
Rauni, the Txukahamei, as they rushed reinforcements to Cachimbo.

Orlando was still sitting on his desk in his blue sweater, with an old khaki
cap on his large head. Sipping endless cups of black coffee, he tried to cope
with the situation. Cachimbo was the next base on the chain of airstrips the
Villas Boas had built across the forest to Manaus, and most of the aeroplanes
flying through that day touched down on our landing ground. One plane left
a copy of the Rio de Janeiro daily, *Correio da Manha*, which had the
following stop-press item on its front page: *The Air Force has sent a
squadron of TC fighters to Cachimbo with teams trained in jungle combat.*

Reason: the plane of the Commandant of the 1st Zone on landing there saw about a hundred Indians in a suspicious attitude.

The radio was blaring news. Aircraft and reinforcements seemed to be flying from all over the forest; from Belem, Bananal, Manaus. Brasilia was issuing calming statements to the press.

'I have the impression that the Cachimbo crisis is turning,' proclaimed Nilho Velhoso of the Indian Protection Service at a press conference. 'I don't believe that with so much military might, the Indians would dare another attack.'

The Indians, we learnt later, had not fired an arrow.

Every now and again some department or organisation would come through on the radio requesting information on the crisis. Could Orlando launch an expedition next week? His replies were cautious. But when he put the switch down: 'They are acting like cowboys – as if there are Indians riding round Cachimbo shooting arrows down the chimneys.'

That night, what had seemed not much more than a glorious farce turned suddenly into tragedy. An aeroplane carrying over 20 military personnel, an official of the Indian Protection Service, and an Indian guide to the 'relief' of Cachimbo, sent out a desperate message: 'Total breakdown in radio compass. Petrol almost nil.'

There was a silence for a few minutes. Every radio operator listening in the black emptiness of Amazonia knew exactly what those words meant. Then came the Brazilian SOS.

'Colleagues. SVH SVH. I inform that 2068 is about to crash-land. We are flying without means . . .'

The ensuing air search over the forest between Manaus and Cachimbo went on for twelve days before a tiny fleck of white was located above the sea of jungle. It was a kite flown by one of the five survivors.

In the panic to send reinforcements to Cachimbo, the plane had taken off with its spare radio compass out of order, and the other had broken down. The plane had flown hopelessly off course until its petrol ran out. Twenty men and an aeroplane had been lost. At least $200,000 had been spent on the air search – and it was uncertain whether the Indians had been hostile.

'Shout Indian and the whole world goes crazy,' said Orlando. 'The *civilizados* fly aeroplanes all over the forest. A brigadier is photographed crouched behind a machine gun. And it is just someone like Takuman looking from the trees.'

Takuman, the Kamayura chief, was in the hut with several other Indians. He smiled.

In the ten years that had passed since my first visit to Xingu, there had been tremendous improvements. It had only required dedication, money, organisation and a series of practical measures to reverse the desperate battle against disease and invaders that I had witnessed in the 1950s. Unknown tribes like the Suya and the Txikao had been contacted before the pioneer frontier arrived – in order to shield them from its bullets and disease. The first impact of civilisation had been softened for newly contacted tribes by introducing them to it slowly – by inoculating them both medically and psychologically. Epidemics had been restricted by insisting that visitors arrive at Xingu's posts with government permits; airstrips had been built at every village so that the sick could be flown out to the new hospital at Posto Leonardo; and the medical campaign had gradually become so successful that Xingu had a rising population in the 1960s. The Parque's equipment now included a number of boats and a small tractor and aeroplane. And these, and the two posts of Leonardo and Diauarum, were run by young Indians who could read and write and were training to take over the administration.

I was 33 years old now and had spent the intervening years working for the BBC, ITN and ATV. At the beginning of 1967 we returned to make a film in Xingu called 'The Tribe that Hides from Man'. A Brazilian photographer, Jesco von Puttkamer, helped at the beginning but the main filming was to be done by three of the best documentary cameramen in England, Charles Stewart, Chris Menges, and Ernie Vincze, whilst Richard Stanley, who arrived with his guitar for the last few weeks, got the Kayabi hooked on country and western singing. Claudio had thoughtfully built for us a large airy hut at the post of Diauarum where my wife Pilly and our six year old daughter, Boojie, mainly stayed. And we had a boat and a budget for a year and Sir Lew Grade – who gave us the money – said in reply to a question from a journalist, 'I don't know what they're doing, but it's costing me a fortune' – which has always seemed to me a good approach to film production.

That was more or less the situation of the Parque and the film unit when the Cachimbo crisis broke. The crisis was to launch the last great Villas Boas expedition to open up the then largest remaining unknown area of Amazonia. And for the film unit, it appeared to be an unrivalled opportunity to be present as the spearhead of development entered the forest. ('If you do the film,' Orlando suggested, 'maybe you will be able to tell us what "a spearhead of development" is?')

In fact, the Villas Boas brothers had come across the camps and trails of the Kreen-Akrore as far back as the early 1950s, when they had been building the airstrip at Cachimbo. At the time, they had decided to leave the tribe a few last years of peace, and they were rarely heard of, except in 1961 when they ambushed and killed a young Englishman called Richard Mason who had cut a trail out of Cachimbo in the hope of exploring the River Iriri. Amongst his party were John Hemming, today Director of the Royal Geographical Society, and Kit Lambert who became manager of 'The Who'. In early 1967, however, the government announced that its two new development roads would be built to pass through Cachimbo, and Orlando had immediately warned of the probability of a Kreen-Akrore attack on the road builders and the urgent need to contact and protect the tribe. Though, at first, he was given little attention, the crisis at Cachimbo produced the funds almost instantly. Yet if Orlando had been able to see into the future and to guess at the enormous tragedy ahead, I doubt he would have accepted the mission. Once, on a journey outside the Parque and close to the mouth of the Xingu, I had accompanied the Villas Boas brothers when they had found the last eight members of the Kararao tribe almost paralysed with fear, lying in their hammocks shivering with flu. A dozen had died in the previous fortnight and 80 percent of the tribe had perished in the two years since they had been contacted by the Indian Protection Service. Moving, almost blindly, out of the hut, I heard Orlando mutter, 'It would have been kind to machine-gun them from the start.' The bitter and very similar thought that the Cachimbo expedition was to place in my mind was that even if the extermination of the Kreen-Akrore tribe had been the deliberate goal of our society, an expedition to 'save' the tribe would have been an essential part of the process.

The clouds of the rainy season were already making reconnaissance difficult when we flew to Cachimbo with Claudio. A Cessna aircraft picked us up, and just beyond the Juruna village we turned to the west, flying up the line of the River Huaia as it ran down from the Cachimbo plateau. It was along this route that the unknown Miahao came every year to steal from the Juruna, and Claudio suspected that they might, in fact, be the same people as the Kreen-Akrore.

The land beneath was at first perfectly flat, a green floor smooth to the horizon. But after ten minutes, it began to crumple into formations of little hills, and gradually the whole area fragmented into ranges with brown outcrops of rock stabbing through the forest. There were abrupt valleys, sudden cliffs, a thousand hiding places – a block of completely unexplored jungle lying between the River Xingu and the River Tapajos. This was the empire of the Kreen-Akrore. It formed a rectangle roughly 350 miles wide and 200 miles long, and was probably the largest unknown area on earth at that time. The Kreen-Akrore had always killed all Indians and all *civilizados* who entered it – with the exception of the Villas Boas, who had first crashlanded a plane on the Cachimbo plateau.

After our plane had landed on that airstrip cleared by Claudio ten years before, we taxied up to a stone building with a corrugated iron roof. Concrete pillars, supporting nothing, stood in marshalled rows beside a concrete path giving an air of order in the jungle. There was a little concrete pool at the side of the path and someone had roughly shaped an egret out of wire, painted it with whitewash and popped it into the pool. A few rocks and other objects had escaped the general clearing, but to include them within the overall climate of discipline, someone had painted them with whitewash. There could be little doubt that Cachimbo was an Air Force base.

'If the Indians come again,' said the sergeant in charge, 'I am going to shoot. I have nothing against Indians, but I cannot take the responsibility for the women and children who are here.' There were loaded rifles in every house, and on the sergeant's orders, no one went out unarmed.

'What can Indians do against stone houses with bolted doors?' Claudio asked. 'Arrows can't get through wire-mesh windows and corrugated iron roofs. One loud bang from a gun and they would run.'

One of the men who had been there during the 'attack' took us out and showed us what had happened. A plane coming in for its first approach had radioed that some animal was blocking the runway. As the base had no cattle, someone had been sent to look. An Indian. The sergeant fired into the air, and to his understandable horror, three groups of about 60 Indians in all got up from the low scrub which surrounded the base and ran across the airstrip. The aeroplane, under the command of an Air Force brigadier, promptly dived and howled a few feet above the heads of the terrified runners, and then turned and swooped again. The Indians fled like deer.

Everything indicated that the 'attackers' had approached in peace and unarmed. When the area was searched after the incident, arrows, clubs and bows had been found, left in bundles on the other side of the airstrip. And there were footprints of women and children. No Indian takes his family to war.

'An irretrievable blunder,' Claudio muttered. 'Not so much the shot in the air, but a monster of a plane roaring and diving at them. They must have been terrified. It will put off the contact for years.'

Next morning we flew out of Cachimbo down the southern line of the River Braco Norte where the stream frothed and foamed in a series of rapids over great slabs of red and brown rock. The rainy season was at the stage when huge black clouds parade in columns across the sky, and our plane was forced to twist and weave between the pillars of rain.

At the River Peixoto, we turned up-river, flying east. 'The site,' Claudio said, 'is on the next northern tributary. Perhaps the one after.'

Fifteen years before, Claudio remembered flying over an unknown Indian village in this area, and, from their traditional enemies, the Txukahamei, he also knew a great deal about the Kreen-Akrore. A branch of the Txukahamei tribe that lived outside the Parque, the Mekrenoti, had in fact only recently attacked the Kreen-Akrore. Using shotguns against Kreen-Akrore bows, they killed nearly 20. And when we had flown to the Mekrenoti village with Claudio to investigate, we had seen four wretched Kreen-Akrore children captured during the massacre – human booty, like the many stone axes and rush baskets the victors had brought back. There was also a fascinating knife made of a Kreen-Akrore wooden handle and a tiny fractured piece of steel. The Kreen-Akrore must have captured the blade in an ambush, and then fractured it to provide as many 'knives' as possible. There was also a curious 'necklace' made of shells and tapir's toe-nails that clattered when worn around the waist. Woven into its centre were some blue and red Czecho-slovakian beads that had been brought into Xingu by Claudio. A Kreen-

Akrore had killed a Txukahamei for those beads. Now a Mekrenoti had killed a Kreen-Akrore to get them back – a reminder of the ping-pong futility of tribal war. It was because of this last attack that Claudio believed that the Kreen-Akrore would have retreated to the southern limits of their area as far from the Mekrenoti as possible.

Ten minutes later, we were over the tributary. We turned and followed it to the north, climbing up over rapids, flying into the plateau. Then we turned and flew down the other bank, Claudio hunched by his window. Once we saw smoke, but it turned out to be rain. Then, suddenly, the pilot heeled the plane in from the river and turned towards a distant hill. Gradually we began to make out a faint crease in the forest. Then, with agonising slowness, it grew into a wall of trees, until there was a sudden flash of emerald. In the dark green of the forest, this light green shone like neon.

'Fantastic!' Claudio shouted. 'An astonishing thing.' The plane veered round, and we piled on top of each other, staring out the window. 'Never, never has there been anything like this. The anthropologists will run to see it.'

We were looking down on a smooth, ordered pattern of geometric gardening. There were circles and ellipses, bisected and sub-divided. Even the Parque's relatively sophisticated Indians, using steel axes and machetes, leave ragged holes in the forest when they cut plantations. It is too much trouble to move the trees from where they fall; they scatter their crops between the stumps, and their plantations look disorganised and shabby. What we were looking at now was – for Amazonia – fantastic. We flew backwards and forwards, staring at the sight below. The outer rings consisted of single rows of banana trees, in beautiful curves and circles. The crosses and double avenues were straight lines of maize, looking like paths over lawns of grass. It was as if we had stumbled on a tropical Versailles.

What purpose could the patterns serve? Why bother to remove the fallen trunks and stumps when, with stone axes, it would be a Homeric task?

On a second flight next day, we found an older plantation to the east. Then, almost immediately, there was another, and another, all in the same pattern as the first, each newer and more clearly defined. Finally, we saw one with three abandoned huts in the centre, and then we were over and past. Concealed by a high ridge of trees, we had flown straight across a village. The plane heeled and we swept back. There was the village. A long double path, a ring of half a dozen huts. Some of the figures standing in the square were brown, but most were painted black. Arrow after arrow rose towards us, and at the summit of their flight, turned over gracefully, catching the sun in a golden flicker of light – messages of Indian resistance, glinting and shimmering just beneath the plane.

Claudio said there was no point in searching any further. The Mekrenoti usually attacked from the north and the Txukahamei from the east. The harassing aeroplanes had always come from Cachimbo in the north-west. Claudio intended to approach from the south – the opposite direction.

During two subsequent flights, Claudio dropped presents on the unknown village – knives, aluminium bowls, small rolls of cloth, rubber balls. These were tied to 'parachutes' of coloured balloons, and on our final flight, the Kreen-Akrore responded. Two large fires sent up a double pillar of black smoke as our string of brightly coloured presents plummeted down.

That double pillar of smoke was the first formal communication between the village below and our civilisation. We all looked at it with awe. It was the beginning of an interchange which could now only develop until this vast, untouched area of Cachimbo was cut by roads and divided into ranches.

'Walking naked, sleeping on the ground, cutting with stone, roaming the wilderness, they are happier down there,' Claudio said, 'than they will be for the next hundred years – even if we succeed in saving them from the road, the epidemics and the Mekrenoti.'

TWO

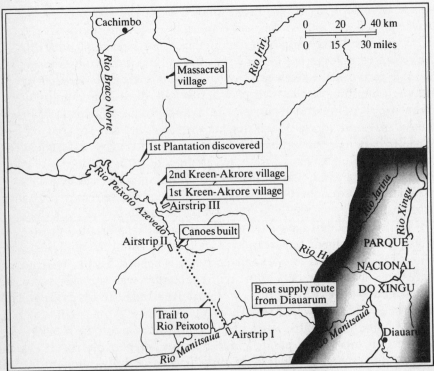

THE KREEN-AKRORE EXPEDITION

Several months later a small party of 20 Indians travelled with Claudio in three boats from the River Xingu up its western tributary, the River Manitsaua-Missu. Ernie Vincze, the cameraman, had flown out to join the expedition for three months; he was unable to get out for six. Whilst, for a

THE SPEARHEAD OF DEVELOPMENT 59

year, I was not to see our son, Xingu. Pilly had been carrying him while she was in the Parque, but as she was having repeated attacks of malaria and was unable to take chloroquin or primaquin while she was pregnant, she had flown back to Ireland.

Two days journey upriver, we built the first of the expedition's three airstrips and began cutting a 60 mile trail across the watershed that divided the Manitsaua-Missu from the River Peixoto Azevedo – the unknown waterway of the Kreen-Akrore. It was to be eight months before we were to emerge, and during this time I was to be led into a deeper and more complex awareness of the forest. Just as hunting with Kaluana had given me a consciousness that I could have acquired no other way, so there is a dimension of jungle that is hard to sense except through the Brazilian technique of approaching an unknown tribe. Initiated by Marshall Rondon at the beginning of the century, and passed on by his officers to the generation of the Villas Boas brothers, and from them to the present generation of Apoena Meirelles (Chapter 3), this tradition probably has no like anywhere else in the world. It is the technique of contacting a people who you cannot speak to, who you never see in the confining fog of forest, and who, almost by instinct in the case of the Kreen-Akrore, kill on sight.

Every day the cutting party pushed the trail forward roughly one kilometre. And in its methodic movement and in the whole strategy of airstrips linked by a trail, the expedition was essentially *civilizado* in nature. Just the appearance of the trail implied something revolutionary in the virgin forest. Our trail slashed through it, gaping at every yard with the yellow wounds of branches, the mauves of sliced lianas, the white sap of the rubber tree which bleeds for hours. An Indian path is less of an intrusion, because the bushes are beaten aside with clubs; our machetes sliced so clean that the track was studded with shoe-height stakes, half-concealed by the debris. Our canvas shoes were stabbed to pieces in a fortnight, and most leather boots were finished in a month.

On the other hand, because we were operating in deep forest and confined by the enveloping vegetation, we were entirely dependent on Indian skills. Wherever we were, one of the expedition's Indians would pause every few minutes to pick a strange sound out of the maze of animal noise. Every track, every broken twig, was examined and assessed. The Indians were the expedition's radar in the forest.

'The monkeys are going down,' Pripuri, one of the Kayabi leaders once whispered to me. 'The monkeys are running on the ground.'

Apparently, another Kayabi had shot some Capuchin monkeys, and the pack had dropped off the trees and escaped through the undergrowth. 'Where the monkeys only know the jaguar, they stay in the trees. But when the monkeys know Indians, they understand his arrows.' Pripuri paused dramatically. 'They drop.'

A day or two later, Pripuri paused at a small sapling bent at waist height. He showed us the definite break in the sapling, and how the top was dropping to the ground. I already knew that no animal except the tapir breaks at this height; but every hunting Indian does, as a matter of course, to mark his trail. Pripuri looked carefully for a tapir's tell-tale tooth marks under the break, and ran his finger up and down to show us that they were not there.

With Cuyabano, another Kayabi, he cast around and discovered a whole line of these broken stems and twigs, moving at a right angle across our trail.

'One man and one boy,' he said, indicating that some of the saplings were broken lower down, at the height of a boy's hand. 'Maybe a month ago.' They could tell by the degree the saplings had dried.

'How do you know it wasn't a Kayabi?' I asked.

'*Civilizados* and Kayabi mark with a knife, Adriano. Truly, the men who walked here were wild Indians.'

And so, from the journey's start, at 60 miles from their village, we and the Kreen-Akrore had begun to feel for each other in the forest. From then on, our party always travelled in convoy, and kept together as much as possible.

'Indians are hunters who kill by surprise,' Claudio said. 'Even when we were outnumbered by 200 Xavantes on the Serra do Roncador, they never charged an alert, well-armed party.' Claudio left presents strung across the cutting head every night; four saucepans, twelve knives, 18 strings of enticingly mauve beads, two strips of cloth.

'Certainly they will refuse them. But presents jolt the mind,' Claudio argued. 'All strangers, according to Kreen-Akrore experience, are enemies. Can a present-giver be an enemy too? It will disturb their psychology, dislocate the reflex to kill.'

It was a similar theory that led Claudio to refuse the Kayabi offer to follow the Kreen-Akrore tracks back to their hunting camp.

'That was the stupidest mistake I ever made – to walk into a Txikao camp. They were all lying in their hammocks under the trees, and not one of them saw me. I was almost up to the hammock of an old man when he opened his eyes. I offered him a red handled machete as a present. And suddenly, what screaming, what running, mothers grabbing children, arrows flying every-where. I would be dead if Cerilo the Kayabi had not been following behind. He fired in the air, and with just that one shot, they were gone. It put the Txikao contact back for eight years.'

For the hundredth time, Claudio laid down the expedition's policy.

'It is a disaster to come upon Indians in the forest. First, they must watch from safety. Then they must have the time to understand. Finally, they must take presents without pressure. And, in the end, the contact must be in an open place, where they are safe and can see. The Juruna would never have held their ground the first time if they had not watched us drop our revolvers in the water.'

As Claudio talked, during those first few weeks on the trail, I began to sense that we were not really manoeuvring with the Kreen-Akrore, but with an imaginary Indian who lived in Claudio's head – a composite Xavante, Juruna, Suya, Txikao – who was somehow materialising on the screen of forest around us. It was Claudio's understanding of this ever-changing image – modified with every action of the Kreen-Akrore – that governed all the steps we took. And it was from this time that the concept of the forest as some sort of a mirror or screen began to return to me in a variety of situations.

Once when we were carrying equipment up the trail from one camp to another, I found an excuse to rest a little longer – the loads were very heavy – by analysing the wall of forest that faced us across the trail. In fact, when looked at closely, 'wall' was a poor description for an infinite variety of leaves in a limitless number of planes. Examining them, I realised that what made vision difficult was not that they formed a wall-like barrier to sight, but that there were infinite variations of light reflecting off an infinite variety of vegetation. The sun was striking through the canopy of branches down into the jungle and occasionally a brilliant shaft hit a leaf facing in my direction, like a mirror aiming the sun into my eyes. An elephant could have stood behind that particular leaf and remained invisible.

On the other hand, in other places there were tunnels through the light and vegetation where it was possible to see for 20 to 30 yards. Over the whole scene, the sunlight ricocheted from one leaf to another, one plane to the next, producing a million variations of brilliance and darkness. For both us and the Kreen-Akrore, this winking screen of forest acted like a porous mirror. In it you never knew whether your gaze would literally or metaphorically penetrate – to reveal the man you sought on the other side – or whether it would be reflected back – mirroring the eyes and, therefore, the motives of the seeker.

Pripuri, the Kayabi, usually swung the lead machete, and every 20 to 30 yards he would pull out the compass that hung around his neck on a nylon cord. His long black hair was topped by a railway man's red cap, and he flourished the compass like a station master's whistle: 340 degrees. Pripuri would line up on a tree and cut towards it.

Claudio followed, hunched and less impressive in a floppy hat and dirty shirt, checking Pripuri's bearings and holding a sack of presents on his shoulder ready for a chance encounter with the Kreen-Akrore. He was followed by Cuyabano, the second Kayabi leader, who widened the trail. Usually, a satchel swung by his side containing a cooked snack of two or three monkeys' heads. A mile behind, a party of a dozen Indians cleaned the cutter's trace into a broad ride along which the supplies of the expedition would flow. And finally, there was the group of four or five who guarded the camp and made up the small convoys that moved the camps from stream to stream. Ernie and I were part of this group beacuse it took half a dozen journeys to move our equipment – camera, recorder, generator, petrol, film, batteries and so on. To reduce the journeys, we made our loads so heavy that we had to get into the haversacks by kneeling on the ground and then heave ourselves up by pulling on the trunk of a tree.

For two months, in dense confining jungle, the trail moved forward at roughly a mile a day. Then, one morning, Pripuri parted the bushes at the cutting head and called out in excitement. Before us was a golden river. The sand was warm and yellow, the water was a soothing green, and a school of fish flicked their tails casually against the current. It was the River Peixoto Azevedo – our first 'view' since the trail had started.

We began our second airstrip close to its southern bank, and almost immediately the Kreen-Akrore approached.

On our second night, Claudio came hurrying back in the dark.

'I was just going out of the camp,' he said, 'when he ran. I know the sound of a tapir or paca. With certainty it was a man. Six or seven steps, then he crouched.'

Next day a message came from the airstrip.

'There is smoke down-river. You must keep at least five in the camp.'

On the third evening, the cooks came running from their sandbank to say that two or three sticks had been thrown at them from across the water.

'Maluware, that's whisky soft-talk,' someone called out to one of the cooks. Maluware was a very civilised Karaja chief from the River Araguaia, who, instead of being jailed for a crime, had been exiled to the Parque. He replied in the dialect of the Araguaia frontier.

'Sirrah, are you not believing that I am receiving sticks in the night?'

Suddenly, we heard club blows coming from across the river. Dark bird shapes, disturbed by the banging, flashed over the water.

'They are approximating,' Maluware whispered.

'It is the classic approach,' Claudio agreed.

Next morning, we crossed to the far bank and looked at the freshly broken branches and the marks where a club had been beaten on a fallen log. Though Claudio's plan had always been to enter the Kreen-Akrore village, the classic technique of the Indian Protection Service was to make a contact at a distance from a village, sometimes as far as 60 miles or more. We were now about 25 miles from the Kreen-Akrore village, and the summons of the clubs could be the opening move.

The next evening, several of the Txukahamei were sitting by the river and a frog was grumbling softly.

Plop. A stick fell into the water.

'What was that?'

'Just a stick,' said Bejai, a Txukahamei who worked with the film unit and helped carry the equipment.

'Where did it come from?'

'Maybe the other side.'

Plop. Plop. Ping. A stone clattered on the pebbles close to me. By now 30 of us had gathered by the river bank, but there was no sound until – rattle, plop. A stone crashed through the branches of the dead tree into the water.

'Don't shine your torches,' Claudio said. 'It may frighten them.' The stones began to come in a spasmodic hail from only 30 yards away. But there was no question of arrows. We all knew that we were watching something like a mime or ritual.

'Don't be careless,' Claudio warned. 'Sometimes a younger one or a stupid mule will shoot on his own.'

Eventually, someone shone a torch on Claudio. Cave-chested and entirely undramatic, he stood up holding an aluminium pan in his hand, and shouted across the water in the Kamayura language.

'Friend,' he called invitingly. 'We are not savage. Come here.'

To this there was no reply. Several of the Kayabi now stood up and shouted in their language; and then Dudiga called in Juruna.

'Bejai, turn on your radio for music.'

A voice suddenly emerged from the air. 'The Pope will be leaving Rome on Thursday . . . Cardinal . . . and Cardinal . . .

The names were indistinguishable, and when Bejai switched off, we found that the pebble-throwers on the other side had lost interest. The throwing had stopped, and there we were, sitting on a sandbank, wondering what it had all been about.

'Perhaps they want us to know that they are not going to attack,' Claudio suggested.

If he was right, it was a remarkably timid act for Indians bred to the internecine warfare of the jungle. We went back to the kitchen, where someone lit the lamp. Then for the next hour we talked about our image of the unknown Indian – about why the Kreen-Akrore had crouched behind their defences for more than a century.

By 1968, the time of our expedition, most of the tribes that remained unknown in Amazonia were probably deliberately hiding from civilisation. Like the Suya, some may have retreated from an attack by other tribes, but most would have fled from a *civilizado* massacre, and this can so dominate the thinking of a tribe that its members will change their way of life and the pattern of their society. For instance, the Urubu and Guaja tribes near the coast appear to have ceased being agricultural societies during the slave-raiding era of the Portuguese and to have broken up into small scavenging groups living off what they could find in the forest.

But, probably the greatest terror in the memory of most tribes is an epidemic. When we had arrived with Orlando and Claudio at the village of the Kararao, the eight survivors of the flu epidemic had been petrified in their hammocks, shivering and sweating, hypnotised by fear, gazing like rabbits at a spectre quite beyond their understanding. If those eight had fled into the forest, they would have carried a group memory of the creeping death that from generation to generation would have been distorted into a nameless haunting evil associated with all strangers.

Something of this sort, I agreed, might explain why the Kreen-Akrore killed all their captives. It could also explain their reluctance to approach. But then why, I asked, the throwing of the stones, and why the banging on the trees?

Claudio shrugged his shoulders and made no direct reply. But one of the strangest features that had always puzzled me in the stories of the Txukahamei tribe was that though most of their tales of civil war ended with the flight of the losing faction, five, sometimes ten years later, the refugees usually returned – often to be clubbed to death by their victorious enemies.

'When Indians can live comfortably anywhere in the forest,' I had asked Rauni, 'why do these people come back when they know they will be killed?'

Indians don't shrug their shoulders. 'Adriano,' Rauni said. 'You ask silly questions.'

Nevertheless, my assumption was that many Indians seem to prefer death to life outside the tribe. From the edge of the forest they watch the gorgeous dances, listen to the magic songs, and one day they can bear it no longer. They step out of the darkness into the light of the village square – to their probable death. Man is a magnet attracting his like, and I felt that this could explain the incident of the stones. In the loneliness of the jungle, the expedition must have had a fascination for the Kreen-Akrore. They had lived for centuries without speaking to any outsider, and here we were, in coloured shirts, raucous with music, bearing presents. As our steel-cut trail stabbed towards them, their village must have become a cockpit of hope, fear and rumour. Its inhabitants must have swung from terror to fascination and back again.

During the coming weeks the airstrip was completed, and Orlando flew in with more Indians from Posto Leonardo. The final party consisted of 36 men including Txukahamei, Kayabi, Trumai, Txikao, Waura and Mehinaku – many of them from tribes that had been contacted by a Villas Boas expedition in the past, and so already aware what a 'contact' was about.

When seven canoes had been burnt and carved out of trees from the forest, all our party and all our supplies were loaded in and we paddled down river.

It was a quiet, secretive waterway. We were high on the headwaters of the Rio Peixoto Azevedo and the stream was barely deep enough for our canoes to pass. Dark walls of jungle formed a narrow gorge, the sky was cut off by a roof of branches, and whole graveyards of fallen trees lay rotting in the water. Often we had to stop and axe our way through. We knew that the Kreen-Akrore never used canoes, and that intruders from the Amazon coming up the Sao Manuel River had always been ambushed at the mouth of the Peixoto Azevedo. It was a possibility that no boat had disturbed this quiet waterway since the beginning of time.

The punt poles dripped and groaned as they bit into the sand. Huge schools of a fish called *matrincha* filed under our hulls, and bicuda shot like torpedoes across the surface, slashing into their victims. Deer, unconcerned, moved occasionally in the shallows, and a tapir once scrambled up a steep bluff.

On the second day, the parties moving down the river bank on either side –

to protect the canoes from ambush – began to find old camps, discarded baskets and broken arrows. And by the fourth day, every sandbank seemed to have its footprint, piece of banana peel, or bunch of timbo lianas for poison fishing. We were in the much-used backyard of the Kreen-Akrore.

By the fifth day, there were so many signs of the Indians that it was obvious we were close.

'That's the tree I marked from the plane,' Claudio stood up in the canoe. 'The village is due east.'

'Are you sure?' Orlando asked.

'It's precisely four kilometres.'

It was one of Claudio's contradictions, that though his memory could be unreliable on other things, he had an astonishing grasp for aerial reconnaissance. Anything seen from the air is, for most people, hard to recognise from the ground. But Claudio was seldom wrong.

To the east, four kilometres away, the Kreen-Akrore village awaited us.

A sandbank backed with a tangle of bamboo made a safe camp-site on the southern shore. The box of presents was unpacked. Mirrors, beads, knives, pans and one symbolic link with the almost weekly gifts which rained down from the sky on the Kreen-Akrore village – a toy aeroplane. Half the party were left to guard the camp, and the rest of us crossed the river and climbed the steep bank. Shotguns and rifles had been left behind, but there were half a dozen revolvers should a warning shot be necessary.

After five dreary months, this was the moment.

Cupionim was in front, cutting the trail. Claudio followed with the compass. Orlando, shirtless, occasionally flicked with a machete to widen the trail, and the rest of us came behind in a long file. It was dark because of the clouds, and the sounds of our movement were muffled by the recent rain. As we advanced, several Kreen-Akrore paths cut across our route, but instead of following them to the village, Claudio went straight over. By arriving from an unexpected direction, he may have hoped for some sort of tactical surprise.

'A cry,' Pripuri halted, pointing to the left. 'First a little cry. It is a boy. Then a big cry. It is his father.'

No other sound followed, and we moved on through a patch of high jungle which was unexpectedly open. Then we came to a stream of clear, amber water running over black leaves, arriving in an area of lower forest. A tree rose above the surrounding jungle, and one of the Kayabi climbed into its highest branches.

'I see no village,' he called softly, 'but the jungle drops.'

Two hours after leaving the river we moved into an old plantation. A tree had been chopped with a stone axe; nuts had been gathered into a pile; some bark was already kneaded into cord. Soon we were passing new mandioca plants and clumps of unripe banana. We were in the garden of the village.

'Give me a pot,' Orlando whispered. 'Pass the mirrors to the front.'

Down the broad Indian trail we advanced, each man holding a present in his hand. Half a dozen logs had been set out as seats under some tall trees, and from here we could just make out a patch of brown banana leaves at the end of the trail.

'The huts.'

A macaw flew off, screaming, and then came back to screech at us again.

'It's tame,' one of the Indians whispered. 'It belongs to the village.'

Orlando's bare belly led the way, forming the spearhead of what must have looked a very odd procession. In his hand he swung an aluminium pot like a thurible, Kretire came next waving a mirror, and Claudio made benedictions with his saucepan.

We came closer, then walked into the village. The doors of the huts faced away from us; it was impossible to tell whether anyone was inside. There were 30 seconds of incredible tension, and then we were crunching over dead leaves that had fallen off the huts. If there had been anyone inside, he would have heard already.

'Look for trails,' Orlando ordered. 'Those without shoes stay where you are.' Bare feet could be confused with Kreen-Akrore footprints.

Kretire, the Txukahamei chief, moved forward. We were on the edge of a rough circle formed by half a dozen huts, and when he reached the centre, he looked round.

'They left running,' he called in a half-whisper. 'But they did not sleep here.'

He pointed to a hole in the ground where a bunch of green bananas had been buried to ripen quickly. The bunch had been freshly dug up, and the lining of green banana leaves had not even begun to dry in the sun.

'With bananas, they run,' Kretire explained succinctly.

'They must have seen us,' Orlando whispered. 'Let's shout in Txikao.' He pointed at the green leaves in the hole and turned to Caraiwa, the Txikao.

'Look, Caraiwa. Look, it was just now. Shout "Venca. Presentes".'

'Venca. Presentes,' Caraiwa shouted, but in Portuguese rather than Txikao.

'Puta merde,' Orlando gasped. 'I know how to shout in Portuguese. But they don't understand it, you mule. Quick, Pripuri, shout Kayabi.'

Pripuri's words rolled away through the jungle. Silence. The words echoed through the trees again. Silence. Later, Kretire showed us the trail down which the bananas had been carried, and Claudio drove two stakes into the ground and hung up a string of gifts on a nylon cord. On another trail, he hung up some more.

Next day, work began on yet another airstrip, and a party stayed behind to protect the camp. About the middle of the afternoon this group suddenly saw three black figures moving across the sand down-river. The Kreen-Akrore walked calmly out of the jungle and stood on the sandbank, 600 yards away. It was a deliberate and frightening confrontation.

Dudiga advanced to the waterline, and shouted in Juruna, waving an axe. There was no response. The Kreen-Akrore stood motionless. Quatara, one of the youngest Kayabi, tried in his language, but his words came out in a nervous whisper.

Across the water on the yellow sandbank, the three black figures stood like a line of Toltec statues. They did not call. They made no gesture. And after a few minutes of tension, they just turned and vanished into the forest.

Kretire sat on the beach looking after them.

'Now they are watching from the jungle,' he said. 'Tomorrow they will come with many men.'

They returned, in fact, two nights later, though unseen by us. The party that checked the village was electrified to find the presents gone.

'Forty-eight knives,' Claudio shouted to those behind. 'And all the little pots.'

Kretire and Pripuri began picking up burnt faggots of wood. 'They came using these as torches,' was Orlando's explanation, but he decided they must have stayed until daylight. 'See the pan they dropped on the path. They ran when they heard us coming.'

All the plastic dolls and most of the mirrors had been broken, and Pripuri suggested that the Kreen-Akrore associated them with witchcraft. The few unbroken mirrors were turned face downwards on the ground, so a passing Kreen-Akrore could not see himself in the glass. But nearly everything else had gone, and, most important of all, the Kreen-Akrore had left four of their clubs for us. They had accepted our gifts, and then had left presents of friendship in return. It was a momentous act. Between their tribe and the rest of the world, it was the first diplomatic exchange.

'This is the beginning,' said Orlando, examining the clubs. 'A contact in three days. That's not impossible.'

He picked up one of the clubs, which was beautifully carved with a blade-like shape at the end. But the other three were just rough staves, with a heavy root forming a kind of hitting knobble like Xavante clubs.

Next morning, Orlando decided to press our advantage. We crossed a log bridge over a small stream and then followed the well-beaten route down which the Kreen-Akrore had fled with the presents. The forest was sodden after a night of rain, and when we glimpsed the dark brown banana leaves ahead, we moved forward gingerly. Four huts. But they were deserted.

The trail crossed the tangled thorn scrub of an old plantation, and on a bough jutting out like a dead finger above our heads we could see the black silhouette of a bird.

'It's a gralha,' Orlando whispered. 'It will cry.'

It did, despite our efforts to tread softly; its harsh, cackling voice carried for miles across the forest. In the next patch of high trees, Pripuri smelt the embers of a fire. Yesterday, he said. Then we found another village of several huts under the trees, and began to realise that the Kreen-Akrore did not have a permanent village, but a number of temporary ones. Their huts were so simple that they could be put up in an hour.

'Every plantation, every hunting place, will have its village,' Orlando said. 'They must move from one to the other.'

The path cut across an overgrown plantation, and we seemed to be on the edge of a major clearing. It was an area of tall, almost park-like trees, and they were decorated with a whole series of animal carvings. In the thick bark, a stone axe had cut the blunt outlines of a tortoise, a deer, a snake, a monkey, a man. We were staring at them, fascinated, when Pripuri pulled Orlando's arm.

'A cry,' he said softly. 'A cry across the village.'

'What will they do?'

Kretire, near by, mimed a club falling. But Claudio and Orlando moved forward. The bushes parted on to an open space about 100 yards in diameter. We advanced into the circle of huts, waving our presents as we had done before. But this time it was like arriving at a picnic after the bull had chased the picnickers away. We saw huge baskets of mandioca, banana, potato. Clubs, bows and stone axes were strewn around. Sleeping mats on the ground still held the dents made by human forms, and there was cotton woven round a woman's spindle. It looked as if the tribe had just jumped to its feet and fled.

Checking the fires, Pripuri said that they had been out for some time, certainly since dawn. The Kreen-Akrore were probably moving deeper into the forest, and had carried out their first loads in the early hours. We had interrupted as they had come back for second loads, and the cry we had heard was probably a scout warning those behind.

We strung up the presents, and left some aluminium pots in the huts. But as we left the village and returned to camp, we knew that the situation had changed. It was only too obvious that now that we had stood in the warm and living home of the Kreen-Akrore, there was no further goal to seek. If they had not welcomed or fought us in their village, they were unlikely to confront us anywhere else. It was obvious that for every step we were taking forward, the Kreen-Akrore had begun to take a step back.

Two months before, when the stones were thrown into the River Peixoto, we had been able to argue that the shyness of the Kreen-Akrore was nothing more than caution. But during our five days' journey on the river, they had been safe and within shouting distance, yet no call had come. Three Kreen-Akrore had stood on a sandbank only 600 yards from our camp; not a word or gesture. Finally, when we had advanced to their first village, they had retreated to the second. And when we advanced to the second, they had retreated again.

The pattern could no longer be ignored, and Claudio said that any further pressure might drive them to the other end of the forest.

We walked back to camp knowing that the positive, direct approach had failed, and that there was now no alternative to the more passive technique practised by the Indian Protection Service. If we could not go to the Kreen-Akrore, then we must attract them to us. And that meant sitting in a place where the Indians could watch us, month in, month out. Only gradually, as they saw that we meant no harm, would their fears subside.

∽⚬∽

Rain is the temper, or the black mood of the jungle. And as we waited, rain either pounded on the roofs of our camp or wrapped us in a grey drizzle. We breathed, we ate, we moved in water. Storms and the passing of storms marked the time of our waiting.

The little stream near the camp had been a foot wide and three inches deep in October, and only a tadpole could have swum in it. By December, it had become a torrent ten yards wide, two yards deep, rushing so fast that anyone who tried to swim was swept away like driftwood. Hundreds of miles of forest were already underwater, and the whole character of the land had visibly begun to change. The animals had gone to higher ground, few birds sang, and it was the *pintado* and the *trairao* – leopards of the water – that hunted under the trees.

As the rain fell, so the Kreen-Akrore watched. Late at night Claudio would rake the loose earth on the airstrip, and next morning there would be footprints, fresh on the dew. A new green arrow was found dug into the ground.

'They were beating the trees.' Pripuri came running up one day. 'They were there, beyond the bridge.'

'What have you done about it, Pripuri?'

'I have withdrawn myself, running.'

So it went, round and round, but without any physical contact, and therefore without any sense of reality. And the rain wore away at our patience, like some spectre of Amazonia, reaching for our minds and health. In the padded cell of the forest, the very claustrophobia of the rain seemed to turn us increasingly back into our minds towards the deep misgivings that lurked there. During the expedition we had been constantly staring across the frontier at the unknown man lurking behind it, and possibly because of the hypnotic tension of the process, I had increasingly come to feel that what lay between us was a two sided screen onto which we both threw our image of the other. Now, as the rain and mass of vegetation pressed on our eyes and spirits, the more I gazed at this screen, the less it showed of the Kreen-Akrore and the more often it became a cruel, sombre mirror of our own motives and interests.

And so it was that during this time, I came to a very bleak assessment of the expedition. In one sense, the objective of our mission was so clearly worthwhile that there was a tendency to look at it uncritically. Unless we reached the Kreen-Akrore before the road, they would be finished by bullets and disease. But if the Villas Boas managed to get to them first, they could be protected from the road, trained to accept inoculations and medicines, and helped during the approaching years of shock and dislocation.

So obvious was all this that one tended to regard the prospectors and the road-builders as the dark force of evil. It was only when you met the prospectors and the rubber tappers who actually did the shooting, that you realised they were humble men driven by necessity to the forest, and they shot from little more than ignorance and fear. Behind them were 15 million near-starving people in the north-east of Brazil, and the government argued that it could not ignore their desperation in the interests of a few hundred Kreen-Akrore.

It was this that led me to reflect that the same government that paid for the Parque's budget, also paid for the road that would later cut off half the Parque; that the department that guaranteed the Indians' land, in some cases, shared the same building as the department that lent money to 'develop' Indian land. And that if international charitable foundations supplemented the low budget of the Villas Boas, so the financial empires which created these foundations provided the market that sent the developers to the forest. In some ways, the killing and the 'saving' were linked, and our expedition was an inevitable part of the process. Ever since the first Europeans came to the Americas, there have always been *civilizados* who were genuine friends of the Indians, men like Las Casas and Rondon, fighting to protect them. Yet the Indians have died at an appalling rate. The idealism of Rondon's group of officers cannot be doubted. But in the cruel light of history, was not the bloodless acquisition of Indian land the final result of their heroism? Once, when I asked Rauni what the Txukahamei would do if they found a small tribe of white men living in the forest, he had said: 'Kill all the men and marry all the women.'

What the rain, and our situation, now placed in my mind was that we too followed this simple evolutionary technique, but the principles that bound our society together made it hard to speak of it with the honesty of Rauni. After all, how could the government crusade to develop the forest of Cachimbo in order to feed the poor, if this meant killing even poorer Kreen-Akrore? And could a world civilisation, expanding across the globe to draw all men into a universal brotherhood, acknowledge that its by-product was the slaughter of Indians? Perhaps it was the unconscious solution of our race to proceed with the ruthlessness of all evolution, but also to send other *civilizados* to work against it – yet never in time, with enough men or enough resources, to make any difference.

This was a much bleaker view of the situation than I'd had at the end of my first visit to Xingu. At that time, I had regarded the Villas Boas brothers as crusaders for a lost cause, but lost because of practical deficiencies such as money, doctors and the lack of legally defined boundaries for Xingu. Now they had all that, or at least much of it, and though the expedition had not contacted the Kreen-Akrore, it had obviously been conducted with skill and success by a combination of Indians and Brazilians working towards a jointly accepted common goal. And yet that was clearly not enough. We all sensed, in our bones, that the Kreen-Akrore were doomed. And why they were doomed was because our civilisation, intent on its current understanding of development, would make no allowances for the forest people that stood in its path.

During the 1980s, a similar situation often confronted the environmental groups campaigning against unsound development projects in Brazil. 'Okay,' the government or the World Bank would say, 'Tell us what to do. Tell us how we can go ahead with the project and also protect the forest and its people.' In the case of the BR364 road (in Chapter 3), the obvious palliatives were money for Indian reserves and a variety of biological and national parks. In the case of Acre (in Chapter 6), the argument was mostly over indigenous colonies and the final compromise was largely over extractive reserves for rubber tappers. In the case of the Kreen-Akrore, what the Villas Boas had asked for were the resources to contact and protect the Indians in advance. In each case, quite genuinely altruistic people were forced to choose between having no influence on what was being planned, and therefore extracting no environmental benefits from it, or compromising with the machinery of development, which meant that they were only mitigating a harmful process which, in principle, they should have fought to stop.

During those months of waiting in the forest, the only course that seemed to be genuinely capable of improving the situation for the Kreen-Akrore was to change the world – and in 1969 that was as depressing a conclusion as anyone could make. That one day environmental lobbyists would quite coolly set out to do that – to force the World Bank to change its, and the world's, economic attitude towards Amazonia and the Third World – was, in the 1960s, something that was unimaginable. All this is obviously an extreme presentation of only one side of the Kreen-Akrore case. But in the light of what followed, it is by no means unfair.

In January 1969, the expedition budget ran out, the Indian Foundation said it had no more money and the whole party was withdrawn to the Parque. No money was forthcoming for another three years, by which time the new development road was about to reach Cachimbo and hordes of prospectors were pulling tons of gold out of the River Peixoto. In 1972, Claudio and another party of Indians from the Parque were then given resources to fly back to the airstrip, and within a few months the Kreen-Akrore called to them across the river. Contact, and peaceful contact, was at last made. But almost immediately the reason became apparent. The Kreen-Akrore were starving. They had contracted an epidemic of flu – probably from contact with some of the prospectors – and half the tribe had died and the rest had been too weak to plant. They had abandoned centuries of isolation because they were desperate for food.

Unfortunately, this first official contact attracted so much publicity that the principal opponent of the Villas Boas brothers, General Bandeira de Mello, resented the support it gave them. He was the military government's head of the Indian agency, FUNAI, and he immediately transferred them – making it manifest that they had been used and manipulated just to make the road possible. A number of less experienced Indian officers rapidly succeeded one another, and the Kreen-Akrore were soon to be seen standing on the road stopping trucks, begging and selling their women as prostitutes. Epidemic after epidemic racked the tribe until the 500 Kreen-Akrore who probably existed when we first entered their village in 1968 were reduced to 79. Finally, with the tribe approaching extinction, a new head of FUNAI permitted the Villas Boas to fly the shattered remnant into the Parque, where adequate food and medical treatment halted the decline.

Today the vast area of forest that belonged to the Kreen-Akrore is largely populated by the cattle of ranchers and land speculators. The River Peixoto Azevedo has been the scene of several enormous gold strikes and the prospector/colonist towns of Matupa and Peixoto de Azevedo stand close beside the river. The huge base of Cachimbo is sealed off as a military zone for testing rockets, and, many newspaper articles have suggested, also for underground nuclear explosions. A satellite photograph of this part of Amazonia in August 1987 showed the greatest conflagration ever recorded, with 6800 foci of fire under a massive pall of smoke. And today, not a single Indian makes a camp-fire or plants corn in what for centuries was the vast and virgin hunting ground of the Kreen-Akrore. If he still wanted it, I could now answer Orlando's question. The spearhead of development had, of course, been us.

What I did not realise at the time was that the hopelessness and despera-tion of such situations are the spurs of evolution – and that this evolution was already taking place inside the Parque Nacional do Xingu.

THREE

One morning in the spring of 1967, I was at the Parque's northern base, the Post of Diauarum, when a canoe slid into the landing place with the news that the Kamayura tribe were to visit Diauarum. The post was a score of thatch huts standing on a bluff above the River Xingu, so I was able to watch the waves of panic, literally, rippling out with the canoes across the river to the surrounding villages.

Living in the 'Pax Romana' of the government maintained Parque, it was easy for visitors like myself to forget that for centuries the valley of Upper Xingu had been a cauldron of invading tribes. Most had arrived withdraw-ing from the advancing whiteman. But where tribe met tribe, they ambushed, fought and massacred. And many of these massacres had been the result of a visit like the one we were about to witness. What was more, the Kamayura – who were now coming to visit us – had, a dozen years before, asked to inspect the guns of some visiting Juruna so that the rest of the Kamayura could club their weaponless visitors. Now the remaining Juruna lived in a village near the post of Diauarum. And this was the first time the Kamayura had been down-river since.

The only person at the post of Diauarum who seemed unconcerned was Claudio.

'It's what the Parque is about,' he said, swinging in his hammock. 'When we first came here, it was a struggle to keep the Indians alive, fighting epidemics, trying to defend their land. But that's over for the time being.'

Claudio brooded on this for several swings of his hammock.

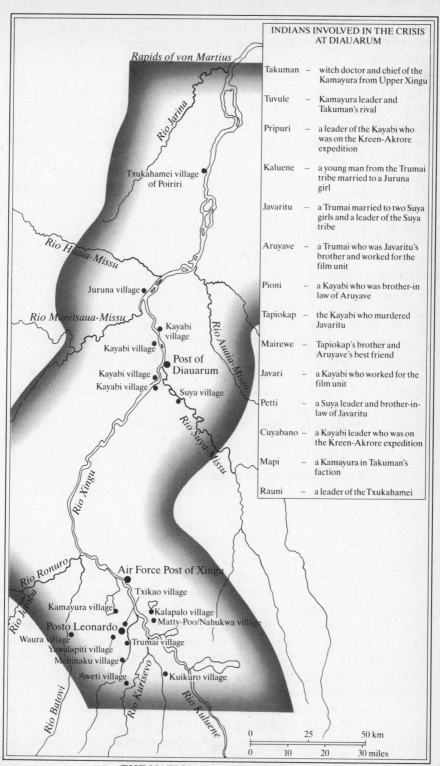

Rapids of von Martius

Rio Jarina

Txukahamei village of Poiriri

Rio Hauia-Missu

Juruna village

Rio Manitsaua-Missu

Kayabi village

Rio Auaia-Missu

Kayabi village

Post of Diauarum

Kayabi village

Kayabi village

Suya village

Rio Suya-Missu

Rio Ronuro

Rio Xingu

Rio Idobu

Air Force Post of Xingu

Txikao village

Kamayura village

Kalapalo village

Posto Leonardo

Matty-Poo/Nahukwa village

Waura village

Trumai village

Yawalapiti village

Mehinaku village

Aweti village

Kuikuro village

Rio Batovi

Rio Kurisevo

Rio Kuluene

INDIANS INVOLVED IN THE CRISIS AT DIAUARUM	
Takuman	witch doctor and chief of the Kamayura from Upper Xingu
Tuvule	Kamayura leader and Takuman's rival
Pripuri	a leader of the Kayabi who was on the Kreen-Akrore expedition
Kaluene	a young man from the Trumai tribe married to a Juruna girl
Javaritu	a Trumai married to two Suya girls and a leader of the Suya tribe
Aruyave	a Trumai who was Javaritu's brother and worked for the film unit
Pioni	a Kayabi who was brother-in law of Aruyave
Tapiokap	the Kayabi who murdered Javaritu
Mairewe	Tapiokap's brother and Aruyave's best friend
Javari	a Kayabi who worked for the film unit
Petti	a Suya leader and brother-in-law of Javaritu
Cuyabano	a Kayabi leader who was on the Kreen-Akrore expedition
Mapi	a Kamayura in Takuman's faction
Rauni	a leader of the Txukahamei

0   25   50 km
0 10 20 30 miles

THE NATIONAL PARK OF XINGU

'Should we keep them in a zoo? Of course not. The Indian must adapt to civilization. But the disturbing thing about civilization is not the atom bomb or the computer. It is the *civilizado* himself. One man alone can destroy a tribe's self-confidence. Unconsciously, he can shatter its confidence.'

He said that this was especially true of the down-river tribes. They had hidden in the forest, and had barely met any strangers until they made friends with either him or his brother. The first task was to teach them to adjust to other people, and obviously it was easier for them to adjust to Indians before they tried to adjust to *civilizados*.

'Of course, it's good that the Kamayura should come,' Claudio ended. 'They are more self-assured and sophisticated, and the meeting could be valuable.'

Two days later a flash appeared on the southern arm of the river. Canoes lie low in the water and are hard to see, but the moisture on a paddle catches the sun like a mirror. Everyone in the post drifted down to watch flash after flash coming down the river. Gradually, we made out several tiny dots that seemed to appear and disappear beneath the water. Eventually they grew bigger and steadier and resolved themselves into three canoes. They crept down the far bank, swung along the contour of the flooded sandbank, then caught the current to sweep across the river and onto the landing place.

Half a dozen men and a few women and children got out. There were packages of food and hammocks, and bows and arrows. It was a typical visiting party, except that the Kamayura themselves were strikingly different from the people of lower Xingu. They wore their hair cut rather like helmets, and they were naked except for bands of cord around their calves and biceps. (In Xingu, it was the Indians with the longest experience of civilization who did not wear clothes, and the most recently contacted tribes that showed visible evidence of *civilizado* influence.) As the Kamayura stepped out of their canoes, they looked lithe, alert, and much more assured than the Indians who were with us on the shore.

'Have you come?' one of the Post's Indians asked.

'I have come,' Takuman, the Kamayura leader, answered. He then walked up the slope to Claudio's hut.

After a few minutes Claudio came out and allotted the visitors a hut.

Thus began the chain of events that was to shatter years of Claudio's work and to bring the Parque to one of its bitterest moments. The paradox of Xingu was that it needed a crusader's determination to hold off the predators of civilisation long enough to give the Indians time to adapt; at the same time, it demanded a self-defeating gentleness of touch to help the Indians adapt without crushing them. How can you attempt to 'save' the Indian, if one of the things you have to save him from is himself?

'How can the Indian be saved?' Claudio would sometimes say to visitors. 'Animals can be saved from extinction because they are content to remain animals. But all humans recognise improvement, and desire the advantages of other men. As soon as there's a shop near here, the Kayabi will load their canoes with mandioca flour and paddle up river. After twenty trips they will buy an outboard motor and make their business more efficient. You will see, it will be the Indians themselves who will break the isolation of the Parque, who will destroy their tribal society. In this cultural sense, how can the Indian be saved from extinction?'

This was the ideological impasse – how to save without destroying – from which the brothers were never to find an outlet. But the confrontation produced such a ferment of ideas in both them and the Indians that the evolution of a new Xingu was already under way.

Next morning we watched the Kamayura scrape away at the weeds and leaves in the middle of the Post. In Upper Xingu, the centre of the village or post is smooth from the continual movement of dancing feet. But on the lower part of the river, the Indians are less preoccupied with ceremonial, and the centre of Diauarum was undanced and very much overgrown.

The Kamayura scraped for several hours until a large area was smooth and clean. Then they began to paint each other with the bright red of *urucu* and the black of the forest dye, *jenipapo*. They painted strong, aggressive designs across their bodies and faces. Walking to and fro, the other Indians pretended not to be too interested.

Suddenly a Kamayura leant forward, staff in hand, chanting in a sombre voice. He stood in the middle of the cleared patch in the centre of the Post, and crouching, flailed the air with a shack-shack. Before him, another Kamayura pounded a thick bamboo pipe on the cleared and beaten ground. And swooping and dancing, leaping and pirouetting, the Kamayura began to rush in and out with leaves on their arms whirling like birds. They yelped and shrieked in joy. But anyone could see that their faces were impassive beneath the paint.

The air is so clear in the middle of the rainy season that it seems to shine like crystal, and the oiled paints on the Kamayura gleamed and flashed in the sun. Their skirts of straw swirled, their feathers waved and shone. The other Indians watched, and there was an occasional rumble of thunder from the rain clouds building up across the river. The chanting grew deeper, the dance more fervent. Something like a bright and formal happiness had begun to gyrate above the black earth in the centre of the Post. Then, finally, the batch of clouds came up overhead, the rain poured down, and the Kamayura stopped to drink the porridge-like liquid which is part of the ritual of the Tawarawana dance. Takuman the chief had been one of the dancers, and he came over and sat down beside me. He had been very friendly during my first visit to Xingu, and now he seemed to be asking for some sort of support in return.

'We have come to talk about that Tuvule.' His face looked sombre. 'When I sit in my village square, all the Kamayura sit at the other end. When I live in the village, they all go and live in the plantations. That Tuvule makes my life sad. So I have come to say to Claudio "Let Tuvule be chief. I will go and live with my brother in law at the Yawalapiti village."'

Takuman's huge shoulders were accentuated by a wrestler's sash of coloured cotton, and his face was armoured by two bars of black paint across the eyes and cheeks. His appearance did not seem to fit the resignation in his words.

'Claudio says to me, "Takuman, you are a great chief. Your father was a great chief. Why are you frightened of a young man?"' The painted snake leapt angrily across Takuman's muscles. '"Claudio," I say, "I am not frightened. I have talked hard to this Tuvule. Do not kill the otter," I say, "Orlando says the otter must not be killed." But Tuvule laughs and lives in the village, pointing and talking about me. All his men have .22 rifles and .38 revolvers. And we have none.' Takuman was talking about Orlando's efforts to save the great river otter of Amazonia from extermination – efforts that were frustrated by the workers at the Air Force base in the Parque, who offered the Indians a gun for every skin, and then smuggled them out. Takuman's point was that he was losing influence by supporting Orlando.

'All Tuvule's men have guns,' he added bitterly. 'And now Tuvule says they will let the otter live.'

That night I told Claudio what Takuman had said and asked if he would take sides.

'Of course it's a temptation,' he snapped. 'To interfere is always a temptation. But we must not. Between *civilizados* and Indians, yes – to correct the balance. But between Indians, interfering ends by crushing.'

Incensed by the idea, he leant forward in his hammock.

'You know that Takuman's father was chief. But do you know that Tuvule's father was one of the greatest chiefs? So his line is purer, and perhaps he will win. What right have I to interfere, just because Takuman is our man?'

Three figures swayed out of the darkness at the other end of the hut, moving to a strange, rhythmic honking, ponderous but also surprisingly gay.

'The lord and owner of rituals, that is a chief,' Claudio said. 'Takuman made those pipes and he is the best pipe-maker in Xingu. But he cannot punish, he has no power, and what authority there is in the village lies with the head of each hut. The chief is just the head-man with most influence. But when we come to a tribe, we *civilizados*, what do we look for? We look for an important man to be the channel of our business. So, of course, we make him more important in the eyes of the tribe, and eventually he becomes just that – a chief. But in the nature of Indian society, it is not so. And in the long run, our interference harms.'

We sipped at tin mugs of Brazilian cane spirit, cachaca, and sat there half the night, listening to the sound of the four-foot, laughing pipes. Most *civilizados* find Indian music monotonous, but Claudio was deeply stirred.

'What magnificence. How beautiful.' His hammock swung with enthusiasm. 'I have been here 20 years, and I have never heard Jacui like this.'

Jacui is the spirit who lives beneath the water, and his pipes are usually sad and sometimes mocking. The pipes may never be seen by women, and that was why the Kamayura were dancing up and down in the concealment of Claudio's hut.

'I told you the Kamayura are a mystic, devious people,' Claudio said. 'That is why I know Takuman has not come about Tuvule.'

When I awoke next morning the Kamayura were, once again, whooping in the dance. They had danced all the previous day and had then piped all night. Now they were dancing again. The whole thing suddenly began to seem to me to be too gay, too incessant and too feverish.

In his cleared space at the centre of the Post, Takuman had become a ring master. On the black earth of Diauarum he was conjuring up a humming-bird world of light and rhythm, and wherever they were, whatever they were doing, the other Indians were hypnotised by his spinning, coloured magic.

Every day in the weeks that followed the tension rose and fell, growing and relaxing according to the clouds in the sky. Early in the morning we would watch these clouds pile up in a great rampart across the other side of the river. Then the water would turn from pewter to slate grey, and as the sky pressed down, the terrific heat became almost unbearable. The 'Eiffel Tower' of Diauarum, a raised platform with half a dozen petrol drums that provided the Post with water, would make exploding noises as the air in the drums expanded. Gradually, the clouds edged across the river. The water turned jet black and the air became so hot that it seemed as solid as glass. Then, a streak of silver lightning, a rush of black waves, the banana leaves clattering like rattles in the wind, and the clouds would lunge across. The rain would pour down, the dancers run, and the pressure drop.

The Indians from the other tribes would paddle in from the surrounding villages, watch, move away, and then return to look again. They seemed fascinated and yet uneasy. The Juruna had lost virtually all their men during their last visit to the Kamayura village. The Suya had been enemies of the Kamayura for almost a century, and in 1960 the up-river Trumai tribe had fled to Diauarum because the Kamayura were about to kill them in vengeance for witchcraft. Even the Kayabi had had a man murdered on a sandbank early in the 1950s.

Pripuri, the Kayabi leader who went on the Kreen-Akrore expedition, was standing near me one day when Takuman stopped dancing and came to watch beside us. After a long pause he said to me, but loud enough for Pripuri to hear: 'Pripuri is a friend. When we are canoeing down the river, Pripuri calls to us, "Come here. Rest in my house."'

Takuman smiled reflectively. 'He gives banana and mandioca and potato, and we rest. But we also know that my enemy Tuvule sent a message to Pripuri to kill me.' Takuman paused for emphasis. 'So we are happy Pripuri is our friend.'

Takuman went back to the dance and Pripuri stood almost rooted to the ground. Claudio said he was the best leader in his tribe, and that he had been one of his right-hand men in building up the Parque. But Takuman, the Kamayura, came from a more subtle and intricate culture, and we could almost watch him playing with the Indians of Lower Xingu like a snake with a rabbit.

'That relative of yours, a few years ago,' I asked Pripuri.

'Was it Takuman who killed him?'

'Not Takuman,' Pripuri replied. 'A relative of his.'

As the days grew hotter and the dancing more intense, the atmosphere seemed Neapolitan with intrigue. The Kamayura had asked to visit the Juruna village. But the Juruna had refused because Takuman was a witch-doctor. Then Pripuri paid Takuman to witch away Diauarum's vampire bats. Recently they had slaughtered all the Post's chickens.

One day, Kaluene, the strongest of the Trumai men, began to put on his paint, and not long after, the whole Trumai tribe was dancing in the cleared space with the Kamayura. The Trumai were the tribe that had fled to Diauarum to escape the Kamayura, and it was Takuman's father who was said to have been killed by Trumai witch-doctors. Yet in the short time since the beginning of the visit, several Trumai girls had yielded to Kamayura wooing, and the two old witch-doctors of the tribe had succumbed to Takuman's flattery. Only they, Takuman told them, truly remembered the ancient legends; they would be much appreciated in their true and ancient home up-river.

The Trumai put on their wings of leaves and their skirts of rushes and danced with the Kamayura. They whooped and chanted, since Tawarawana was really their dance and their spirit. They had originally brought him from the east, and had taught his dance to the other Indians of Upper Xingu. Now these last descendants of a tribe that numbered only 20, the guardians of an ancient language like no other in South America, were dancing with their declared enemies. They stamped on the black earth of the post, black from the refuse and blood and buried bones of countless ancient villages before them. The last had been that of the Suya tribe, until one night the Txukahamei had rushed out of the surrounding forest and clubbed most of them to death.

Claudio came out of his hut to watch in the battering sunlight. He was stooping, and he looked worried. If the friendship of the dance could become a friendship of reality . . .

The only Trumai not there was the witch-doctor's son. He was ill, lying all day in the gloom of his hut crippled with, I think, paralytic arthritis. Indians tend to conceal the sick, much as we hide a corpse. His limbs were wasted into sticks, joined unnaturally by knobs at the knees and elbows, and his father would say: 'Every day I have to go out fishing because I have no son to fish.'

He called his son ugly and unbeautiful, and we knew that Claudio was watchful in case the father's resentment reached the stage where he might kill. If the Trumai left the village and went up-river, Claudio could not watch so closely.

Across the river, the temper of the clouds was rising, and as the heat beat its way into the body and rose to the eyes, the tension seemed to grow alive within each person. There was Takuman, his face visored in black, his body painted like a leopard. Once the greatest wrestler, now the greatest witch-doctor. What did he seek in this dancing myth?

There was Kaluene, the strongest of the Trumai who could out-wrestle Takuman. He had two Juruna wives, and stole and beat his women. With arms like wings, he looked happy, floating on the music. The Trumai girls danced with their hair completely covering their faces, and with little rush tails sticking up behind. One of them had a pale skin; she had been kept from the light of day in the traditional six months seclusion of puberty.

The river was like a sheet of plate-glass, so polished that the sun seemed to skate across its surface. The light was so vivid that the Kamayura shone like coloured fire. Everyone was turning and gazing at the clouds, waiting for that first moment when the rain would pour down – an expected but unpredictable release. The tension of all the sky would sheet down into one narrow column of rain. It would drop here, or two miles away. Why? Why, for years, did the chickens increase, until suddenly the vampires massacred them? Why was this Indian struck by magic and that tribe wiped out by disease?

At the time, I explained all the tension as nothing more than imagination stimulated by the unknown. The arrival of the Kamayura had released Indian fears inherited from thousands of years of jungle fighting. But since then I have begun to suspect that we were watching something as close to the ancient pattern of war and festival as I would ever see. And what makes an Indian war hard to understand is our concept of absolute hostility. To the Xinguano, war is a sport, with trophies for the victor. They spy on an enemy for years, then attack and kill, capture and marry his women. Even when the arrows are flying there is a game-like intimacy between the opponents, and they shout each other's names, learnt from captives or spying on the enemy. Often the periods of war are interrupted by periods of festival when the enemies dance in each other's villages.

In the great isolation of Amazonia, where hundreds of miles of forest insulate the tribes from each other, war is one human group reaching out to another in the excitement of death. The excitement is increased when you walk in paint and music through the ranks of your enemy. You blaze in colour, vibrate to music, tingle with the imminent possibility of death. And, of course, many of the dances, like the spear-hurling Javari, are merely a sublimation of battle.

War is a communion with other men. So is a festival. And so Takuman danced. And so the Trumai were hypnotised, and danced, too. Until a few days later a distant whoop came floating across the roof of the forest.

'Suya!' the Indians shouted. 'Suya! Suya!'

The Kamayura had asked to visit the Suya village. Now, everyone said, the Suya were coming to Diauarum to forestall that visit. Takuman was a witch-doctor, and one of the limitations of Xingu magic is that the witch-doctor's packet of medicine actually has to be placed in the village to be witched. Whoop after whoop travelled faintly over the mile of forest between the tributary Suya-Missu and the main arm of the Xingu. Eventually nine canoes debouched into the main river, paddling fast. One Suya, painted red and black, stood up in the canoe waving his hand to blow the rain clouds away; the others whooped and whooped while they paddled, racing to beat the rain.

As they came into the shore, we saw that Javaritu was seated in the bow of the first canoe, cross-legged and red with *urucu*. He was a trusted henchman and ally of Claudio's, reliable, watchful, a man of obvious moral strength. If Kaluene could be called the Achilles of the Trumai tribe, Javaritu was the Suya's Ulysses. He had married two Suya girls, and though as a Trumai and an outsider he could never be their chief, everyone knew that he virtually carried the group by his sense and steadiness. Javaritu stepped out of the canoe, and soon his deep voice was chanting the Tawarawana, and the Suya were dancing with him. Thus on the bright *civilizado* stage of the post, there were now five tribes – the Kamayura, Trumai and Suya swirling in the dance, the Kayabi and Juruna watching. The sun beat down. The dust rose above the oil drums on the water tower.

Claudio turned to me. 'For fifty years,' he said, 'the Suya hid on their river. From all Indians, all *civilizados*. When we contacted them, they were so disturbed that they stopped planting. Do you realise what that means? For thousands of years the Suya had planted mandioca – it is the basis of their existence. Then we come, and it takes two seasons to teach them to start planting again. That is how cataclysmic was their meeting with strangers, how important it is that they should learn to associate with other tribes.'

That night the Post shook to a new dance, one that was part of the Feast of the Dead. Chanting in deep, rhythmic voices, the Indians moved from hut to hut, round and round the Post. Not only the Kamayura, but also the Trumai and Suya, who had fought in Upper Xingu and had partly absorbed its culture. And the Juruna and the Kayabi, too, who had no part in that culture at all.

It was a remarkable crumbling of tribal barriers, a merging of isolated and hostile peoples. In the face of the approaching whiteman, it was their inter-tribal hostility that was the Indians' greatest weakness. Now the five tribes danced together from the hut of one tribe to the hut of another, as sheets of lightning flickered in the distance.

So it had been in the last days of the buffalo on the Great Plains to the north. Desperate, pressed by the whiteman, the prairie tribes of America had been drawn by the Ghost dance into a common and increasing friendship. For those prairie Indians, the innovation had come too late. For the tribes of the Xingu, we all hoped that it would come in time.

Indians sometimes dance for a week or even longer, but there are always one or two who slip away to catch fish or fetch mandioca. Amongst those who set out in their canoes next morning were Javaritu, the Trumai who lived with the Suya, and Tapiokap the Kayabi.

In the middle of the afternoon, a low wailing began to ebb and flow across the post, and when we asked what was the matter, we were told that it came from the wives of Javaritu. They were crying because he had not come back. And no one has ever explained why the wives should have been alarmed so early. It was as if everyone seemed to be aware that the mounting pressure of the storm had at last discharged its lightning.

Next day Javaritu's brother strapped on his revolver. Aruyave lived with us in the 'film hut' and looked after the film unit's outboard motors and generator. He picked up a .22 rifle and took our boat up to the Suya village saying that if his brother's canoe had sunk, he would be waiting on the bank, and if Javaritu had gone back to the village, he would be glad of a tow.

Aruyave returned that night. He had seen nothing except a cloud of vultures circling over a sector of the forest.

Claudio called us to his hut and tried to persuade Aruyave that it was more likely that his brother had broken a leg, or had been wounded by a snake or jaguar. He was probably lying helpless in the jungle, and Claudio promised that he would send all the canoes next day, and they would find him. Aruyave and the other Trumai did not argue. They just said that Kaluene, who had left on the same day for the Juruna village, was also dead.

By the next night Claudio was beginning to face a situation approaching hysteria amongst the Trumai. Whenever I went to see him, there were always two or three dark figures in a corner of the hut, and Claudio would be talking to them, his white shirt looking ghostly in the darkness.

'Javaritu was Claudio's friend,' one of the Trumai said. 'But we are weak and other tribes are more important. Claudio will let them kill us.'

Aruyave had gone to where the vultures were hovering and had found only a dead tapir. But still the state of panic grew. Then news arrived that Kaluene, the other missing Trumai, was indeed dead; he had gone to the Juruna village on the morning Javaritu went fishing, and after beating his wife, had tried to seduce a girl in the plantation. A young Juruna boy who was a relative of the girl had hit from behind with a branch and had then clubbed him to death. It was a terrible end but an expected one. Several Indians had told us that only Claudio's intervention over the last few months had kept Kaluene from being murdered. But the rumour that came with the news was that the killer had a new .22 rifle, and there was no one else who could have brought it down river except the Kamayura.

Almost immediately the Kamayura left Diauarum, paddling their three canoes swiftly up-river. That night, shot after shot exploded in the dark.

'Who is it?'

'It's Aruyave, the brother of Javaritu.'

'What's he shooting at?'

'He is shooting at the night.'

During the next few days the little group of Trumai swung from anger to fear and back again. But the only one who seemed likely to act was Aruyave, and he was only 18. Whether the killing of Kaluene had or had not been deliberately provoked, the Trumai had lost their two most effective men. And the sick young chief spoke for all of them when he said: 'We will go upstream. Why should we hide? We will go to our old village and the Kamayura will kill us. We will die in our home.'

Claudio countered by talking calmly and confidently. The Trumai were safe while he was there; an attack on the Post was unthinkable. In any case, there was no definite news to indicate that Javaritu had been murdered. As always, Claudio faced the situation quietly. When he was not talking to the Indians, he would be playing with one of their children. And on the occasions when he left his hut he seemed to move absent-mindedly, like an ageing academic. Was it possible that this spectacled, very gentle recluse could really contain the crisis?

That his methods had kept the Trumai under control was shown a few days later. Claudio was needed for a more urgent crisis in another part of the Parque, and a plane had come to take him to Posto Leonardo. Immediately he had gone, most of the Kayabi went back to their village. That night, the tension in the Post seemed greater than usual. The crickets whined, the frogs croaked, no one appeared to be asleep.

Then Javari, the second of the two Indians who lived and worked with us, told Aruyave that he knew where his brother, Javaritu, was buried. The tension was explained. Apparently the murderer had talked, and the leader of his tribe, the Kayabi, had chosen Javari to pass on the information. Next morning the old Trumai witch-doctor paddled off in his canoe and later reported to Aruyave: 'It is a small grave. They have cut off the head and the arms and the legs.'

That afternoon, a crowd packed into the radio hut at the time of the daily link-up with the Posto Leonardo. Aruyave shouted into the microphone: 'I am going to get the body.'

'Aruyave, do you hear me?' Claudio's voice was distorted in the speaker. 'You must take Cuyabano or Pripuri.' They were Claudio's most trusted men in the Kayabi tribe. He must have hoped they would guarantee the Trumai's safety.

'I will not take one of the tribe that killed him,' Aruyave replied

'That's an order, Aruyave!'

Aruyave's heavy Trumai face became heavier. 'That is not an order I will obey.'

Claudio had virtually brought up Aruyave since he had been orphaned as a boy, and had great personal authority.

'Aruyave, do you hear me,' he repeated. 'I order you to obey.'

'I do not obey.'

The speaker sputtered as Claudio switched off, 100 miles away, and everyone filed out of the hut.

Next morning, the black earth of a grave was fresh outside the Trumai hut, a deep round hole extended at the bottom so that a body could lie facing east. We assembled by the landing place, and I saw that all the Trumai had guns.

But if it was meant to be a war party, then it was a tragic sight. Here was the entire fighting power of the great Trumai tribe who, a century before, had poured into Xingu like a horde of Attila. At that time, they had four or five villages. Now their battle strength consisted of Aruyave, two feeble old witch-doctors, a ten year old boy, Diauarum's cook, and another man who was in his thirties but a bit simple. There were two outsiders; one was a Juruna who had married a Trumai girl and was thus related to the dead man's wives. The other was Petti, a Suya, who, also through the wives, was the dead man's brother-in-law. Aruyave was the only effective man beside the two outsiders.

I had been asked to go, and so had Aurore, a French anthropologist working in Diauarum. Aurore because she worked with the Trumai, and I because Aruyave worked with me. Respecting Claudio's principles, we could not interfere, but at least we would be there to show our sorrow. Years before, Javaritu had been my guide on a month-long trip to the River Batovi, and he had remained a reliable, understanding friend ever since.

Javari, who worked with us, was the only member of the Kayabi tribe that had committed the murder. He had been invited because he had given the news. But I wondered whether he had done this out of friendship, or because the leaders of the Kayabi had asked him to do so – and if the latter was the reason, was it because of some plan, which, like the motives of the murder, I did not understand?

We got into the boat and, using the outboard, towed two smaller canoes up the Xingu. On the right bank of the River Suya-Missu we transferred to the two canoes we had been towing, and soon arrived at a lake filled with a sea of green and yellow grass. Then we paddled in white fields of *aguape*, as graceful as lily leaves, curving like the fingers of a Siamese dancer. It is from these leaves that the Indians distil their crystalline salt.

We skirted an area of dry land, and suddenly there was a canoe ahead. As we approached, we saw that it was half-full of water. There were bright patches where bullets had splintered chips of wood from the side. The old witch-doctor pointed.

'They shot him here. He ran there.' He knew from the tracks and broken rushes he had examined the day before. I could not understand Trumai, but Javari, who was sitting beside me in the canoe, quietly repeated the version he had heard from the Kayabi.

'This was the fishing place of Javaritu, the murdered. He came from over there.' Javari pointed to a gap in the rushes. 'Tapiokap the murderer is in a canoe over there, and calls "Stop. Stop. Come and talk to me." But Javaritu has fear and paddles away. "I must catch fish for my nephew," he says. "Pah", Tapiokap raised his .22. "Pah. Pah," he shoots two bullets in Javaritu's back. Javaritu falls and the canoe turns into the water. Over there Javaritu stands with the water around his stomach. "Why do you do this?" he calls. Tapiokap fires two more, here and here.' Javari pointed at his chest. 'Then the bullets are finished and Tapiokap takes a shotgun. Javaritu calls on Pripuri. He calls on Cuyabano. He calls on all the Kayabi, his friends.'

This was the worst part of the story – the thought of Javaritu begging for his life in the shallow swamp. Unlike most Indians, he usually never asked for anything, not even a fish-hook.

'Javaritu calls,' Javari went on, 'but Tapiokap shoots here,' indicating his throat. 'And the water swallows him.'

This account differed from the old Trumai witch-doctor's. In his version there appeared to have been two attackers, and apparently Javaritu fired back. But whatever the details, Javaritu had been shot down without mercy.

One of the Trumai started to wail a moaning chant. The Suya brother-in-law sobbed. Aruyave, the brother, bent to his knees and bowed his head. All the others were silent. Then Aruyave and the cook, the only close relatives, began to dig beside some mauve flowers in a patch of jungle that was very bright with sunlight. When the loosened earth released a smell of decay, the other Trumai turned and sat in the canoes. Aruyave continued scraping softly with his hoe, answering questions that were called up to him.

'Is the head still there?'

'It has not been cut.'

'Are the arms off?'

'The arms are here.'

'Is there flesh?'

'The flesh is here.'

Apparently it was the possibility of mutilation that had most disturbed the Trumai. Reassured, the two witch-doctors paddled away in one of the canoes, and Aruyave continued slowly performing his last duty to his brother. Soon he would be torn between the tribal obligation of revenge and the *civilizado* principle of compassion. It therefore seemed incredible that at this moment he should remember one of Claudio's lessons. He came over to me.

'Is it dangerous to touch?' he asked.

'No, Aruyave. But you should wash afterwards.'

He went back to the grave and gently covered the body, now black with moisture. He came over to me again.

'Can you give me .20 bore cartridges? I want to make a present to my brother-in-law. I have always liked the Suya. Now I hate the Kayabi and like the Suya more.'

The men of the Suya tribe, with their large lip-discs, can appear brutal or frightening at a distance; but they have very gentle eyes and charming, child-like faces. Petti, the brother-in-law, was standing a few yards away, much more noticeably upset than anyone else, even more than Aruyave, whose face was heavy and did not show much expression. The murdered man was not even a blood relative of Petti's, but Javaritu's commonsense had helped and guided the Suya through the most difficult years of their early contact with civilisation. Like children, the Suya felt helpless and deprived by his death. Tears were running down Petti's face.

The body was wrapped in a red hammock and laid in a canoe. Aruyave got in, and paddled away through the trees and across the expanse of rushes. His voice rose in a strange, wailing chant that was one of the most tragic and beautiful sounds I have ever heard. An Indian song of mourning is emotion finding instant release, a wild and spontaneous sound which can never be repeated afterwards. Aruyave poured out his sorrow as he paddled his brother's body through the waves of rushes and past the nodding flowers of the *aguape*. His song flowed and flowed. It was a spilling tragedy, like the release of blood.

Claudio returned to Diauarum a few days later and he talked night after night, session after session, with Tapiokap, the murderer. Afterwards he would call us for a drink, and occasionally his frustration showed.

'All Tapiokap says is, "It was just so, Claudio. In the lake I talked to Javaritu. Then I went and killed him. Just so, Claudio."'

'But that is ugly, man. Is there no better reason?'

'No, I am like that.'

'But that is beast-like, Tapiokap.'

'Claudio, such I am. I am just like that.'

At these times Claudio would appear at his most controlled and rational. He said that most Indians were quite open about what we regard as their weaker or more evil motives. 'If he's a coward, he just says, "I was frightened. I ran away." Or if she's killed a child, she just says, "I did not want it. I buried it." The Indian is a more natural man,' Claudio repeated more than once. 'And we have to remind ourselves of it. He behaves according to his nature, without limit.'

It seemed as if Claudio was restating his theories to remind himself that they were the truth, and that no amount of disappointment could modify that truth.

Could it have been as meaningless as that? A psychopathic killer roaming the forest, excited by the dancing and tension?

The summer of Xingu is a time of dry days and desert nights, and during this period nothing changed. The rain drained off, leaving the sandbanks clean and yellow, and the duck flew in, calling happily, as if trying to make us forget the tragedy. All the sandspits seemed to have their pairs of jaribou storks standing about in neatly married couples, and even anacondas were easier to see as the water fell and the pools grew clearer. It was at this time that my family, Boojie and Pilly, flew in to join us. And for three months Pilly carried our unborn son – the son I was not to see for a year – as we travelled the crystalline rivers of Upper Xingu, visiting village after village for festival after festival.

Towards the end of the dry season, there is a week of light showers which ripen the fruit of the Caju. And it was in this gentle time of the Cajuinha that a Kamayura canoe came down the river carrying one of Takuman's more rebellious henchmen called Mapi. He stepped out of his canoe wearing a cast-off Air Force uniform, white gym shoes, and a light blue forage cap.

'A bad element,' Claudio muttered as we watched. 'Always intriguing and hanging around the Air Force Post.'

But Mapi proved to be an effective emissary. After months of vacillation the Trumai tribe agreed to abandon the Post and travel up-river to join the Kamayura.

'It's not the Trumai the Kamayura want,' Claudio grumbled, 'but the women. Four beautiful girls, and they are short of women. Takuman will probably have one. She's the daughter of a Kamayura and was promised long ago.'

And so the Trumai were about to break up as a tribe. The three young men, including Aruyave, were married to Suya women and would have to stay in Diauarum. The girls would go up-river to marry Kamayura. And that would leave two old men, two boys, an old woman and a cripple to continue the ceremonies of the tribe.

'Why does the young chief agree? Even if he is a cripple.'

'He says, "I am going to die. I leave it to my father."'

'Why does the witch-doctor agree when the Kamayura once threatened to kill him?'

'He's a vain old fool. They tell him he is the only one who knows the legends.'

If I had not already learnt something of the strange magnetism that links an Indian to his enemy, it would have been a baffling decision.

A few days later, Claudio stood on the black mud bank of the Post and watched the frustration of years of work for the Trumai. He was lending a canoe. He had given bullets, fishing-line and other supplies. But it was a bitter moment.

The break-up of a tribe does not necessarily imply the death of its members, but it does mean the end of a culture. And an Indian's vitality is connected with his understanding of himself through that culture. He works and lives, hunts, marries and dances because his ancestors did so before, because his children will do so after. He can live in someone else's village, but, like colonial government, it degrades a man and saps his vitality. For 25 years one of the main features of Claudio's work had been the prevention of the very thing that was about to happen.

The Kamayura and Trumai loaded themselves into three canoes. With his head shaved like a Buddhist monk, the crippled young chief sat propped between them.

'Goodbye.' His face was wry with suffering. 'Maybe Tapiokap is roaring, waiting for us in the middle of the way.'

In the weeks that followed, Aruyave, the murdered man's brother, occasionally walked about the Post with his .38 strapped to his waist. And one day Tapiokap arrived, as if daring his avenger to kill. Shouting and struggling, Tapiokap had to be rushed off to one end of the Post before

Aruyave could get his gun from his hut. It was like a scene from an Italian opera. But it led to a killing – and a killing that threatened the Parque's future. In Javaritu, Claudio had lost a man who worked within the Suya tribe, so it had been the tribe, rather than the administration of the Parque, that was the loser. But Aruyave was one of the three boys who had been virtually adopted by the Villas Boas and who now ran all the day-to-day administration of the Parque. Everyone hoped that eventually they would become the leaders of some sort of modernised Indian society.

These three boys were Aruyave, Mairewe, and Pioni. Pioni was a Kayabi who was married to Aruyave's sister, and so he was not only Aruyave's brother-in-law but also the murdered Javaritu's. This gave him an obligation to kill Tapiokap in vengeance. But even worse, a vicious stroke of fate had made the last of the trio the brother of the murderer, Tapiokap. Mairewe was about 20 years old and Aruyave's closest friend. But by tribal custom, if Aruyave or Pioni executed Tapiokap, then Mairewe would be equally obliged to kill them.

And so Claudio went on talking in his hut, week after week. He had deliberately educated the three boys, Mairewe, Pioni and Aruyave, so that they were not divorced from the Indians they were being trained to administer. Thus, though one part of their minds agreed that it was tragic to kill a fellow Indian, another part reacted in a typically tribal way. A relative's obligation is the elimination of the murderer, and this is essential to the whole pattern of interlocking duties which forms a tribe's culture.

Claudio, for once, seemed very tempted to interfere; possibly he was thinking of removing the murderer, Tapiokap, from the situation by force. For he kept saying: 'Interfere? Certainly not. It's the temptation of all civilizados. You see the approaching disaster, and by a swift act of surgery you think you can save the Indian from himself. Then, of course, it's not the Indian who recognises the problem and finds its solution. And the next time the problem appears, he is no further towards solving it. They become the passive morons of civilisation, waiting for decisions to be taken on their behalf. Amazonia is full of them – witless, detribalised, remnants of a once vital people.'

At the end of the summer we flew out of the Parque with Orlando and Claudio to spend six weeks on a government expedition near the mouth of the Xingu. When we got back, the murderer, Tapiokap, was dead.

'My people are sad,' began the Kayabi who told us. 'Pioni has killed the brother of himself.' (Tapiokap and Pioni were members of the same Kayabi group.) 'Pioni took a canoe across the river, and he took a mosquito net to the village. "Look," he says, "Claudio has left a net, but it is too small for me." So he gives it to the brother of himself. "Come," that Pioni says. "We will go to the Post and I will arrange ammunition for you." On the way, he shoots, then cuts the stomach so the body will lie under the water where no one can see it.'

On Claudio's order, Pioni and Aruyave were now at Posto Leonardo, and Mairewe, the brother of Tapiokap, was 100 miles away at Diauarum.

Every day we would hear the killer and his potential avenger talking to each other in the emasculated language of the radio.

'Diauarum calling Leonardo. Diauarum calling Leonardo.'

'Leonardo replying. Leonardo replying. All well here. All well. Do you need a doctor? What about supplies?'

The subject that chained them like prisoners to each other was never mentioned.

Once Claudio flew Pioni down for a few hours and asked Mairewe to talk to him in a hut. They wept and embraced and said that they came from the same grandfather. But Claudio kept them apart, and he still went on talking and talking to the other Kayabi.

'That Tapiokap was mad. Just look what lunacy he did among the Kayabi. He killed the father of . . .' (I didn't catch the name.) 'Was it with an axe?'

'It was an axe.'

'There, you see, you are lucky to be without him. And now Pioni is sad. He is a Kayabi but he cannot talk to the Kayabi. He wants to come to Diauarum, but he cannot pass amongst his relatives. Surely the Kayabi should not kill him?'

Sitting in the dark, I wondered if this time Claudio would succeed, if this would be the occasion when the chain of revenge and counter-revenge would be broken by the Indians themselves. With such justice on the side of Pioni, with so much intelligence in the mind of Mairewe . . .

The rest of the tragedy soon revealed itself in Upper Xingu. All the Trumai girls had been married off, and though at first the old witch-doctors were honoured guests at the Kamayura village, gradually their hosts forgot to bring even their daily fish and mandioca. The two old men made their way over to the Post of Leonardo, where they built a hut and lived for a few years, a small fragment of a tribe waiting to pass into extinction.

'Takuman, look at the Trumai,' Claudio reproached, when we flew to Leonardo after the expedition. 'They have no plantation, they have no house. They are no longer a family, and you say you called them upriver to save them from Tapiokap.'

Takuman, the Kamayura chief, was wily enough to reverse Claudio's own arguments.

'Claudio, I am an Indian,' he said calmly. 'Don't talk to me like a *civilizado*.'

But of course he did, and so increasingly did the other Indians. For they were already adapting to the needs of survival in our rapidly encroaching civilisation.

Looking back, it seems to me that what we had been watching was one of the moments of great trauma that lead up to evolutionary change. Claudio had encouraged the Kamayura to come down river because, like everyone else, he was conscious of Xingu's need for unity in the face of the approaching frontier. But after decades of attrition between the Upper and Lower Xingu tribes, it was very difficult to see how the Indians could achieve that unity. Over the previous one or two centuries, however, the Upper

Xinguanos had, in fact, produced a common culture amongst their eight originally hostile tribes, and I have come to believe that Takuman's visit to Diauarum was an initial, tentative step in a similar bonding process between Upper and Lower Xingu. After decades of fear and hatred, the Kamayura formally travelled down river to visit the Lower Xinguanos, and though we all saw at once the enormous upheaval that this caused, it was only much more gradually that its more positive results emerged.

In 1973, the Villas Boas brothers retired to live in Sao Paulo, Claudio an exhausted, nearly shattered man. He and Orlando were then succeeded as administrators of the Parque by a number of anthropologists who criticised aspects of their policy. Later, when the administrators were Indians, some of them also spoke out against the paternalism of the Villas Boas. Whatever the rights and wrongs, it now seems – with the benefit of hindsight – that the details of policy in Xingu were much less important than the general climate which made possible the gradual coming together of the tribes – the social cohesion and unity which eventually helped the Xinguanos to fight their battles for themselves under common leaders. In the 1970s, these involved a whole series of demonstrations and political actions in the capital, Brasilia. But their greatest victory was probably in August 1980 when the Txuka-hamei, led by Rauni, but supported by all the Xinguanos, won back the northern part of the Parque that had been cut off in 1971.

Until that time, the ranchers who had acquired this part of the Txuka-hamei's traditional territory, had cut down the forest with impunity. But in 1980, Rauni warned a chain-saw gang that if they went on cutting Txuka-hamei forest, they would be killed. When the warning was ignored, he gathered together a large party of Txukahamei, and painted black and carrying warclubs, and supported by the Suya, Juruna and Kayabi, they killed eleven workers. Obviously any reprisal by the ranchers would have been murder. But Indians were then legally minors and not considered responsible for a crime. So, though the controversy held the headlines for a week, Rauni's threat to continue killing anyone cutting down Txukahamei forest produced an impasse. Cutting teams, understandably, became un-available. Eventually the government indemnified the ranchers and returned much of the northern part of the Parque to the Indians.

Until then, I had always looked at the destruction of Amazonia from a *civilizado*'s self-centered point of view: the forest was being destroyed by the process of development, so it was that process and its *civilizado* proponents that would have to change if the Amazon forest was to survive. It didn't occur to me that the forest – or at least its human occupants – could themselves evolve, so that they might unite and face the threat of the frontier by offering an alternative way of handling the forest more attractive to our world than that of the developers.

As far as I know, the Parque do Xingu was the first society of forest peoples in Amazonia to confront the frontier by struggling toward its own unity, and then to use that unity to become a political force acting in its own interests. And the Xinguanos were to be so successful in the 1970s that their example was to be one of the inspirations behind the formation, in 1980, of Brazil's Indian Federation – the Uniao das Nacoes Indigenas.

'The success of Xingu', says Ailton Krenak, UNI's leader, 'created an umbrella under which the weaker Brazilian tribes were able to come together and to grow. Xingu formed a temperature that produced the rain which created the large plantation in which UNI was born. Now UNI has national and regional offices across the country and when Xingu is attacked, UNI and all the other tribes help Xingu.'

In 1980, few people believed that the scattered tribes of Brazil, which had seldom shown any significant unity in the previous centuries, could develop into a genuinely cohesive force. Many, therefore, dismissed the Union of Indian Nations as a public relations front – the ideal face that the Indian would like to present to the nation of Brazil, but one contrary to his ancient separatist traditions. Yet again, however, the necessity of the frontier was to turn a shell built out of great need into a functioning political organisation.

It is significant that when the *seringueiros* were later struggling towards their own similar 'birth' as a political force, Ailton Krenak was to be one of the people who helped them.

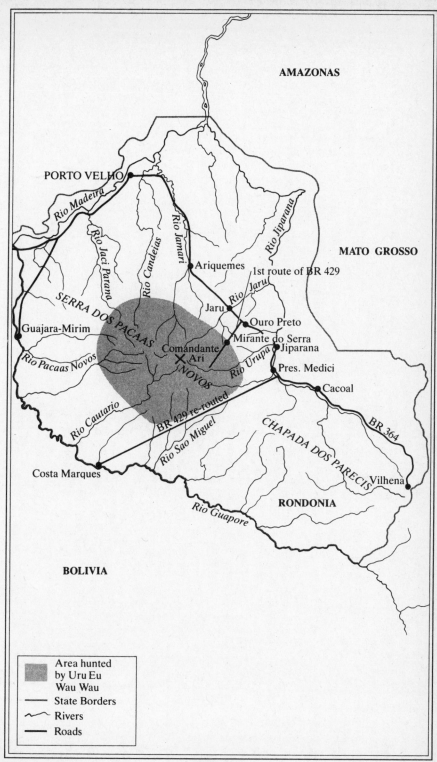

AMAZONAS

PORTO VELHO

Rio Madeira

Rio Jaci Parana

Rio Candeias

Rio Jamari

MATO GROSSO

SERRA DOS PACAAS

Ariquemes

1st route of BR 429

Rio Jaru

Jaru

Ouro Preto

Guajara-Mirim

Mirante do Serra

Rio Pacaas Novos

Comandante Ari

NOVOS

Jiparana

Rio Urupa

Pres. Medici

Cacoal

Rio Cautario

BR 429 re-routed

Rio Sao Miguel

CHAPADA DOS PARECIS

BR 364

Costa Marques

Vilhena

Rio Guapore

RONDONIA

BOLIVIA

	Area hunted by Uru Eu Wau Wau
	State Borders
	Rivers
	Roads

RONDONIA

three

THE FRONTIER ARRIVES

RONDONIA
1980–4

During the 1970s, the whole pace of Amazonian development increased. At the beginning of the decade, the two development roads in the centre of the basin joined up at Cachimbo and went through to the southern side of the River Amazon, opening up the north of Mato Grosso and the west of Para. Of these two, the BRo80 cut the northern part of the Parque do Xingu in 1971, and the part north and east of the road was divided into lots and sold to ranchers and speculators. The frontier had arrived and the battle over the integrity of the Parque had been lost.

At roughly the same time, the military President, General Medici, visited drought victims in the barren North-East of Brazil and in an emotional speech he made what seems to have been an unpremeditated, or at least unresearched, promise to help the landless poor. Only ten days later, in June 1970, it was announced that the Trans-Amazon highway would be driven from the North-East of Brazil westwards across the Amazon basin to the frontier of Peru. It would be accompanied by what was called the National Integration Programme. This would open up 'a peopleless land for a landless people,' settling 100,000 colonist families over five years with an ultimate goal of one million. This road and colonisation programme were to be the forerunners of the great development projects of the 1980s, and, from the beginning, there seems to have been hardly a pretence at checking whether the land was suitable, the colonists adaptable, or the scheme in any way viable. By the end of 1974, only 5717 families had been settled, of the projected 100,000, and of these, 17 percent had already abandoned their land. And so, in the middle of the decade, the government changed its stance, once again giving greater emphasis to large ranches as a means of developing the forest.

Over the next few years the ranching programme proved to be an even greater debacle. Of the 94 subsidised ranches later studied in a government survey, only three were regarded as in any way economically viable. The report calculated that the government had lost $40 million in unreclaimable tax incentives, and that a third of the pasture was already degraded or returning to secondary forest. And so, at the end of the decade of the '70s, the yo-yo of Amazonian policy swung once more back to colonisation projects.

The biggest of these was located in the Western Amazon in what were reputed to be the better soils of the State of Rondonia. It was called the Polonoroeste project – the north-west pole project – and was budgeted at one and a half billion dollars, of which nearly half a billion was to come from a massive World Bank loan. But in addition, there was a $60 billion development project based on minerals in the Eastern Amazon, half a dozen enormous dams were in various stages of construction, a quarter of a million freelance prospectors were ransacking the forest from one end to the other, and land speculation was rife all over Amazonia. At the end of the 1970s, it looked as if the Amazon forest could well disappear with the twentieth century.

And so it was that, in January 1980, we launched our project to film a whole decade in Amazonia – 'The Decade of Destruction.' It was to be a co-production with the Catholic University of Goias who would distribute the films in Brazil.

ONE

'The two were lying there stuck with arrows. Shot down in the shallows, with arrows sticking out of them in every direction.' Chico brushed a tear away with the back of his hand.

'"My sons," I said when I went hunting. "Go to the river and clean the fish." And so I had gone, taking the shotgun with me. Now I know the Indians must have been lying there, on the edge of the forest, watching – waiting for me to go so the boys would be unarmed.' The tears were pouring down Chico Prestes's face.

'Half an hour later, when I came back to the clearing, there were tracks everywhere – barefoot ones. My God, there was chaos in the hut. Everything gone. I shouted my sons' names, "Luis! Dimes! Fabio!" And then I heard a faint, tired voice. I ran to the river bank. And there they lay, in the shallow water, full of arrows.'

Chico Prestes had the broad, sturdy build of the modern Amazonian frontiersman. But as he sat, surrounded by his neighbours, he looked caved in on himself as though hollowed out by tragedy.

It was January, 1980, and we were in the frontier town of Ariquemes in the State of Rondonia. The government land agency, INCRA, was here giving landless families free blocks of forest of between 50 to 100 hectares as part of the great Polonoroeste development project. But though INCRA had surveyed and marked out Chico's plot, they had not told him that FUNAI had 'interdicted' the region – that the government's own Indian Agency had officially declared it the territory of an unknown and warlike tribe. It was, as I discovered, a tragedy typical of the 1980s – a government department hurling colonists quite blindly to disaster.

'Luis, my eldest, was lying on the ground,' Chico went on. 'And I could see leaves in his mouth when he said, "Father, the Indians shot us," and then, "I am going to die."'

'"Nonsense," I said. "Have faith in God." And after I looked around, "Where is your brother? Little Fabio."'

'"Father, Father," he said. "He was there on the sandbank fishing. When we ran, he must have stayed there."'

'So I ran to the sandbank, shouting, "Fabio. Fabio." There was nothing. Just silence. And then I saw tracks. Prints of three Indians running on the sand. They were running, and then they came back. They must have been carrying him because they went straight to the forest.'

'"They have taken my son," I cried. "My poor little creature, they have taken him."' The tears welled out of Chico's eyes and he seemed to collapse further in on himself. 'So I stayed there without knowing what to do. All alone, except for God, and my two wounded sons.' The paralysis that had overwhelmed Chico appeared to halt him again so that he could hardly speak.

'Fabinho will be seven years old in February,' said Chico's wife, Raimunda. She was broadly built, and gave the impression of being more capable of dealing with the situation than Chico. 'But Fabio is strong, and maybe he will survive – even though he is living with beasts.'

'I pulled one arrow from Luis,' Chico continued, 'and then tried to pull the other.'

'"Father, don't pull," Luis groaned. "I can't stand it." Then he said, "I will tell you how it happened. Ten minutes after you left, we were cleaning the fish when we heard a sound behind our backs. We thought it was you returning. Still kneeling, we looked around. And there behind, it was black with Indians, 25 to 30 all with bows drawn."'

The Uru Eu Wau Wau tribe – or the Urupa, Arara, or Black Mouths, as they were known in different areas – was then probably the largest of the unknown groups remaining in Amazonia, estimated at that time at somewhere between 500 and 1000 Indians. They had been locked in incessant conflict with the rubber tappers of Rondonia for over 70 years, raiding down the rivers that flow out of the Serra dos Pacaas Novos. It was they who had kept this vast block of forest out of the hands of the developers.

'As the poor boys ran,' Chico went on, 'the Indians shot them down. Dimes later told me that even with his face lying in the water he could still see one Indian with a head-dress – the chief. When he spoke only one came forward for the service.' Chico hesitated, nervously again, 'The service to dispatch them in the water. He chopped Dimes on the neck with a machete and Luis as well. Then they went to get the little one.'

'The cut,' Raimunda, his mother, said, 'was through to the bone. When you looked, you could see the bone. The doctor said another half centimetre and it would have cut the vein in his neck.'

'The Indians had taken my bag and Luis's,' Chico said, 'but they had only thrown the cartridges and pills of medicine on the ground. So I collected the cartridges in the hut and went back to the river calling for Fabinho. Saying to myself, "What am I going to do? What am I going to do?" and calling "Fabinho. Fabinho." Running up and down like a madman with the gun in my hand, wondering what to do. Then I remembered the boat and brought it up. The eldest, he crawled to it and fell within the boat. Then, the younger, I carried to the front. Two hours later my son Luis, my oldest, died. And so I paddled on alone, with one dead and one alive, until I arrived at the first colonist house. It was they who helped me get to the road and bring Dimes by car to the hospital here.'

Both the hospital and Chico's home were in the rapidly growing town of Ariquemes, which is located on the River Jamari 70 kilometres below Chico's plot. And at the time of our arrival, the town was seething with stories of Uru Eu Wau Wau cruelty and cunning.

Survivors of other Indian attacks had reported that the leader was a bald Brazilian (Indians don't go bald) and looked like a North-easterner from the coastal state of Ceara. And so widespread were these rumours of a white chief that they had attracted the attention of Brazil's military intelligence. The Servico Nacional de Informacoes wanted to send two officers into the area because it was close to the border of Bolivia where Che Guevara had crossed to start his ill-fated guerrilla campaign. Could the Uru Eu Wau Wau attacks, the intelligence officers wanted to know, be the cover for a secret Communist base serving both Bolivia and Brazil?

It was in this bizarre climate that the Indian Agency, FUNAI, launched its 30 man Uru Eu Wau Wau expedition. The date was January 1980, and the leader was Apoena Meirelles. His father, Francisco Meirelles, had been as well known as the Villas Boas brothers and was one of the FUNAI officials who had decided to leave the Uru Eu Wau Wau in peace for as long as possible. But now, public meetings were being held in Ariquemes to avenge Chico Prestes and to 'clean' the forest for development. And colonists, skin-hunters, prospectors, mineral companies, loggers and land speculators were pressing in from every direction. 'One way or another,' Apoena said, 'isolation for the Uru Eu Wau Wau is a thing of the past.'

Day after day, we heaved our four boats in the pouring rain through a torrent of violent water. Apoena was making his journey at the height of the rainy season, because there was more water to allow passage over the rocks. But we lost a boat and an outboard motor in the first week, and the journey was to cost three boats and two outboard motors in roughly two months. Our nine metre aluminium boats were ideal for carrying through the forest.

But when caught by rocks and held broadside to the river, they buckled like silver paper.

The film unit accompanied the expedition in its own aluminium boat. And as our project was a co-production with a Brazilian University, our unit began as a British-Brazilian hybrid which became entirely Brazilian (except for myself) within two years. In fact, so many different people were to come and go over the decade that it's confusing to name them all (except in the acknowledgements at the end). The head of the Brazilian side of the co-production, however, was Mario Arruda whose father had been a rubber tapper and who had been brought up in Amazonia.

One day, resting by a set of rapids near the old Seringal Monte Negro, Mario said, 'I don't think we should think of the Indians and *seringueiros* as completely hostile.' 'Monte Negro was where a *seringueiro* called Antonio Pezinho worked 30 years ago. One day, he came across an Indian camp somewhere in the forest, and instead of running away he took off all his clothes. He made a drink with fruit and water, and then sat in the centre of the clearing playing a flute. Finally, when the Indians surrounded him with their bows drawn, he calmly offered the chief a drink. The chief knocked the bowl aside. So Antonio filled another calabash, drank from it, and then offered it to the chief again. This time the chief smiled and drank, and from that day, Antonio began to live with the Uru Eu Wau Wau. I heard this story from one of the *seringueiros* Antonio would approach in the forest to ask for tobacco. (Unlike most other Indians, the Uru Eu Wau Wau don't grow tobacco.) Finally, during a rubber-tapper raid against an Uru Eu Wau Wau village, he was shot down while firing his bow against the *seringueiros*, standing back to back, with his Indian friends. I think we'll find,' Mario concluded, 'that these Indians have a good understanding of *civilizados*. And that we'll hear more of their bald white chief.'

Within a month, two FUNAI posts had been built to block colonists moving up the Rivers Jamari and Nova Floresta, and an airstrip was being levelled in the grass clearing of the old *seringal*, Antuerpia. Then, with half a dozen Surui Indians, Apoena Meirelles set out to follow the Uru Eu Wau Wau raiding party.

Our two boats travelled upstream, moving slowly, as the Surui checked the clues on either side. Then, on the third day, we came to a clear patch of river bank that looked worn with use.

Anini, the Surui in the bows, leapt ashore.

'Fish scales,' he called softly. 'And many bones.'

With the Surui in front, searching for tracks, we walked into a large clearing under the forest canopy.

'Many houses,' Anini called back. The huts were crude lean-tos covered with wild banana leaves. But the ten we found contained little more than the ashes of dead fires and one or two broken calabashes. The rain was dripping quietly, and the place had a gloomy, abandoned feel.

'They come down from the *serra* where the streams are too small for fish,' Apoena said. 'This is their fishing place. Probably also, they left their women and children here when they attacked the colonists. Look,' Apoena pointed at a broad trail that went into the forest in a south-easterly direction. 'That's the direction of the village I found from the air.'

As we were hanging up presents across this trail, one of the Surui called to Apoena. 'A tin,' he hissed dramatically. 'A tin of the baby fish.'

There were, in fact, a total of three startlingly yellow sardine tins. They were lying beside a cracked tortoise shell, in the ashes of an old fire, and they had obviously been opened roughly with a knife. They looked completely wrong in an Indian camp – like toast and marmalade in a Tibetan monastery.

'Apoena, surely even the Uru Eu Wau Wau haven't learnt to eat sardines?'

'It was probably the boy, Fabio,' Apoena said.

'Yes, surely the boy,' Hugo, one of the FUNAI men agreed. 'They must have carried the tins for him to eat.'

But searching the camp next morning, we discovered an empty box of .38 bullets under some leaves, and two sodden boxes nearby that had once contained .22 rifle bullets. Even if the Indians had carried sardines for little Fabio, why should they carry bullets for guns they didn't know how to use?

The question, and the doubt that it raised, were to change our journey into something very different – an investigation into the secretive underworld of the forest and its brutal raids and massacres.

When we got back to Ariquemes, at the beginning of March, we spent a few days getting to know the old part of the town. The new sector had been laid out by the Land Agency, and was divided into commercial and residential areas with homogeneous plots. The older part, however, was strung out haphazardly along the river and road, and mainly consisted of shanty bars and brothels serving illegal prospectors and skin hunters.

'There are rivers of gold in the *serra*,' the prospectors complained, 'but we can't go there because of the Indians. Why doesn't FUNAI move them somewhere else? It's the government's duty to get them out of the way.' Lust for gold, skins and land lay behind much of the resentment against the Indians. But there was a deeper, underlying hatred accumulated over years of raid and counter-raid. 'The Indians are beasts,' we were told. 'If a puma attacks, we can kill it. But if we defend ourselves against the Indians, the government puts us in jail.'

It was in these bars that our guess was eventually confirmed. Chico Prestes, shortly after his son was kidnapped, had organised a party of half a dozen men – led by a well-known Indian hunter – and had set out to rescue Fabio. Nearly everyone in Ariquemes supported him. 'It was his own son? Every father would do what he did.'

Chico's house was beside the largest brothel, the Boite Paulista, in the old part of town. The verandah faced onto the street, and it was here that Mario told Chico about our journey and that we knew he had taken the same route up the River Jamari. He then opened his shoulder bag.

'Do you recognise this?' Mario said as dramatically as Hercule Poirot – and produced the sardine tin.

'Well,' Chico replied practically, 'where did you get it?'

'In an Indian camp on the headwaters of the Jamari, more or less ten minutes before it branches to the west.'

'Tell me another thing. Was there a tortoise shell there?'

'Yes.'

'Then it's ours,' Chico said calmly.

'So this was yours!' Mario plonked the tin on the table, a little like a prosecutor filing evidence.

'Yes, sir. It was us.' Chico's openess was unexpected. 'We were avoiding hunting so as not to alert the Indians. We ate the tortoise and the sardines before we followed the Indian trail into the *serra*.'

'And this box of .38 revolver bullets?'

'That's ours too.'

Once Mario had got Chico to make this admission, he moved directly to the point. 'Listen, Chico. On this trip you made with these six men, you didn't by any chance bump into an Indian – have a clash with them? That could make the contact much more difficult.'

'No sir, we didn't.' Chico spoke with conviction. 'From the camp we travelled for twelve hours, and it was only after we came off the plateau that we began to run into fresh tracks, and then found a plantation where they came for mandioca. Our leader said, "they must hunt here all the time because game is scarce. If we go on, we will certainly bump into their village." And so,' Chico concluded, 'we turned back.'

This did not ring very true. After all, Chico's purpose had been to rescue his son. Was it likely they would turn back just as they were getting close? 'But didn't you see any Indians?' Mario insisted. 'You implied earlier that one of you startled an Indian in the forest.'

'One man thought he did,' Chico's reply was confused. 'But he didn't. We arrived at the plantation at nightfall, and went back because we had no more food.'

'Even if they did kill Indians,' Raimunda, his wife, interrupted, her eyes grim. 'What of it? It's nothing after they killed our child.'

'Ave Maria,' Chico sighed. And for years, that was all we managed to get out of him.

But, that night we did learn two other things.

First of all, the neighbours told us that Dimes, the wounded nine year old who had been moved from hospital to a larger one in Manaus, had tragically, and very unexpectedly, died. 'The wound in his neck suddenly inflamed,' Chico said. 'It must have been Indian poison on the arrow. We thought he was coming home in a few days, and then, suddenly, he was dead.'

'Ah, God release me,' Raimunda said. 'I would have finished my life if they hadn't restrained me. I went almost mad. First, my oldest son killed barbarously, without a chance to defend himself. A boy so strong, with so much courage, finished. Then Dimes, who was crazy to leave hospital, who we all thought was cured, dead before I could get to the hospital. And little Fabio, still out there suffering in the forest, living with beasts. For, the Indian is a beast to me. And no one can say definitely whether Fabinho is alive or not. For me, it's worse than if he were dead.'

It was this need to resolve what had happened to Fabio – even more urgent since the death of Dimes – that was to open a door that had been firmly bolted against us.

Unlike most of the other colonists in the area, who were mainly from the south or north-east of Brazil, Chico had been born in Rondonia and had spent most of his 43 years working as a rubber tapper. It was his experience in the forest that had made his rescue mission possible. Now he told us that he had just received a message from other *seringueiros* on the River Jaru. A shirt had been found on an Indian trail, and it might be Fabio's.

Chico asked for help in checking the story, and we offered to take him to the River Jaru. At least it would break his paralysis of inaction and self-doubt. 'Since they killed my sons,' he would say, 'I cannot work, I cannot sleep, I cannot think, I cannot do anything.' It was Raimunda who was supporting the family by taking in washing and cooking lunch for the girls in the brothel next door.

Three weeks later, Chico steered our aluminium boat with a 25 h.p. outboard motor up the River Jaru. There were fewer rapids than on the Jamari, and we often passed the huts of *seringueiros* standing on the river bank. It was to be my first real visit to a *seringueiro* area. On the next day we walked through the forest down a series of broad trails which are called 'varadouros' by the *seringueiros*. They had the peaceful feel of ancient pathways. New trails, freshly cut in jungle, are jagged with the sliced stumps of saplings, whilst the ground is unmoulded by the passage of human feet. *Varadouros*, on the other hand, are usually broad enough for two loaded mules to pass each other, and, under the soaring trees, they have the graceful look of Cistercian alleyways – cool and inspiring. Every few minutes there would be a rubber tree, cut with a cross-hatched herring bone pattern that often reached from knee level to twice the height of a man. Usually one cut would be white from a recent slash, oozing its sticky milk into a little tin at the bottom. And there was something about these well-worn trails and well-cared-for trees that spoke of a different relationship between man and the forest. I noticed, for instance, that it is hard for a *seringueiro* to pass one of these ancient scarred trunks without unconsciously stroking its mossy bark – very much like a farmer pats his cow.

After three or four hours, we arrived at a palm-thatch hut in a small clearing from which emerged a tubby *seringueiro* called Antonio.

'The shirt?' Chico asked anxiously. 'Please show me the shirt.'

Antonio went back into his hut and brought back a dirty piece of brownish check material.

Turning it round and round in his hands, Chico looked at it hopefully, and then with faltering disappointment. 'It's not the child's.'

THE FRONTIER ARRIVES 101

'No?'

'It's not the child's,' Chico said despondently. 'Nor does it belong to either of the two that died. This is too small for my eldest son. And I don't remember the other with a shirt like this.' Chico handed it back. 'Where did you find it?'

'It was a long way from here,' Antonio replied, 'in the middle of their trail on the day they ransacked my house. They probably dropped it because they were carrying too much. My whole house was cleaned out.' Antonio waved across the broad, airy hut.

'They took everything, even the mattress. They left me without clothes even to go shopping in the town. All I had,' he laughed, 'was the dirty work-shirt on my back. It was after that, when we were following their trail, that I found the shirt.'

As he and Chico talked, it became apparent that though the *seringueiros* were very vulnerable in their isolated houses, they were by no means helpless. Antonio knew how to track the Indians, and had not lacked the courage to set out after them.

He told us that earlier on that day of the raid, he had been bleeding rubber when he suddenly became aware that two Indians were close. One was signalling to the other through the underbrush, pointing to the tree that Antonio was working on. Then they began to manoeuvre sideways, to get at him from the rear. Antonio leapt up and ran through the jungle, and, by bad luck, ran straight into the Indian camp, knocking over a pan of honey. The few startled Indians in the camp fled in one direction. And Antonio had pounded off in the other – to his hut. It was then that he discovered it had been looted.

That night we stayed with the middleman who bought rubber from the *seringueiros* in the area. When the rubber price had fallen and the banks stopped financing the crop, the great *seringais* on the River Jaru – Canarana, Sao Domingos, Sao Francisco – had broken up and the owners had left the forest. Many of the *seringueiros* had nowhere to go, however, and stayed on as small-holders extracting rubber as a part-time activity. Who now bought rubber and brought in supplies was usually an ex-foreman or a *seringueiro* who had the natural qualities of a leader – like Alfredo de Santos. He was known as Alfredao – the great or big Alfredo. His sombre eyes left you with a feeling of latent violence.

'They kidnapped your son to become their chief,' Alfredao told Chico. 'As he grows up, they will watch to see if he runs away. And if he doesn't, they will give him a woman, and let him rule them.' He was obviously trying to console Chico.

'What he is saying is right,' Chico said. 'They captured him to make him a chief.'

'And why would a white man want to be the Indians' chief?' I asked.

'They have many women and much food. And they don't work.' Alfredao's face was rough, almost wizened, from many years in the forest. 'If I want something, I have to work or owe money – like all *seringueiros*. But they just hunt and steal. They take everything we have – pots, pans, axes, flour. Once they even stole a gramophone.'

'Have they already had a white chief?'

'Yes. They have some very pale people amongst them.' Alfredao's hooded eyes showed that, despite his compassion for Chico, he was uneasy about what we might ask him.

'How do you know that,' I asked.

'Because I have seen them.' Alfredao's eyes glinted with irritation. 'I spoke to the chief but he told me to go.'

'Why didn't he shoot you?'

'Because when you show friendship, they don't shoot. I said "friend" in their language. But he just beat the ground with his foot and ordered me to go.'

'Do you think they would exchange Chico's child for presents?'

'Only if they are tamed,' Alfredao said grimly. 'When they are civilised, they may hand him over. But now? For presents? No.'

Alfredao went into his hut and that night Chico talked to him by the light of a small oil lamp until the early hours of the morning. Next day Chico asked me if we could have a talk away from the hut, under the fruit trees in the clearing. With his voice lowered, he asked if I would provide the money for an expedition to rescue his son. Its leader would be Alfredao.

'But Chico, Apoena is already angry about your first expedition. If you bump into the Indians, you will have to defend yourselves. And if you kill an Indian that will make peaceful contact even more difficult. They might even get angry and kill your son.'

'But they won't see us,' Chico said. 'Alfredao can pass amongst the Indians without them seeing.'

'Chico, how can he? He is not invisible.'

'With an *oracao* [an incantation or prayer that derives from the half-magic religious practices of the north-east of Brazil], he can pass amongst them without being seen. Look, they attack everyone around here, but they never attack one of Alfredao's rubber tappers'. Chico waved around the clearing where several *seringueiros* were sitting. 'He even has an Indian woman he captured.' Chico nodded towards Alfredao's wife washing dishes down by the river. 'And they still don't attack him.'

'But Chico, if he captured her, that means he must have been on raids against the Indians.'

'He led some of the attacks,' Chico said decisively. 'That's why he thinks he can get my son back.'

And so the iron gate began to swing. The explanation for Alfredao's authority amongst the *seringueiros*, the reason why he knew so much about the Indians, was that he had planned and carried out raids against them. Under Brazilian law at that time, an Indian was considered a minor under tutelage and was not held responsible for his crimes. But a *seringueiro* who killed Indians could be brought to trial by the Indian Agency, FUNAI. A blanket of secrecy, therefore, covered all their raids.

A *seringueiro's* work usually begins at dawn when he sets out to cut the trees on one of his trails. Later in the day he returns to collect the milky liquid that has oozed into a tin at the bottom of each cut, and, finally, in the afternoon, this is poured through the smoke of burning *babacu* nuts. The white, rubber-milk becomes tacky in the smoke and vulcanizes as it is poured onto a growing elastic ball rotating above the fire. It was as Alfredao helped a *seringueiro* rotate this rubber ball that I suggested that he could assist the process of understanding and therefore contacting, the Uru Eu Wau Wau by telling us about these raids.

'I knew of a man nick-named Ossada,' Alfredao started slowly. From his resigned expression, he knew exactly where we were leading him. But for Chico's sake he did not want to be unhelpful. 'He was a *patrao* opening up a *seringal* in this area and I passed through an Indian village where Ossada had ground up the Indians.' Alfredao's eyes gleamed at the word 'ground'. 'In 1962, there were many attacks against the Indians and they were fleeing from one side of the *serra* to the other. Ossada sent 20 men after them, and, on the other side of the *serra* on the headwaters of the Rio Cautario, they minced the Indians up.'

'Can you guess how many were killed?'

'There were bones scattered all around. Maybe 50 bodies or more. They opened fire on them, then burnt the huts and everything in them. Nothing was left but the bones and a pile of pots. Fourteen big pots, all shot through with bullet holes.'

A few days later, when Chico was talking about the *seringueiros* who put out presents and then shot from ambush as the Indians collected them, Alfredao added, 'That was Ze Milton. He was the *patrao* of the Muqui *seringal*, and sent out many raids. Most were led by Paraguaiano who was a professional Indian killer, hired from one *seringal* to another to wipe out the tribes.' Alfredao was weighing out rice for a *seringueiro* as he talked.

'Can you guess how many Indians they killed on the Muqui?'

'Many. More than a hundred.'

'Did they capture Indian women?'

'No. Their orders were just to kill. They were not trying to capture women to learn the language. They didn't want to tame them like we did.' Alfredao looked across the hut towards his wife, Maria, who was cooking on the stove. She had attractive features, and the stocky body and long straight hair of an Indian woman. For the past few days we had watched her caring for her two, equally Indian-looking, sons. And now Alfredao had provided an opportunity to ask about her.

'So Maria was captured to learn the Uru Eu Wau Wau language?'

'No,' Alfredao said. 'Her mother was.'

That day we did not press any further. But I had begun to sense that Alfredao felt some sort of affinity for the Indians. Like the Indian, the *seringueiro's* life depends on his love and knowledge of the forest; and much of that knowledge – for instance, bleeding rubber – had originally been learnt from the Indians. In the past Alfredao may have taken part in raids because he was paid by a *patrao*. But now that the *patroes* had left the forest, he must have been wondering whether it was in his interests to go on making the Indian his enemy?

'It was a very brutal time under the *patrao*,' Alfredao told us. 'Sometimes there were a dozen *seringueiros* tied to the trees – men who didn't work or who tried to sell their rubber elsewhere. We would be told to cut ten sticks of *goiaba* for each of them. *Goiaba* is strong and pliant and we would have to beat each man until all ten sticks were broken. Sometimes it killed them.'

Gradually, over several conversations about the Indians and the forests, Alfredao told us how he had captured Maria.

'The first time I led a raid was in 1962. We went with 23 men and arrived at nightfall. So we had to wait till dawn before we caught one.'

'How many Indians were killed?'

'Only one. But we caught an old woman. A strong one and clever,' Alfredao smiled, and avoided the issue of the dead Indian. 'In fact, she was so strong and clever that she escaped.' Alfredao laughed. 'On the journey back she kept saying she had to urinate and she would go out of the camp and crouch down and then come back. A little later she would go again, but each time a little further. And the last time, more or less at nine o'clock at night, when she crouched, she just crawled away into the forest. We searched for her with torches,' Alfredao shook his head smiling, 'but never found her.'

'So we had to go back, but with only twelve men. And we again arrived at night and had to wait until the break of morning before we caught two.'

'How many did you kill?'

Alfredao did not look at me and never actually said that any had been killed.

'After we fired, six were left on the ground. Then we took away the two women we had captured, one with a little boy and a girl.'

'Why didn't they escape?'

'Because I brought them all the time on a chain. At night I put the two women in hammocks, close to each other, and passed the chain from the leg of one to the leg of the other.' Alfredao's tone was a strange mixture of the raider's harshness and an older man's more questioning reflection. 'That was how we travelled until we arrived at Seringal Sao Domingos. There, Dona Laura, the wife of the owner, gave a dress to Maria to cover her. But Maria put both her hands on it and tore it.' Alfredao glanced at her and laughed. 'She split the whole dress and threw it. But Dona Laura gave another dress and Maria's mother didn't let her tear it.'

'That night, when I said here's the chain to put on your foot, Maria's mother looked so sad, that I agreed not to put it on. And then they were so happy that they spent the whole night talking – teaching me their language. They hardly slept from joy.' Alfredao's face reflected both pleasure and sadness at the memory. 'I kept telling everyone that soon I would be able to speak to the Indians in the jungle and stop the fighting.'

'But on the next day when we arrived at Seringal Canarana, everyone was sick with flu. And two nights later, Maria's mother asked for 'Tata'. It's the

Indian's word for fire. She was cold because she was sickening. So I put some sand in a tin, and built a fire in it and put it under her hammock, warming her shoulders. Then Chico Affonso applied many injections for pneumonia. But it was no use. Maria's mother, Diacui, died. Then six days later, the other woman died, and the boy too. Only Maria survived.' Alfredao seemed genuinely sad, and it was apparent that he was talking now not just to help Chico, but from an inner need of his own. 'The two women never tried to run away.' He insisted. 'Never. They went everywhere with me. Where I went they followed. If I went into a room and shut the door, they banged until I let them enter. They didn't want to escape in any way.' Alfredao was clearly proud that he had been liked by the Indian women, and some part of his reputation seemed to derive from this.

'And the Uru Eu Wau Wau never tried to rescue the women?'

'Never. They roam around here, very close. But they never come into our clearing.'

'Why not?'

'They watch me in the forest. They know who I am.' Alfredao looked round darkly at three or four of his *seringueiros* who were listening. 'They never kill any of the *seringueiros* who work with me.' Part of his control over them seemed to depend on their belief in his magical powers and the protection these gave them.

Now that colonists were moving up the River Jaru, however, Alfredao's system and the history of his *seringal* seemed somewhat irrelevant. An INCRA survey trace had halted only three kilometres from Alfredao's house, and his whole area had been surveyed and then demarcated into plots. Colonists were already cutting down the forest a dozen kilometres away, and within the next year Alfredao expected to be swamped and most of his rubber trees cut down. I wondered, therefore, if Alfredao was re-evaluating his relationship with the Indians in the light of these changes.

'Maria.' This seemed a tactful moment to start talking to her. 'Do you want to leave this place?'

'No. It's beautiful. We have many crops and fruits.'

'Is that the reason you moved upriver when the *seringais* collapsed?'

'No,' It was Alfredao who replied. 'It was to be closer to the Indians. To see if they would approach us. But they never did.'

'Maria, can you remember your mother?'

'No.'

'Wouldn't you like to meet your brother or sister?'

'Yes.' Maria said simply.

'We will visit them,' Alfredao added, 'after they are pacified. When they are civilised, Maria and I will talk to them.' And with that enigmatic statement, our visit ended.

For us, the trip with Chico had provided an unexpected glimpse of another way of life in the jungle and one that, despite the horrifying brutality of the raids, revealed much in common between the *seringueiros* and the Indian. Their battles had been over rival uses of the forest. But now that the forest itself was menaced, their interests were closer and their rivalry might disappear.

As for Chico, though the trip had produced no expedition to rescue his son, it did answer one of his most frequent questions. 'Why should the Indians want to kill them?' he would repeat pathetically. 'The poor boys had never even seen an Indian.'

'Vengeance!' Alfredao had been quite definite. He then explained why.

In November 1978, a party of skin-hunters had come down the River Jaru, out of Uru Eu Wau Wau territory, with a pile of ocelot skins. They had been led by a professional hunter called Atanasio and had spent the night at Alfredao's house. Three or four days later, the Uru Eu Wau Wau had raided from the same direction and, on November the 16th and 17th, killed a *seringueiro* (not one of Alfredao's) – who was found with eight arrows in his body – and a woman – who was found in another hut under the bed. Her two young daughters were discovered alive, beside her, holding the arrows projecting from her body. The hunter, Atanasio, was not seen again until October 1979 – when he emerged with another party. He said that they had travelled up the River Jamari to hunt in Indian territory, but that they had clashed with the Uru Eu Wau Wau. Atanasio swore he would never enter their area again. A week later, on October the 26th 1979, the Indians had back-tracked along Atanasio's entry route into their territory – down the Jamari River – and had killed Chico's sons. 'Maybe that ocelot hunter was really hunting,' Alfredao concluded. 'But possibly he was also paid by land speculators to kill Indians and drive them off the land.'

A few months later, we located Atanasio, the professional hunter of ocelots, and he proved to be an alert and very wary man. After two meetings, we decided that our only chance of finding anything out was to film one of his hunting trips. And since Chico would have made Atanasio suspicious, he decided not to come.

An ocelot has the most valuable pelt in the forest, worth more than its larger relative, the jaguar. The delicate fur, if punctured by a bullet, is unsaleable. And so Atanasio's technique was to shoot a monkey or some other bait, and then drag its bleeding body along the ground for half a kilometre in either direction. We watched as he tied the monkey to a tree in the centre of this scented trail, at the height that an ocelot could reach by leaping from the ground. Where the ocelot's feet would fall back to the ground, he dug a shallow hole. As he set the spring trap, he explained that if badly sited, the savage teeth could spoil the ocelot's skin. Also that if the spring was too powerful, it could break the leg making it easier for the ocelot to chew through its own foot and escape. Camouflaged with leaf mould, the trap was left indistinguishable from the forest floor.

On the first day and night, Atanasio talked about his hunting experiences but not about the Indians. But on the second morning, we found an ocelot snarling and tearing at the trap that had closed on its right leg.

Atanasio clubbed the head, so as not to damage the skin, and as he skinned the body and pegged the pelt, he began to talk expansively.

'These skins are worth 3000 cruzeiros ($50),' he said with satisfaction. 'Where the cats are many, I don't look for gold. Just catch 40, 60, 80. At 3000 per skin,' he smiled broadly, 'that's a lot of money. And if you sell in Bolivia, the price is even better.' (The trade in ocelot skins is illegal in Brazil, and mainly goes through Bolivia.)

'So, how many ocelots have you killed?'

'More than 1000. Sometimes four in a night, 30 in a journey.' Atanasio was obviously much more commercially orientated than most of the *seringueiros* we had met.

'On your last journey, how many did you kill?'

'Fifteen.' I noticed that this was less than usual, and that it might indicate an interrupted journey.

'That journey was where?'

'The River Jaru.' Exactly as Alfredao had said.

'The cats are getting scarce now that the forests are coming down,' Atanasio explained. 'I started in Para, near the Belem-Brasilia road. Then I had to go to Mato Grosso. And now, even here in Rondonia, the forests are beginning to finish. It's only where the Indians hold back the plague of colonists that there are any ocelots left. So for a professional hunter like me, the journey is only profitable where there are Indians.'

'Where's that?'

'The headwaters of the Jamari on the Serra dos Pacaas Novos.'

'Oh? When were you there?'

'Ah,' Atanasio's tone changed and he looked wily, 'I haven't been there yet. That's just where it would be profitable to go.' He had remembered to be careful, and I changed the subject.

As he finished skinning the ocelot, Atanasio cut off its ears, putting one inside the other. He then threw them away with his left hand. 'That makes the ocelot's mate come looking for it during the night,' he explained smiling. 'The Canella Indians taught me.'

'Do you use a lot of magic in your hunting?'

'It needs courage to confront the jungle,' Atanasio agreed grimly, 'to be hidden from the Indians. But I have the help of Caboclinho da Mata.' (This is one of the spirits of the folklore of the north-east of Brazil, which has similar origins and ceremonies to voodoo). 'There is a prayer for Caboclinho to protect you from the Indians. For you to see the Indian and the Indians not to see you. You wash your clothes with the blood of an animal. Then, fasting, you bathe very early in the morning with a liquid boiled from leaves. Afterwards the Indians don't see you.'

'When was the last time an Indian passed without seeing you?'

'I passed some Indians on the Upper Jaru. I hid behind a branch and put leaves in front of my face.' Atanasio showed us how he held a branch in front of his face, the leaves emphasising his predatory, hunter's eyes. 'When I looked through the leaves, they didn't see me.'

'How many Indians were there?'

'Two men and two women, carrying a wild pig. They were naked with only a G string made of lianas.'

'Were they close?'

'Very close.'

I then put the key question. 'When was this?'

'That time was 1978. Then in '79, they were very close to me again, because they stole a bush turkey I had killed.'

'What month was that?'

'It was October '79.' The same month as Chico's sons were killed.

'Did you leave because you were frightened?'

'No,' Atanasio became casual and he covered his tracks again, 'just because my food ran out. *Seringueiros* shoot at the Indians, but if I see their trails or camps, I just divert to one side. So the Indians know I don't want to quarrel with them and leave me alone.'

Though we stayed for several more days, that's all we got out of Atanasio. And if we had not known the precise dates of the Indian attacks, and the fact that Atanasio had come out just before both attacks, we would not have put two and two together. But when we related what we had heard, neither Chico, Alfredao, nor the other *seringueiros*, had any doubt. Atanasio was indubitably a professional hunter. But he had also been paid to attack the Indians – probably by people interested in their land. The speculators would have hoped that the Indians' retaliation would incite a major reprisal expedition – and that this would lead to the extermination of the tribe.

Despite Atanasio's almost piratical way of life, I noticed once again that he had learnt much of his trade from Indians. And that he spoke of them without any of the venom that he used for the colonists. The survival of his ocelots depended on Indian reserves. And what he and Alfredao obviously shared with the Indian was their expertise in the forest and the livelihood it provided. Ever looking for something positive in the depressing devastation of Amazonia, I wondered whether these very different peoples of the forest could ever band together in defence of their common environment.

And then the cruelty and bloodshed of their history made me think again.

After our journey through the *seringais* with Chico, we lent him some money to take his boat to the great gold strike on the Rio Madeira. There he could quickly revive his fortunes and morale by hiring out the boat. But malaria struck before he could go, and when next we saw him, he was emaciated with a swollen belly. The doctor, fearing that Chico's spleen would burst, had operated.

I have often noticed that malaria seems to break out during periods of great emotional or physical strain. And the self doubt which first gripped Chico when he found his sons shot with arrows, now seemed to grip him ever more firmly. From time to time he would take his boat to the tin mines on the edge of Uru Eu Wau Wau territory, and make some money transporting prospectors. But his failure to resolve the fate of Fabio was bleeding his energy and life away. His malaria, over the months, was to come back again and again.

From time to time, during the expedition to contact the Uru Eu Wau Wau, we would fly out to show Chico pieces of cloth that we found in their camps. But none matched the shirt and shorts Fabio had been wearing. Once, however, we brought arrows that had been shot at Vicente Rios, our cameraman. And comparing them with those shot at his sons, Chico confirmed that they were definitely the same. Each Indian makes his arrows in a different way, and one from both incidents had been made by the same man.

'Fabinho never went bare-foot in Ariquemes,' Dona Raimunda interrupted, 'and his feet were very soft. I hate to think of him without shoes, walking in the jungle.'

'I took that INCRA plot to leave a place in the world for my sons,' Chico said almost to himself. 'And now that they are gone, I cannot bear to look at it.'

As Chico weakened, Dona Raimunda, by contrast, seemed to grow broader and more determined – from necessity. She still made money by washing clothes and by renting two rooms across their yard to the girls in the brothel next door. Beside the main dance hall of the Boite Paulista, there was a long narrow wooden shed, which looked like a chicken battery, with a dozen small coop-like rooms for the girls to receive their clients. The two rooms in Chico's yard were large and less utilitarian, and we would sometimes arrive in the morning to find a petrol lorry or a refrigerated meat van parked outside while its driver slept off the night. This close and daily dependence, on both his wife and the brothel, seemed to diminish Chico. He gradually got weaker and the attacks of malaria became more frequent.

In August 1983, Chico returned from the tin mines for the last time and went into hospital with another bout of malaria. Within four days this developed into cerebral malaria and Dona Raimunda was called two hours before he died. In his delirium all that he talked about was Fabinho.

Some months later, Dona Raimunda said, 'Now that Chico's dead, and they cannot arrest him, I will tell you about the raid.'

'They went up the River Jamari,' she said, 'until they could go no further. Then they followed the Indian trail past many camps and unused villages which had scrub growing in the middle. After several days the leader, Raimundo, said that they were close. The path was beaten clear and there were many footprints. So he left Chico with four men and went ahead with one man, until coming round a bend in the path, he was suddenly face to face with an Indian coming the other way. He shot him. If the Indian ran, he would warn the others. So he shot him. When they ran up, the Indian was still alive with his hand up, asking them not to kill. But Raimundo killed him with the revolver saying that by one death, at least, they would be avenged. They took his head-dress and belt and necklace and went back to get Chico to attack the village. But when they returned to where the body was, it was gone and the Indians were all around in the jungle, shrieking. One calling here, another there, hidden in the bushes. The men crouched back to back to defend themselves. Chico saw two run from behind a tree. Then he saw another and fired. He didn't kill him outright because the Indian went on running. When night came, they crept away, travelling all night until they reached the boat at dawn, and returned to Ariquemes.'

As contacts between the Indian Agency expedition and the different Uru Eu Wau Wau nomadic groups developed, it became increasingly unlikely that any of their bands could still be hiding a kidnapped boy. And when Indian interpreters eventually spoke some of their language, the Uru Eu Wau Wau admitted that they had killed Fabinho soon after he was kidnapped. 'He cried all the time,' they explained, matter of factly, 'so we killed him.' Eventually they showed some of the FUNAI people where they claimed to have left the body. But as there were no bones, and each Uru Eu Wau Wau accused another of the killing – all Indians expect killings to be avenged – it was very hard to be certain what had happened. Dona Raimunda, and some *seringueiros*, still hope that Fabinho is alive.

Tragedy after tragedy had racked the Prestes family from the day that they had accepted their government plot. So, for us, they became a symbol of all the other tortured families taking part in the violent change along the frontier. And thus my thoughts kept returning to the *seringueiros* Chico had introduced us to. More than most invaders of Amazonia, the original rubber-tappers had been led – you could say almost blind-folded – into the forest. Most had been fleeing from poverty and starvation in the north-east of Brazil, and many were lent money during a famine by the *patrao* of a *seringal*. They had never seen a forest. They had no idea what they were getting into. But, once they had fallen into the debt slavery of the *seringal*, few were able to buy their passage out. And so, they had stayed on – for generations. Finally when the rubber price fell and even the *patroes* quit, the *seringueiros* had been left to moulder in the forest. However, from an ecological point of view, to moulder is to adapt to your environment. And many of the *seringueiros* we visited had managed to transform themselves into forest small-holders, eating well from mandioca, corn and rice plantations. Their houses were surrounded by fruit trees. Most raised ducks, pigs and chickens. Some had half a dozen cows. Fish or game were never lacking. And, for money, they bled rubber and collected Brazil nuts.

It was a healthy way of life and a sustainable use of forest. And yet everywhere we went in Rondonia the forests of the *seringueiros* were being demolished by colonists who earned less, lived worse, and practised a type of agriculture that was completely unsustainable. Even when the land agency recognised the *seringueiros*' squatters rights, they usually gave them plots of only 50 to 100 hectares. And because rubber trees grow at a distance from each other in the forest, the average *seringueiro* has to have 300 to 500 hectares to make a living. So in the central part of Rondonia, most sold their title deeds and moved to the slums of Porto Velho and Manaus – without an audible protest. Within two years of our visit to Alfredao, all the forest of all his *seringueiros* had been wiped out. And the house where Chico had examined the shirt that might have been his son's, had become the town of Tarrylandia.

At the time, it seemed to me that though the *seringueiros* had learnt to understand and use the forest as well as the Indian, what they had not developed was a new vision of themselves that would enable them to defend their rights. The *seringueiro* still thought of himself as a poor Brazilian driven by misfortune to the jungle and was crippled by a lack of confidence similar to Chico's. Unlike the Indian, who saw himself as part of an ancient social unit which had the right – if not the ability – to defend itself and its land, all *seringueiros* conceived of themselves as part of Brazilian society and, therefore, unconsciously accepted that their differences with INCRA and the colonists derived from their own backwardness. And so, though they obviously had one of the few tried solutions for the utilisation of Amazonia, it seemed, in 1980, unlikely that they would ever be able to defend it.

Perhaps it is part of the inherent nature of a frontier that what is necessary but improbable rapidly becomes an achievable, accepted fact. For within half a dozen years, *seringueiros* like Alfredao were leading a nationally organised, political movement, and their closest and most supportive allies were to be their ancient enemies the Indians.

TWO

On May the 14th, 1980, Apoena Meirelles, with half a dozen Surui Indians, landed on the golden plateau of the Serra dos Pacaas Novos – the heartland of the Uru Eu Wau Wau. The savannah grass was blowing in the mountain wind, and all around were the red, box-like mesas that form the crest of the Amazonian watershed. The sheer cliffs we had seen on Mount Roraima, 2000 kilometres to the north, were repeated here on the southern lip of the Amazon basin. And during our aerial reconnaissance, we had flown past waterfalls floating on the wind, falling in drifting lines to the forest hundreds of yards below. We had found concealed gorges and a series of what looked like deep caverns. The southern watershed of the Amazon was the ancient migration route of the Indian into the eastern part of South America; and if these rock cavities were like others to the east, their walls would be alive with drawings of hunting men and animals in pigments of ochre, red and black. The heartland of the Uru Eu Wau Wau had the sort of unexpected beauty which inspires legend.

The Serra dos Pacaas Novos, however, was by no means unknown to *civilizados*. Only a few years before, an expedition from CPRM, the government's mineral prospecting agency, had – with a surveyor's blinkered disregard – cut a survey trace up into the *serra*, straight through an Uru Eu Wau Wau village and then down into the Guapore valley on the other side. It was they who had told Apoena that a plane could land on the grassland of the eastern plateau. Before that, a military expedition, training army troops in jungle survival, had chopped its way onto the plateau looking, no doubt, for the El Dorado of the intelligence agencies, Che Guevara's secret base. While, for two decades, prospectors for gold, tin and diamonds had been launching expeditions into the mountains. 'Massacred by *seringueiros*, harassed by prospectors, steam-rollered by government expeditions, what,' Apoena wondered, 'will the Uru Eu Wau Wau make of people who walk around hanging up presents?'

Within a few hours of landing, we had built a camp site in a stretch of riverine jungle that ran across the savannah along the banks of a clear stream. And over the next few weeks, we discovered that these narrow strips of forest along the streambeds usually contained Uru Eu Wau Wau trails or camp sites. We would find the shells of nuts, or discarded baskets, or a broken arrow beside the trails, whilst the camps under the trees were simple lean-to huts which any passing Uru Eu Wau Wau could make waterproof with a covering of fresh leaves.

In most places, the savannah that runs along the crest of the watershed is about five kilometres wide, with tropical forest falling away into the valleys on either side. Every now and again, however, the grass is broken by a sheer rock massif, and it was after climbing one of these, that one of our Surui guides saw a thin wisp of smoke rising out of the forest. It was early in a morning brilliant with bands of yellow and blue macaws flying between the mesas, and we all came over to stare. It was our first living sign of the Uru Eu Wau Wau.

Some time later, exploring in this direction, we found a well-beaten trail in deep forest. There were feathers where a bush turkey had been plucked, spare palm fronds where someone had made a basket, and strips of bark that had been collected for medicinal use. Gradually the trail grew broader and the woodland more open, until we came out into a sunlit plantation bright with mandioca, potato, papaya, pumpkin, cotton and *urucu*. From the size of the mandioca roots, it was two years old. And on the other side, the trail went straight into a permanent camp under the trees. There were three large huts where the Uru Eu Wau Wau had left some of their belongings. Ears of corn were tied to the rafters, probably for replanting. There were also bamboo for arrows, an old bow, bits of cloth, metal pots, and even a battered coffee pot. But the ash in the fires was damp and cold, and the nearby stream suggested why. The water was down to a trickle. 'This is why Uru Eu Wau Wau attacks are mainly during the summer,' said Ze Bel, the official leader of the expedition. (Apoena, as district head of FUNAI, had to spend most of his time in Porto Velho.) 'When the streams on the *serra* dry up, the Uru Eu Wau Wau go down to the valleys to fish – and to steal from the *seringueiros*. Then when the rains begin again, they come back to sow their crops.' Ze Bel hung up a variety of axes, machetes and pots in the centre of the village. 'Until the Uru Eu Wau Wau start taking our presents,' he concluded, 'there is not much more we can do.'

Soon after, we flew out with Ze Bel to discover what the Uru Eu Wau Wau were up to in the surrounding forests. And this was to become the pattern of the next two years. For though all the action took place on the high plateau, the reasons for the action lay in the forests around. The expedition's newly-built post of Comandante Ari was in open savannah, ideal for a contact. It was only two hours walk from the nearest Uru Eu Wau Wau village, and now all the trails on the tableland were clanking with pots, machetes and knives blowing against each other in the mountain wind, calling to the Indians. It was here that the initial attacks, the passing of the first present, the long process of contact and adaptation, would take place. And yet everyone at the post was, metaphorically, always looking over his shoulder. When the Uru Eu Wau Wau changed their tactics, we would discover later that it was because of a new road or wave of colonists. And once when a helicopter flew over – probably to supply a secret gold mine to the south – Baiano-Maia, the head of the post, said, 'In a week there will be a clash with prospectors; in a month arrows will be flying between these huts.' The frontier had become a noose for the Uru Eu Wau Wau; every time this noose tightened on the Indians, the post of Comandante Ari inevitably felt it jerk.

When we flew out, we travelled to the town of Ouro Preto, which had been founded in 1970 by INCRA. The area around was the first to be colonised in Rondonia; from it, the State Government of Rondonia was driving the BR429 road southwards, to open up the whole of the untouched valley of the River Guapore which forms the frontier with Bolivia. 'The road will be Rondonia's access to Bolivia, the Pacific and the Japanese market,' one of Ouro Preto's more visionary businessmen enthused.

It was as the rains began, in October 1980, that we heard rumours that this road had started to penetrate Indian territory. We set out to see where it had got to.

The initial part was laid with gravel and ran through an area where the farms looked more developed. Many had wire fences and houses built from boards and corrugated iron. After the first 50 kilometres, however, the road began to degenerate into a dirt track winding through forest. Bulldozers had pushed the trees and undergrowth to either side, and the streams had been roughly bridged by placing in them a type of Amazonian treetrunk which is hollow in the centre. These natural wooden drains channelled the water, and earth had been bulldozed over them to complete the culvert. Small patches of forest had also been burnt and in these clearings a number of colonists were setting up temporary huts covered with tarpaulin. Their clearings were still black with ash, and had the desperate look of a vegetable patch in a bombed out city.

After 84 kilometres, we came out on the Rio Urupa, which is the next river running out of the Serra dos Pacaas Novos to the east of Alfredao's Rio Jaru.

Here the roadbuilders had set up four large huts to live in, and two or three bulldozers were being repaired. A bridge of huge Amazonian logs spanned the river which we knew to be within the normal hunting range of the Uru Eu Wau Wau. We were, therefore, astonished to learn that the roadhead was nearly 20 kilometres beyond the bridge, and heading in the direction of the eastern village of the Uru Eu Wau Wau.

On the other side of the bridge, there were no colonists, and the road was little more than a tunnel drilled through living forest. Dripping vegetation brushed our windscreen for kilometre after kilometre. Once a deer leapt across our bonnet. Another time, we stopped to allow a tortoise to plod its way from one forest wall to the other.

Eventually, 99 kilometres from its start, the BR429 road came to an abrupt stop before a solid wall of forest. Facing it were three bulldozers. A push from the lead bulldozer brought down the tree immediately ahead. Groaning and whining, branches flailing as they tore from the surrounding foliage, it crashed to the ground in a confetti-like shower of leaves. The bigger trees sometimes required two bulldozers together, one pushing behind the other. But Amazonian roots are spread close to the surface in order to absorb the nutrients from decaying leaves. And since the forest shields the trees from the wind, most giants keel over with ease – their roots popping out like corks from a champagne bottle. The lead bulldozer then moved onto the next tree, while the second bulldozer pushed the felled trunks and foliage to either side. Finally, a large tractor with V-like blades, scraped off the top soil and left a smooth track wide enough for a truck. 'We are moving,' one of the bulldozer drivers said, 'at about one kilometre a day. In two months, God willing, we will be putting this road into Costa Marques on the Rio Guapore.'

'Aren't you frightened of the Indians?' asked Vicente, our Brazilian cameraman.

'No. This is their hunting area and there is a camp close by. We will keep on cutting through their villages until we get off the *serra*.

The camp nearby proved to be like the others we had found near the Post of Comandante Ari. Half a dozen huts with a number of tapirs' skulls lying close to the fires. The man who took us there was a colonist working with the road crew. 'A naked Indian ran out when we first arrived,' he said. 'But now, with all the noise they don't come back.'

Obviously no one in the road team questioned whether they should be driving Indians out of their camps. Their job was to bulldoze exactly along that survey line, and the forest did not exist for them, except as a blank space around a surveyor's trace.

From what the roadbuilders said, an Uru Eu Wau Wau village was only 30 kilometres ahead to the south. So immediately we flew back with Ze Bel to the Post of Comandante Ari. And within a day, the head of the post, Baiano-Maia, started cutting a trail to the south and east. If he could set up a FUNAI camp in the path of the road, he would refuse to let the bulldozers pass. And it would not be easy for the State Government to order a Federal

Government department not to observe its constitutional obligation to protect Indian land.

But two days later, everything changed. November the 9th was a day of rest, and the whole cutting party was at the post when we heard shouts and the sound of desperate, pounding feet. When I got to the door, the tallest Surui, Meresor, was panting and pointing to the east. 'I went to the bushes over there,' he gasped, 'and where I went to urinate, there were many Indians – crawling in the grass.' 'How many?'

'Like this,' Meresor held up two hands.

'Did they shoot?'

'I ran before they could get up.'

'Perhaps,' Baiano-Maia speculated, 'that means they came in peace.'

The answer came three hours later. After a heavy rainstorm, that blew great sheets of water into our hut, Maoira, another of the Surui, went to wash in the stream about 20 yards away. It was in the opposite direction from where Meresor had seen the Indians. But it was only 30 yards from the wall of forest. When the post had been built, 100 yards of forest had been cleared along the stream to provide a clear view of 50 yards in every direction. 50 yards is outside the effective range of an Indian bow. But the rest of the original forest still stretched along the stream to the north and south. Since the washing place was 20 yards from the post, Maoira's back was just within arrow range of the southern wall of jungle. While he crouched to soap his legs, he was concealed by the stream-bank. But when he lifted to soap his body, he suddenly saw a dozen Indians, with bows bent, creeping towards him. With a terrified shout which catapulted me and everyone else from our hammocks, Maoira hurled himself out of the streambed and ran rig-zagging, arrows flying, up the path. As I reached the door, he was already pounding into the post, and Meresor and two other Surui were running forward to cover him with their guns.

'I saw them as I ran out,' Meresor said. 'Many Indians. With hammocks round their waists.'

'Did they wear anything else?'

'No. But one was bald.'

'Bald?'

'Bald!' Meresor said decisively. 'Like here,' and he touched a bald patch on Mario's head. The white chief we had heard about in the rumours was back!

Walking down the path, we found ten arrows, vicious with carved, jagged barbs, stuck in the earth on either side of the path along which Maoira had run. Their undersides were coated with a blackish substance that the Surui believed was poison. Maoira was lucky not to have been hit. Carefully examining the forest, the Surui then told us that the Uru Eu Wau Wau had crept up during the rain and had sat for a couple of hours, waiting for the first person to come out to wash. They counted 24 places where men had sat.

In that eerie, tawny sunset, Baiano-Maia posted sentries and radioed Apoena for permission to abandon the trail to the road.

'They must think we are roadbuilders,' he argued. 'They're too frightened to attack the bulldozers. So they shoot at us.'

At four thirty next morning, everyone was moving about in a grey, sullen dawn. 'See,' Maoira said, pointing at footprints in the rain-softened earth. 'They roamed around during the night. They want to know if they hit me.'

For the next few nights, the post was tense as the Uru Eu Wau Wau crept about – during great storms of violent thunder – trying to peer into our three well-barred huts. In the morning the Surui would come out and examine the tracks. They already knew several Uru Eu Wau Wau from their different footprints. On November the 11th, an arrow was fired high into the sky so that it dropped close to some Surui moving about in the middle of the post. And on November the 14th, another Surui surprised a party of Uru Eu Wau Wau trying to creep up to the post from the wall of jungle to the north. As he ran, the Indians let out a series of frightening guttural roars. On the next day, Ze Bel spotted another group creeping through the bushes to the east, and though he and Baiano-Maia walked towards them waving presents, the reply was a flight of arrows and a cacophony of shouts which none of our Indians could understand. There was then a lull for several weeks.

This was to be the pattern for the next five months. Constant attacks succeeded by an interval of two or three weeks when the Uru Eu Wau Wau probably went hunting or to their plantations. The problem for the expedition was how to maintain its position, offering presents in the face of attack, without anyone being hit. For not only would that damage – obviously – the target, but also the hopes of contact. Expecting revenge, the Uru Eu Wau Wau would disappear for months. The orders, therefore, were to walk around visibly alert and armed, and to make it appear difficult for the Uru Eu Wau Wau to attack.

At this time, we also found out that their aggressive tactics could no longer be attributed to the roadbuilders. Immediately after we had driven back from our journey to the road head, we had – by accident – met a World Bank official in one of the frontier towns. Denis Mahar was surprised to hear about the road; the Governor of Rondonia had assured him that no road would be driven into Uru Eu Wau Wau territory. So on the next day he had flown over the roadhead, and when he got to Brasilia had insisted that the roadbuilding should stop. One of the key conditions, for the approval of the World Bank loan for the development of Rondonia was protection of Indians. And neither the State nor the Federal Government wanted to lose half a billion dollars.

The next attack came on December the 3rd and was possibly the most revealing. After lunch, everyone had retired to their hammocks, including Lauro the cook, whose hammock was slung in the kitchen. It was the hut closest to the northern wall of forest. Suddenly twelve arrows hit the palm thatch wall, some sticking in the wall, but others passing straight through – just above and below Lauro's hammock. At his shout, Ze Bel and several Surui ran out to see one of the Uru Eu Wau Wau, on the edge of the scrub, prancing round and round in spirals, waving his bow with both hands above his head. He seemed to be chanting in a triumphal dance.

'I don't think they wanted to kill you,' Apoena said to Lauro. 'If they had, they wouldn't have just fired arrows at a wall. This seems more playful, as if they were trying to scare or test us.' Lauro tried, rather unsuccessfully, to look convinced. But Apoena returned the twelve arrows to the Uru Eu Wau Wau, hanging them up beside their presents in the northern patch of forest. If the dummy attack was a sort of test, then the return of the arrows was a similar form of reply.

There followed a further lull until December the 30th. It was a clear, bright day, and a plane was expected about eleven thirty in the morning. Half the people of the post were at the airstrip, when three Uru Eu Wau Wau, who must have been waiting for a moment of reduced watchfulness, crept out of the southern jungle. They managed to cross the intervening 50 yards without being seen. Silently they came up to the nearest hut and peered into the window, presumably with the intention of shooting anyone inside. With the luck of all the Uru Eu Wau Wau's potential victims, Vicente Rios, our cameraman, was addressing a letter in the corner of the hut where the window shutter made it impossible for them to see him. So the leader whispered to the two behind and started to creep along the wall. Thinking the whisperer was a Surui, Vicente glanced up through the chinks in the log wall. A naked body. Then an arrow bent onto a bow. An Uru Eu Wau Wau was within nine inches of Vicente's nose.

As silently as possible, he rose out of his chair and moved towards the door in the opposite wall of the hut. But as he crept out, the Uru Eu Wau Wau let out their terrifying guttural roars. Vicente ran for the next hut, where I was lying in my hammock.

Few sounds are more paralysing than the Uru Eu Wau Wau's gorilla-like roar. As I heard them, and Vicente calling my name, I leapt for one of the guns that were dotted round all the huts for this sort of emergency. For what seemed an eternity, I fumbled getting the .38 out of its holster, seeing – through the logs – Vicente slip and fall in a pool of mud, just as three arrows flashed over his head. They thumped into the logs on the right side of the door. In moments of sudden emergency, I am the sort of person who usually does the wrong thing. But somehow, in the second before they fired again, I managed to get out of the door, waving the revolver above my shoulder. On the other side of Vicente, the three Uru Eu Wau Wau had their bows drawn for the finishing shot. For a split second we all seemed to freeze into statues of ourselves. And that's how – for once – I can answer one of the most frequent questions about Amazonia. 'Where, precisely, is the frontier?' Of course, there are thousands of frontiers between our society and the unknown, all over the forest – and each is constantly moving. But for that split second, the frontier between our world system and the Uru Eu Wau Wau was on a line precisely seven and a half yards from me and seven and a half yards from the Uru Eu Wau Wau. In the next moment, two Surui armed with shotguns came pounding round the side of the hut and the Uru Eu Wau Wau were gone, leaping with huge kangaroo bounds over the logs that lay between us and the forest. Almost paralysed, we all stared at the scene. If Vicente had not slipped, the arrows would have plunged deep into his back. It took a lot of force just to pull them out of the logs by the door. Once again, a living target at the post of Comandante Ari had been amazingly lucky. And once again, the Surui who tracked the three men out of the forest and then back again, noticed something almost playful in their tactics. The attack had been lethal. But to attempt to shoot through a hut window rather than from ambush on the savannah, implied a spirit of challenge – like a dare from one gangland leader to another.

A few years later, we learnt from the Uru Eu Wau Wau themselves that during this period there had been a difference of opinion between two of their groups. The group of Caninde had wanted to go on attacking, and the group of Careca had wanted to make peace. It was Careca's group, led by his sons, which had carried out this last attack, and they told Caninde that these strangers were different. 'They don't try to kill, even when they're attacked.' Obviously, at the time, we did not know this.

'They are very courageous,' Ze Bel said. 'It's a miracle no-one has been killed. We must put up barbed wire like FUNAI's Arara expedition.' The problem, as Ze Bel saw it, was that the Uru Eu Wau Wau were obviously watching closely, and could probably identify each individual. If they killed or wounded someone, they, like all Indians, would expect revenge. And they might believe the people they had shot at were also waiting to get their own back. In either case the Uru Eu Wau Wau would vanish.

Ze Bel immediately transferred everyone who had been shot at, and brought in more Surui. There then followed a gap of ten days until, on January the 11th, we heard that the Indians had taken all the presents from all the sites where they had been hung. It was the first of the steps towards peaceful contact, and these began to develop with increasing speed and increasing acceptance of presents until, 60 days later, a first Uru Eu Wau Wau received a first machete, directly from the hand of the head of the post, Baiano-Maia.

As soon as the rains began to fall off, we travelled up the BR429 road to check if the Uru Eu Wau Wau had been attacking people settled along it. But there had been no sign of Indians for several months.

What astonished us was the speed of the colonist invasion. Kilometre 58, on our previous visit a few months before, had been solid forest without a house or clearing. Now it was a small village with three dozen houses and its own shop. The bar had a kerosene refrigerator and a pool table. The curtain of our frontier play had almost literally gone down on a forest and come up on a town. The shopkeeper, a migrant from Rio Grande do Sul, told us that Kilometre 58 was marked on the Land Agency's maps as the town of Mirante do Serra and he pointed out the patches of dense forest where soon the petrol station, the school and the sawmill would stand.

At the River Urupa, the abandoned roadbuilders' camp had been taken over by a colonist, and all the way from Kilometre 58 to the end of the road there were many small clearings with makeshift houses. It was as if a column of ants had arrived and was chewing at the forest. A recent arrival, Gaucho, had driven a truck from Rio Grande do Sul, not only with all his furniture, his stove and double bed, but with enough food for a year – including a dozen sacks of beans, 150 packets of mate tea and 60 tins of pig fat. The colonist at the head of the road was a small man called Goiano who seemed unconcerned about the Indians. 'In the dry time, they were hunting here all the time. And once, when they were watching my hut, I heard one laughing – very clearly.'

'Have you never seen them?'

'I was over there, and I saw six men, all strong and naked, crossing the water,' he pointed to the high bank above the stream. 'They were carrying bunches of arrows and one had a bundle of something under his arm.'

Goiano had a very crude hut of logs and thatch, and we were sitting in front of it while he made coffee. The clearing around us was littered with the rubble of deforestation, and looked, as usual, like a bomb site.

'Is life here,' I asked, 'better than where you came from?'

'In Mato Grosso, I had nothing,' Goiano replied. 'I worked without the right to put a cow to grass or even to raise a pig. The rancher wouldn't let me. If I planted anything, I had to give half the crop to him.'

'But you made enough to eat?'

'Very badly.' Goiano laughed. 'Just rice and beans. But then,' Goiano paused significantly, 'I heard they were giving away land in Rondonia.'

'How much did you bring with you?'

'How much money?' Goiano laughed once more. 'After we arrived and I had had a coffee, it was all gone. But I got this plot from the Land Agency. And even though it's difficult,' he waved round the shambles of the clearing, 'even though the Indians are dangerous and there's the risk of malaria, it's better here than there.'

A bit further back, two large families had huts facing each other across the road. Half a dozen children were playing amongst the tree stumps and many had ugly sores on their faces. I asked the mothers whether they weren't concerned for their children.

'I'm frightened,' Dona Maria said, 'but what can I do?'

'To own something,' Dona Gemira, her neighbour interrupted, 'You have to endure the tiger's breath. Before we only lived on the land of others. One year here. One year there. They never gave us land to plant. In Rondonia, we're suffering in the jaguar's mouth. But even if we fall, perhaps we'll come out winners in the end.'

Dona Maria's husband, Renato, was an impressive, active man who had grown up in Parana and had already migrated once to Mato Grosso. He invited us in for a coffee. The hut was small and rudimentary, but Dona Maria kept it immaculately swept.

'Here,' Renato repeated, 'you work for yourself. Plant today, to eat tomorrow. So I believe life here will be better than there. In Mato Grosso, I had to give 40 percent of what I harvested to the owner. 40 percent of all the cotton, beans, rice, everything. We worked hard, just to get enough to eat, and there was no land to pass on to your sons,' he indicated his two very blond boys who were about 12 and 14 years old. Many of the colonists were visibly the descendants of German or Polish migrants. When they stood, in torn jeans, in front of their huts, with their fair hair gleaming in the sun, it was remarkable how they resembled photographs of the frontier families that settled on the north American prairies.

Everyone along the road was full of optimism and looking forward to the dry season, when they would clear forest and later plant rice, corn and mandioca. As a cash crop, Renato had decided on coffee, which he had cultivated in Parana. Goiano was hoping to get seeds from the government for a plantation of rubber. And yet, if any of them had taken a close look at an INCRA colonisation map, it would not have been difficult to predict the disaster that was to come. For the maps were striking evidence of the blindness of officialdom to the forest. The colonisation projects were divided up into a rigid chessboard pattern. Every four kilometres a side road branched off the main road, and each colonist received a plot exactly 500 metres fronting along the road by 2000 metres in depth, or 250 metres by 1000 in depth. The maps revealed no allowance for the terrain, its rivers and mountains. The pattern had been conceived on a drawing board and was plonked straight down on the Amazonian forest without any reference to its nature or individuality. Above all, no attempt had been made to cater for the areas of good and bad soil.

March the 10th was the day of Baiano-Maia's first contact with the Uru Eu Wau Wau, and a week later, the film unit flew back into Comandante Ari.

'The contact started,' Baiano-Maia explained, 'with them shouting from the savannah. So we walked out waving presents. One of the Surui, Ibaroba, took off his shirt and trousers so they could see he was an Indian. Then the leader of the Uru Eu Wau Wau came forward holding a machete in one hand and showing five fingers with the other. I guessed what he wanted,' Baiano-Maia was pleased with his deduction, 'five more machetes. When Ibaroba, another Surui and I got closer, the leader backed away. He was big and painted in red and black. So the Surui stopped, and I went on. The leader watched me until I stopped with the machetes held out. Then he came forward – alone. He took the first machete from my hand, and then another – without a tremor.'

The two Surui put their presents in the hands of four Uru Eu Wau Wau, and then the Uru Eu Wau Wau turned around and went back to the men watching from the bushes. It had taken less than five minutes. But from that moment the future of the Serra dos Pacaas Novos was decided.

Two days later, the Uru Eu Wau Wau returned, but this time with their women and children – a particularly good sign. They all accepted presents, and Apoena decided that the contact was going well enough to be recorded. His instructions were that filming was to be carried out only with telephoto lenses, from concealment, inside the huts.

On March the 18th, the Uru Eu Wau Wau returned, once more led by the chief, who had accepted the presents. We later found out that his name was Caninde. He brought with him seven men, four women and two boys, and they came closer than before, right up to the huts. Caninde asked for 'ibameri' (machete) and 'ibope' (pots), and when they had each received one, he walked, with amazing self-assurance, into an unlocked hut and demanded one of the Surui's hammocks. This was refused because Apoena had ordered that no clothing or personal possessions were to be given away – to avoid passing on flu or some other disease.

'Never in my life have I seen uncontacted Indians so polite,' Baiano-Maia said. 'They ask permission for everything they do.'

Nevertheless, the men remained constantly alert, drawing their bows at any unexpected sound. The women usually stood further back. They were paler and less broadly built than most Indian women, the result – presumably – of interbreeding with captured *seringueiro* children.

When the next party of Uru Eu Wau Wau visited, their leader was Careca, the mysterious, bald chief Meresor had seen on the first attack. He made friends, almost immediately, with Lauro the cook, who had features typical of the north-east of Brazil, and a skin that was paler than any Indian. When the bald-headed Indian and the bald-headed Brazilian stood side by side, they looked like brothers. The white chief of the Uru Eu Wau Wau had been explained at last. He was obviously a *seringueiro*'s kidnapped child.

'At last, the contact seems to be going well,' Ze Bel said. 'In a few years, if nothing goes wrong, we will speak their language. Then we can start to teach them to accept medicine and keep away from the colonists. But will we be in time? The colonists are all around, and we haven't the men or the resources to keep them out.' In fact, it was to take half a dozen years to acquire sufficient influence over the Indians to help protect them, and, from the start the colonists were milling all around.

In April, our team flew out from Comandante Ari and travelled again up the BR429 road. And on the day before our arrival, the Uru Eu Wau Wau raided Goiano's hut. He was in Ouro Preto and the five men staying in his house were away cutting forest.

'They took our five hammocks and all our clothes.' The man who told us, Gaucho, was wildly excited. 'With all our money in the pockets. What use is money to them? They took the best pot, the plates, the spoons, everything. The night before, when they were roaming around, the dog barked so much, nobody could sleep. That is where they killed it,' he said pointing dramatically, 'and cut off its head – to pull out its teeth.'

When we passed Dona Maria's house, she told us that Renato, her husband, was away, and that she was terrified for the children.

'The Indians won't kill the children, will they?' she implored. 'We suffer so much already, and I am so frightened for the little ones. But God must know,' she started to sob, 'what He is doing.'

We could do nothing but share Maria's concern. Two men on the Novo Mundo river to the east had just been shot by the Uru Eu Wau Wau as they were cutting forest for a rancher. A rubber tapper had recently been killed on the Rio Sao Miguel. And a man had been killed, and his wife shot in the face, while clearing a plantation near Rolim de Mouro. The Uru Eu Wau Wau might be making peace with the Indian Agency, but anyone cutting forest in their territory seemed to be at considerable risk. Why then was INCRA, the land agency, sending Brazil's poorest and most humble people into their territory, pushing them directly into conflict with the original even poorer inhabitants of the land? Even if INCRA lacked the foresight to realise that this might cause trouble, even if they failed to hear the warnings of the government's own Indian department, surely the deaths of Chico Prestes's three sons was undeniable and recent evidence of what could happen. Yet the Land Agency kept marking out plots in Indian territory and the colonists went on accepting them. And it was this fact probably more than any other – this courting of disaster with deliberate institutionalised blindness – that forced me to take a harder look at what was happening.

In general, I had become very conscious of a change of rhythm from the 1950s and '60s. Isolated in the forest, the events we had filmed at that time had had a timeless quality about them, and my approach had been more reflective. Now, hurrying from one corner of Rondonia to another, desperately trying to keep up with accelerating developments, it was often months before there was a pause and the time to think about what we were filming. Certainly, something on the frontier seemed to be very seriously wrong. What was less easy, however, was to understand the reason why.

In June, Renato started to clear his land. First he cut the undergrowth with a billhook and then he used a chainsaw to fell all the trees in a rectangle of six hectares. The trunks and underbrush were left to dry during the summer months, and at the end of August – using a strip of car tyre tied to a stick – Maria and Renato fired their land. Dry as tinder, encouraged by a light wind, the six hectares became a conflagration that poured, literally, hundreds of tons of carbon into the sky, transferring much of the forest's wealth to the atmosphere above. For days, everything was black with ash.

The last week of August and the first week of September was the very dry and hot period, before the first showers of the rainy season, when everyone burnt. As we drove up and down the BR429, columns of smoke rose around us like a battlefield. Sometimes, flames lashed so hard across the road that we had to reverse the car to avoid it catching fire, and often a conflagration would get out of control and consume another colonist's crops or house. Once, when we were with one of Renato's neighbours, the wind suddenly veered and in 60 seconds a whip-lash of flame transformed his house into a shimmering skeleton of itself. We would find singed animals creeping across the road. We lived with the taste of smoke in our mouths and the breath of flame on our skin. That fortnight in the summer of 1981 was the apocalypse of the BR429.

Afterwards a breathless hush seemed to hang over the land. The smog was so dense that trucks appeared and disappeared like ghosts, trailing vast clouds of powdery dust. All planes were grounded by the government, and satellite photographs showed a grey pall hanging over the whole of northern Brazil. When eventually we were allowed to fly, the pilots had to peer through a porridge-like fog, until several days of rain washed the smoke back into the ground.

It is the ashes of the forest that, in the first year after felling, produce a good crop for traditional jungle peasants, the *caboclos*. Despite Amazonia's usually poor soils, the nutrients contained in the ash make slash and burn agriculture possible. But no *caboclo* would have chosen Renato's sandy, arid soil. It was so poor that within the first weeks it was obvious something was wrong.

During the following months, Renato and Maria watched their corn wither and die. Some of the 2000 coffee seedlings survived, but none grew higher than a foot. Maria became depressed. The children acquired sores. Renato fought doggedly on.

'What will happen to Renato and the other colonists,' I asked Gabriel de Lima Ferreira, a researcher for Brazil's National Institute for Amazonian Research.

'If it's the same as in earlier colonisation projects in Amazonia,' Gabriel replied, 'it will be a process of migrating agriculture within their own plots, cutting more forest every year and exhausting the soil. In real terms they will get poorer and may eventually be obliged to sell – usually to a big landowner who will combine a number of small-holdings into a ranch. He pays for the land, but what he gets is a title deed and the jungle already half-tamed. All the breaking-in, all the risks, all the malaria, have been taken by the colonist.'

Gabriel later became Rondonia's State Secretary for Agriculture. His prediction was remarkably accurate.

After struggling for a year, Maria and Renato abandoned their land – like Gaucho, like Goiano and like most of their neighbours. 'The soil produced nothing,' Renato explained when we found him working on someone else's farm. 'I planted corn. And the ears came out tiny. Rice should produce a large bushel. There, it was minute. I planted 40 litres to harvest four sacks. The coffee was so yellow, it looked as if it was burnt, and after a year it was only 20 centimetres high. Working with that soil destroyed hope. So much toil and so much difficulty. And now we are worse off than before – sharecroppers, giving 50 percent to the landowner.'

'I had always wanted a piece of land,' Maria added, 'and we went there with so much hope. But all the children got sick. Five malarias. My youngest nearly died. We fought and laboured, and suffered. And we have come out of it worse than if we had never gone.'

In Xingu, what I had seen was a ruthless attack on Indian land by ranchers and speculators. But at least it had made sense and profits for them. Evolution was allowing a very small Indian economic system to be overwhelmed by the most powerful one the world had ever seen.

But here, in Rondonia, colonists and the Land Agency were marching into the forest to their own immediate loss. No one seemed to gain, and the forest which had provided a good living for Alfredao and the *seringueiros* was gone virtually for ever. For though it takes only 20 years of lying fallow under pioneer scrub for the soil to recover sufficiently for another crop, and only 60 to 70 years for the biomass to return to the same weight of trees as before, it requires hundreds of years for the return of the same rich blend of species as a normal block of Amazonian forest.

And so, it was from this time that I began to think of the colonists and developers as people walking backwards into the forest. They were entering a completely new environment, but the colonists barely seemed to look at it. When a colonist arrived at his title-deeded rectangle of virgin *hilaea*, what he saw was a European-type farm, which he had usually left behind in the south of Brazil, and which he could regain here in Amazonia, if only he could get the tropical vegetation off it. In a similar way, the vision of the Land Agency was a map, traced on some drawing board in Brasilia, and rigidly divided into a chequer board pattern to be plonked down onto a tropical forest, regardless of its swamps and rivers, regardless of the Indians and *seringueiros* who already lived within it.

And so I began to have the feeling that we had entered a completely new phase of Amazonian development. The history of Amazonia may have been littered with visionaries like Ford and Ludwig who fruitlessly tried to impose some dream or vision on the forest. But here was a government and a whole society marching into the forest with the manic zest of a lemming migration, hypnotised by an obsession which was even more difficult than the lemmings' to understand. We seemed to have arrived at one of the frontier's dead-ends, where the forest mirrored the absurdity of the society confronting it. Therefore, from the end of 1981, I started to broaden the scope of what we were filming in order to seek different angles and other opinions on what was happening.

THREE

In 1981, there were relatively few voices in Brazil speaking out against the destruction in Amazonia, and certainly the best known was that of Jose Lutzenberger. He had campaigned for a dozen years against pesticides and chemical agriculture in the south of Brazil. And as he had done this in television debates at the height of the military repression – when most other criticism was suppressed – it had made him a national figure recognisable almost anywhere in the country. Once, when I was with him in his somewhat mangy Volkswagen beetle and he absentmindedly overtook a bus while talking with both hands in the air, we were waved into the kerb by a policeman on a motorbike. He came up to the car and lowered himself ponderously to the driver's window. And then, as he saw Lutz, he stopped and smiled. 'So, it's you, Professor,' he said. 'Well you can go on.' And then after a pause. 'You get them – so our children can live in a better world.'

Towards the end of 1981, Lutz joined us in Rondonia, and we started making a film which tried to explain what was going wrong with the colonisation and development programme. 'What we are seeing is nothing new,' Lutz said, when he visited the BR429 road with us. 'This sort of colonisation started in the nineteenth century when the first Emperor of Brazil married a Hapsburg. Princess Leopoldina encouraged German, Italian and Polish peasants to migrate to Rio Grande do Sul in the south of Brazil where each – like my great grandparents – received their own piece of land.' Lutz still lives in Rio Grande do Sul, and his house is full of his father's paintings and etchings illustrating this period of peasant colonisation. 'The land was good and they developed a really healthy peasant agriculture. But a hundred years later, by the second World War, Rio Grande do Sul had been completely deforested and the sons of the colonists began to look for land in the neighbouring state of Parana.'

'That time, however, it took only a generation to deforest the whole of Parana, and by the 1970s, smallholders' land was being bought up and combined into huge mechanised farms. Government subsidies and international bank loans always favour intensive agriculture based on machines, fertilisers and pesticides. After the small man has cut down the forest and made the land cultivable,' Lutz concluded, 'the whole bias of Brazilian agriculture is to push him out and to concentrate his land into large industrial farms.'

And so it was that the colonist farmers who had taken 100 years to deforest Rio Grande do Sul, then 30 years to deforest Parana and Mato Grosso, were now moving up the BR429 road. With the invention of the motor saw, it would take just a decade to strip Rondonia. Then the frontier would roll on.

In the south of Brazil, the capitalization and mechanization of agriculture had pushed millions of people off the land. The government's own estimate for Brazil's landless poor was about twelve million. Their hunger for land led to invasion of ranches, hundreds of murders a year, immense pressure for land reform, and a violent situation that could easily explode into revolution or anarchy. This was Brazil's greatest social problem, and Amazonia was a sort of safety valve for it, where the most desperate and the most adventurous people – who might otherwise become political leaders – could find an outlet. By dumping the rural poor in the jungle, the military government could both postpone land reform in the south and occupy Amazonia against possible foreign conquest – one of the generals' most persistent neuroses. And whether the colonist did or did not do well in the forest was almost irrelevant to the thinking behind this policy.

Dr Philip Fearnside was another of the scientists we started to film at this period. He began his research with the Trans-Amazon road project in the 1970s and is often described as the best environmentalist/social scientist working in Amazonia.

When I said that I found it difficult to understand the apparent futility of what we were filming, Philip suggested that it made more sense if we looked at it in terms of land speculation rather than agriculture. 'Both at the level of the individual colonist, and at the level of the area as a whole, each person expects to make most of his money by selling his plot rather than by the beef or any other product that is produced while he holds it.' Philip nodded towards a family whose data he and his researcher, Gabriel, were collecting near the main road close to Ouro Preto. 'Last year they said they made less than 100,000 cruzeiros (under $1,000). But they expect to sell half their plot (100 hectares) for three million cruzeiros (roughly $30,000) because it's close to the main road. So it would take many years of production to equal what they can make from the increase in the value of the land.' The poverty of the land was, therefore, not absolutely critical to them. What they required from the soil was enough food and cash in hand to live on for the few years before they sold.

One of the trends revealed by Philip's and Gabriel's research was that most colonists planted rice or corn in their first year, and then turned the land over to grass – because pasture was the cheapest way of keeping land in a marketable form. And every year the grass had to be burnt to hold back the pioneer scrub seeded from the surrounding forest. Thus, every year the exposed soil was baked by the tropical sun and its scarce nutrients leeched out by the rain. During the first year, one hectare was usually enough to feed a cow, but after five years, four or five hectares were required.

When we visited the 30,000 hectare Rio Candeias ranch belonging to the de Zorzi group from Rio Grande do Sul, they had 2000 hectares of grass which had been planted six years before. Most of it was shoulder high with scrub, and they were using bulldozers to scrape it away and plant new grass. The bulldozers damaged and compacted the top soil and the ranch vet told Lutz that, though the newly planted grass might initially support one to two head per hectare, the annual decline was very great.

In 1983, their semi-abandoned pasture was invaded by squatters, and though, at first, the de Zorzi group resisted, they eventually gave up the struggle. Cocoa, coffee and rubber did not seem to be doing much better. In theory, three crops are more suited to a tropical forest, and cocoa and rubber are Amazonian in origin. The trouble was that, when cocoa plantations (which did well in Africa and Bahia) and rubber monocultures (which flourished in Malaya and Sao Paulo) were transported back to the Amazon, they were also coming home to the breeding ground of their species's diseases. In the forest, the mass of intervening vegetation isolates each individual of a species from its like and so limits the spread of disease. But in the plantations of Rondonia, one diseased tree meant an epidemic. Hugo Frey was the largest agriculturalist in Rondonia with a model 15,000 hectare farm that, during the early 1980s, was often featured in magazine articles. Frey's family are the biggest producers of apples in the south of Brazil, and they had considerable experience in large scale tree farming. Yet, when we visited him, he had just ploughed up 200 hectares of rubber and 200 hectares of cocoa.

'It's a very bitter experience to build up a project which, after years of work, doesn't produce,' he said grimly, looking over his ploughed up rubber plantation. 'Twelve years ago we were encouraged – with subsidies from government agencies – to plant cocoa and rubber at a time when the behaviour of all types of agriculture were unknown in Amazonia. Now we know that neither cocoa nor rubber do well here. We were encouraged to plant when there had not been sufficient research to produce strains that could resist tropical disease. In 1986, we expected 30,000 arrobas (a Brazilian agricultural measurement) of coffee. We only got 5000. It's a disaster, not just for us, but for the whole state.'

Like the colonist, however, the low yields of the large agriculturalist were not absolutely critical to their financial success. By Brazilian law, any large company can invest 25 percent of the taxes it owes the government in an Amazonian project; and 75 percent of the investment in a project can be provided in this way. Since the money would otherwise be lost, what is of prime importance to the company is not that the farm should make a profit, but that the farm should be resaleable. Speculation was Rondonia's principal industry, and, in the 1980s, it seemed a business completely blind to what it was handling. Like the market for gold, art and stamp collections, land was valued not according to what it could produce, but according to its paper worth in relationship to the national and international market. During a time when Brazil's inflation could rise several hundred percent a year, land was not only a good hedge against inflation, but a very profitable investment. For instance, the real value of pasture land in Rondonia – discounting inflation – soared from 4000 to 10,000 cruzados per hectare between 1984 and 1986.

And so it was, that during 1982, we began to acquire a very different picture of what was happening in Rondonia. In the past, I had thought of intruders in the Amazon basin as blind, but, at least, they had just been invaders of the forest. What we were watching in Rondonia, however, was the absorption of the forest by another system that was not even conscious of what it was consuming. The speculation frontier seemed like a giant, spinning top, gyrating in ever wider circles, devouring all the land from Parana to Rondonia. How good the soil was, what the land grew, were almost irrelevant, so long as it served as collateral for pieces of paper acceptable on the land market – as long as it justified a tax discount or government subsidy.

And as I became aware of this destructive system based on phony finance, so my interest turned towards the ultimate source of much of that finance – one of the world's controlling economic institutions – the World Bank.

FOUR

It was an accident that I heard about the Polonoroeste loan – the loan for the north-west development pole – before most of the people in the World Bank itself. A rumour that it was under consideration was leaked to a local paper in Rondonia while I was there in the summer of 1979. And when I rang Robert Goodland, the ecological officer of the Bank, he invited me to visit him on my way through Washington.

The Bank is a squat, stolid group of buildings with the maze-like corridors of a labyrinth. When I opened the door, I was surprised to finding getting on to a dozen people waiting in a small conference room. They included Robert Skillings, who was head of the Brazil department and later to become the chief advocate of the loan, Robert Goodland and the anthropologist, Maritta Koch-Weser. Apparently the loan had only just begun to be discussed between the Bank's local officer and the State Governments of Rondonia and Mato Grosso, and most people in the room seemed to know as little about it as I did. Despite this, I left that windowless, claustrophobic space feeling that Skillings – a professional roadbuilder – was determined to push the loan through, and that Goodland and Koch-Weser, the ecologist and anthropologist, had their professional reservations.

The main part of the Polonoroeste loan – $240 million – was for the paving of the BR364 highway, which runs from the south of Brazil into the Amazonian states of Mato Grosso and Rondonia. This was the dirt road originally commissioned by Juscelino Kubitschek, the President who built Brasilia and launched Brazil's north and westward thrust into the Amazon. But now, with every rainy season, thousands of trucks were marooned for days in a sea of mud, with their produce rotting in the heat. Truckers would dump dead cows to decompose by the side of the road. Refrigerated vans carrying frozen chickens would lose their whole consignment when the refrigerating fuel ran out. And several times our pick-up was stuck all night with a line of trucks in front and a line of trucks behind – which was the reason we seldom travelled without food, water and cachaca, the Brazilian cane spirit. Waving down a truck with a rope and a bottle of cachaca in your hand was the best way of getting out of mud.

It was to remove this wet season bottleneck, and to lower freight rates in order to make export agriculture more viable in the West of Amazonia, that the BR364 was to be paved. A further $200 million of the World Bank's money was to be for feeder roads, health programmes and rural development. The Bank's staff must have hoped that such a loan would be welcome to everyone.

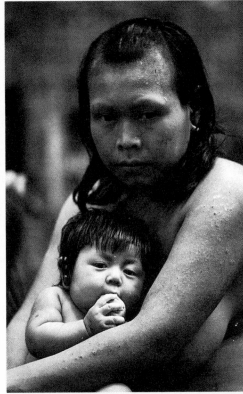

Members of the Txukahamei tribe. *Chris Men*

(Facing page) Orlando and Claudio descending the River Peixoto Azevedo. (Previous page) The start of deforestation. *Adrian Cowell*

(Left) Making the canoes. *Adrian Cowell*

(Below) Loading the canoes. *Adrian Cowell*

(Facing page above) Entering the Kreen-Akrore village. *Adrian Cowell*

(Below) Kreen-Akrore clubs left in exchange for the expedition's presents. *Adrian Cowell*

(Left) Chico Prestes. *Adrian Cowell*

(Below) Chico's family. Fabio – who was kidnapped – and his eldest brother Luis – who was killed – are on the right. *Chico Prestes*

(Bottom left) Alfredo, Maria – the captured Uru Eu Wau Wau girl – and their sons. *Adrian Cowell*

(Facing page) The expedition travelling up the River Jamari. *Adrian Cowell*

Members of the Uru Eu Wa[...]
Wau tribe. *Vicente Rios and*
Adrian Cowell

Deforestation – before and after. *Adrian Cowell*

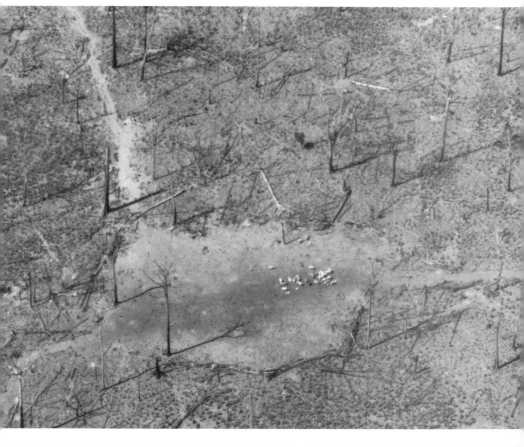

(This page) Gaucho, a colonist, clears his land. *Adrian Cowell*
(Facing page) Burning the forest. *Adrian Cowell*

(Facing page above) Unloading charcoal at the COSIPAR blast furnace for pig iron. *Adrian Cowell*

(Below) Serra Pelada. *Adrian Cowell*

(This page right) Jova during a prospecting trip in the Serra dos Carajas. *Vicente Rios*

(Below) *Garimpeiros* washing gold. *Adrian Cowell*

(Above left) Chico when we started filming with him in 1986. *Adrian Cowell*; (Above right) Chico shortly before his death, worn down by months of intimidation from Darli. *Vicente Rios*; (Right) Darli. *Adrian Cowell*; (Above) Genesio. *Vicente Rios*

(Facing page above) Ilza Mendes before the door where Chico was shot. *Vicente Rios*; (Below) Chico's funeral. *Vicente Rios*

Squatters practising for an
ambush. *Adrian Cowell*
(Below) The funeral of a squatter murdered
by the ranch's gunmen. *Adrian Cowell*

From its inception, however, the Polonoroeste loan attracted violent opposition. 'We understand that the World Bank is about to approve a loan of $330 million for the Polonoroeste Project in Brazil,' began a letter from Survival International (USA) to the President of the World Bank. 'The Bank, however, has not yet found a way to guarantee adequate protection for the 8000 Indians of this region. This is especially serious in view of the fact that a number of the Indian groups in the Project area are still isolated and not in permanent contact with the national society. If it goes ahead with the loan, the Bank will be knowingly participating in the destruction of the livelihood and the lives of hundreds of defenseless human beings.' Neither this, nor any subsequent attack, was to be aimed against the paving of the BR364 itself. The paving of the main trunk highway into the north-west of Brazil was inevitable someday. What its critics objected to was that the loan brought the paving forward before there was sufficient machinery to protect the Indians or the environment from the development it would cause.

In fact, the Polonoroeste loan made more provision than any previous loan for the interests of the tribal people in its area. Probably because of the early controversy, over $10 million was allocated to Amerindian affairs in the Polonoroeste budget. But the Indian Agency, FUNAI, was to spend most of this on hardware such as jeeps, tractors, aeroplanes, schools and hospital buildings without resolving the fundamental problem of Indian survival in the face of colonisation and development. Despite the loan, most of the Indian reserves were to be invaded by prospectors, squatters and timber extracters, and epidemic after epidemic was to ravage the Uru Eu Wau Wau and the other tribes in the area.

If Project Polonoroeste is carried out, concluded a report from David Price, a consultant anthropologist contracted by the World Bank, *land values will rise vertiginously, there will be a new influx of settlers, and the pressures on the native population will be redoubled. More than 8000 Indians in Mato Grosso and Rondonia will be affected. To entrust their welfare to the FUNAI as it is now constituted would be criminal.*

When the Bank had such an assessment from its own consultant right from the start, it was natural to enquire why it went ahead. 'Their initial reaction was to essentially suppress the distribution of my report within the Bank itself,' was Price's answer. 'In a serious sense, I don't think they paid much attention . . . I think that the Bank knows that it's going to give a certain amount of money to certain regions or certain countries every year, and the projects that it supposedly gives the money to are merely pretexts. And I think that all the consultancy and all the evaluation that is done is by way of window dressing.'

This alarming conclusion was to be born out by the attention the Bank paid to its soil experts and its staff ecologist over the Polonoroeste project. D. C. Pickering, Assistant Director of the Agriculture and Rural Development Department, wrote: *It would be unwise at the present time to assume that most of such lands would be suitable for development for agriculture.* But the most trenchant warning of all came from Robert Goodland. From the very first survey mission, in the autumn of 1979, Goodland, the Bank's ecological officer and an expert on Amazonian ecology, had opposed the loan. *One of the main justifications for the highway proposal is to facilitate access of agricultural surpluses to markets*, he wrote at the beginning of 1980, nearly two years before the loan agreement was signed. *Although this may appear superficially reasonable, it creates major environmental implications which are here outlined.* In the stiff, economic terminology of a Bank report, Goodland went on: *Facilitating access to markets promotes market-orientated resource management. The outcome of this policy relegates the study area to supplying food to the south of Brazil. This is less desirable than increased self-reliance for the people of the area, and inappropriate for the resource base . . . Food production in the study area represents a conversion of the resource – forest and some soil fertility – into a short-lived export surplus. Rice occupied practically half the cultivated area and this is dangerous since most of the soils are unsuited to annual cropping. Easing market access – paving highways – promotes production of spoilable surplus, an inadvisable form of land management for this region.*

Goodland concluded as strongly as a Bank report can. *The aim of this section has been to suggest that the type of agricultural development constrained by highway construction may not be entirely appropriate for the region, and is potentially damaging to the Amerindians . . . worsening the migratory flux and wasteful of intermediate sparsely populated areas and of petroleum and natural resources.* And then in muted bureaucratese, he enquired mildly, *How the highway would act as a catalyst for the orderly occupation, colonization and use of the land, remains to be clarified, since the mission received views contrary to this assertion.* All in all, it would have been difficult to make a more accurate forcast of what happened over the next ten years. I, therefore, found it very difficult to understand why such an assessment went unheeded.

Goodland is tall, spectacled, works in the Bank from six thirty in the morning until five in the evening and, at that time, walked to and from his Washington office with the loping stride of a nomadic Indian. He had set up Brasilia University's environmental department and was an authority on the problems of development in the Amazonian forest. He was, in fact, so demonstrably right on the need to protect both the environment and the Indians, and his reminders of what was wrong with the loan became so discomforting to Skillings and the road department, that for four years he was specifically forbidden to return to Rondonia. Already bemused by the chaos in Rondonia, and now even more perplexed by the Bank's inability to see what was happening, I felt that here the World Bank achieved what must be an epitome of blindness, or possibly the gold medal for backwards walking into the forest – the officer paid by the Bank to avoid environmental disasters was formally forbidden to prevent the Bank leaping into the greatest environmental disaster of its history.

On December the 15th, 1981, the loan agreement was signed. On the 13th of September, 1984, the road was inaugurated. On September 19th, 1984,

Congressional hearings were already being held about the devastation it was causing. And in the spring of 1985, Congressional criticism forced the Bank to suspend, temporarily, its payments on the Polonoroeste loan. Finally, in May 1987, Barber Conable, the President of the Bank, made a speech at a dinner held in Washington's Sheraton Carlton Hotel in which he admitted the Bank's mistakes.

There was little else he could do. When Rondonia was elevated from a Federal Territory to a fully fledged State in 1982, its then Governor, who had lobbied for the World Bank loan, made this appeal: 'Come, Brazilians from all over Brazil. Come, men of all peoples. Rondonia offers you work, solidarity, respect. Bring us your hopes and dreams.' Only four years later, in 1986, the next Governor complained: 'Rondonia is being trampled down by a migration of 180,000 people per year. The great problem Rondonia faces today is the devastation of our state.' New arrivals were living as share-croppers on the land of earlier colonists, and as soon as a road into a new area was rumoured, it was like the Klondike – people scrabbling over each other to mark out a patch of land before the Land Agency's surveyors arrived.

Looking at the statistical results of the development programme in Rondonia, deforestation, which had only amounted to two percent of the state at the start of the decade had consumed roughly a quarter by the end. And according to a Rondonia Government report, 60 percent of this deforested area is now scrub on its way back to secondary forest. After Brazil's biggest agricultural colonisation programme three-quarters of Rondonia's population now lives in the towns – much of it in slums. And to take the specific case of Renato and the BR429 road, over 80 percent of the plots along the route between Mirante de Serra and the River Urupa had been sold or had changed hands as early as 1986. The local rice miller in Ouro Preto had bought 29 plots in two areas of the BR429 combining them into two ranches. In Renato's area the process of speculation and capitalisation predicted by Lutz and Philip Fearnside had got under way within the first few years.

What Barber Conable had to say about all this on May the 5th, 1987 was: 'Inevitably the Bank has also stumbled. For instance, a more recent Brazilian project, known as Polonoroeste, was a sobering example of an environmentally sound effort' – a number of the professional environmentalists sitting in the banqueting hall smiled – 'which went wrong. The Bank misread the human, institutional and physical realities of the jungle and the frontier. A road which benefited small farmers also became a highway for logging companies. Protective measures to shelter fragile land and tribal people were carefully planned. They were not, however, executed with enough vigour. In some cases the dynamics of the frontier got out of control. Polonoroeste teaches many lessons. A basic truth is that ambitious environmental design requires realistic analysis of the enforcement mechanisms in place and in prospect.'

Conable then went on to announce a number of world-wide reforms intended to prevent the Bank repeating another Polonoroeste. What he did not refer to, nor did anyone else, was that virtually everything that had gone wrong had been predicted by one or other of the Bank's experts, and particularly by Robert Goodland, who was at a corner table at the dinner.

'How could the Bank be so blind,' I asked later under one of the Carlton's chandeliers, 'when the problems of Amazonia had been pointed out to them in Bank reports by Bank experts employed to do just that.'

'No banker,' replied Bruce Rich, who had led the campaign against the Bank, 'ever gets promotion by not lending money – by not making a loan. Each has some sort of quota, though now they tend to deny this. So the underlying tendency of the system is always to meet or exceed that quota. The whole debt crisis stems from this.'

This reminded me of a conversation I had once had in the World Bank with John Malone, who appeared to be in charge of the negotiations about enforcing the clauses of the Polonoroeste loan agreement. When Jose Lutzenberger, who was also at the meeting, suggested cutting off the loan, Malone's reply was revealing. The Bank's problem, he said, was not how to cut off loans but how to make more of them.

What he was referring to was the fact that in 1985 the countries of Latin America and the Caribbean borrowed $18 billion dollars, but their repayments on previous loans amounted to $32 billion dollars. Latin America had thus become not an importer but a net exporter of capital. She was financing the developed world to the tune of $14 billion dollars per year. The whole financial system would eventually grind itself into dislocation unless some way was found for channelling more money to the Third World. Since the World Bank could normally only lend money for specific projects, what Malone was saying was that its problem was how to find more projects, rather than how to cut off existing ones.

And so it seemed that the momentum of the Bank's financial machine, the need to lend money to Brazil as its debt developed, had over-ridden the practical warnings of its specialists who had visited Rondonia and Mato Grosso. In a very similar way, the Brazilian government's need to defuse Brazil's rural tension and the hunger of speculators in the landmarket, had made Rondonia's unsuitability for colonisation almost irrelevant. It was as if a whole army of catatonic fanatics had marched into the forest, with eyes so riveted on some messianic vision that they were completely unaware of everything around them. And once again Amazonia had rudely shaken the intruder, shattered the World Bank's bureaucratic dream.

But this time, though the Bank and the colonist lost, the prime loser, of course, was the forest. And, by 1985, it was obvious that unless something was done quickly, there would soon be no forest left.

And yet, as the canopy flared and the 100 year-old trunks slowly inciner-ated into ash, as the purest air on earth gave way to smog, and the lush tropical forest was replaced by the blown sands of its arid floor, I felt more optimistic than I had been in Xingu with the Villas Boas brothers. Then it had seemed as if the only way to improve the situation for Xingu was to do the impossible – to change the world and the economic and political system that challenged the forest. Now I had met the people who had developed the political machinery to do precisely that. After years of despondency in Amazonia, it was a heady time.

During my first period of filming in Washington in 1984, I had met Bruce Rich who was the lobbyist leading the campaign against the World Bank. Bruce is small, bearded and has a capacity to concentrate on a single objective that would induce awe in a bulldog. In 1983, he, together with Brent Blackwelder of the Environmental Policy Institute, and Barbara Bramble, head of the National Wildlife Federation's Internation Programme, had – with remarkable boldness – decided to seek a way to change the objective and methods of international economic development in the Third World, in particular the damage it did to the environment. Together they had agreed to concentrate their attack on the World Bank because it was, more or less, the economic standard bearer of the First World, and its policies were followed by most bankers. But it was Bruce who had decided to concentrate the campaign against the Polonoroeste loan. And it was he who had narrowed the controversy from the overall principle of whether the loan should ever have been granted in the first place, to the more limited, but much more proveable, issue of whether the protective clauses in the World Bank's own loan agreement with Brazil were being enforced. If they were not, and if the Bank took no action to enforce them, then it proved that they had just been thrown in as a sop for Congress and the environmentalists.

When Bruce testified in Congress, it was usually for his own Natural Resources Defence Council but also for the National Wildlife Federation. With over five million members, the Federation was by far the largest environmental organisation in America; the head of its international programme, Barbara Bramble, used their voting strength to support and sometimes to defend Bruce. She was the diplomat who held together a coalition of environmental groups which, besides Brent Blackwelder of the Environmental Policy Institute, included Craig van Note of Monitor. Altogether, at that time there were probably not more than a handful of people in half a dozen organisations involved in what was to become a historic campaign.

When Bruce asked me to testify at hearings before the Congressional Subcommittee on Natural Resources, I had agreed that he could show one of our films. But I suggested that it would be more effective if Jose Lutzenberger testified on behalf of his and other Brazilian environmental organisations. And the Chairman of the Subcommittee, Congressman James Scheuer, was so impressed with what Lutz had to say, that he immediately wrote – through the US Treasury – to the World Bank . . .

To express my deep concern over the progress and impact of Brazil's Integrated Development Program for the Northwest region (the 'Polonoroeste project.') It was when this letter received a dismissive reply that Bruce achieved his first breakthrough. He took the reply to Senator Robert Kasten who was the Chairman of the powerful Appropriations Committee's Sub-committee on Foreign Operations – powerful because it oversaw, and could cut off, the US contribution to the World Bank. This amounted to 19 percent of all its funds. So concerned was the Senator by the Bank's dismissal of Rondonia's problems that he wrote to the President of the Bank describing their reply as *at best a brush-off, but frankly more correctly described as an insult.* He then added a barely veiled threat. *As you know better than anyone else, securing support for US contributions to multilateral development institutions is difficult at best. That the World Bank would respond in such a cavalier fashion to groups and individuals who would otherwise support their program is most difficult to understand.*

Soon after, the Bank suspended payments on its Polonoroeste loan. This almost immediately produced the demarcation of the Uru Eu Wau Wau reserve. However, the Bank used this as justification to resume payments again. And when nothing was done for years to expel squatters inside the demarcated reserve, or to stop the BR429 road being driven into the barren lands of the Guapore valley, or to enforce the other clauses in protection of the environment and the Indians, the environmentalists and Senator Kasten took a number of further steps which were to lead to a 20 percent reduction of the US contribution to the World Bank. 'Nothing so concentrates a banker's mind,' Bruce commented, 'as being separated from his money.' And so, for the first time, I was seeing an Amazonian situation improved by someone trying to change the way the world system impacted on the forest. Half a dozen overworked people in a variety of environmental organizations had found a lever to force the World Bank – the developed world's financial arm – to pay attention to facts. It was a historic breakthrough, and was immediately recognised by environmental groups all over the world as such. It was one lesson that did not go unheeded.

In the spring of 1985, the Threshold Foundation held a weekend strategy meeting to plan the launching of a world-wide tropical forest campaign. It was at a farm on top of a pine forested mountain in West Virginia where the cool wind and the open spaces between the trees could not have been in greater contrast to Amazonia. And yet it is surprising how much that has happened since was first outlined then. Bruce Rich described his plan to widen the campaign against the World Bank to Indonesia, Asia and Africa. He proposed to get European environmental groups to put similar pressure on their governments, so that not just the United States, but a majority of the Bank's voting strength could be swung on environmental issues. And he also suggested September 1986 as the date for the first public demonstration outside the World Bank's annual meeting in Washington.

Friends of the Earth (US) had sent Randy Hayes to the meeting and he outlined his plan to set up the Rain Forest Action Network. Its first campaign would be against the Burger King chain for importing beef grown on deforested land in Central America. (They eventually forced Burger King to stop their imports.) Catherine Caufield, author of *In the Rain Forest*, brought from the Friends of the Earth (UK) a very detailed plan for their campaign directed at the international timber trade. (This was to be successful in South-East Asia, but less important in Amazonia where logging is a secondary, but not primary, cause of deforestation.)

I was attending the meeting to work out how to combine our filming in Amazonia with filming some parts of the campaign. My only contribution was to point out that most previous environmental campaigns, against whaling, for instance, had been about issues that could be decided in the First World. But as tropical forests were in the Third World, everything depended on political decisions in those countries. It was thus essential to get the support of Third World environmental organisations from the beginning and afterwards to keep them involved.

At that meeting was Steve Schwartzman, a band guitarist turned anthropologist who had worked with the Kreen-Akrore in Xingu and who had later helped Bruce Rich on the Indian issues of the Polonoroeste campaign. He spoke good Portuguese, was diplomatic, got on well with many of the pro-Indian and environmental groups in Brazil, and was asked to act as the liaison with them. The Beldon and Threshold Foundations financed his first trip to get Brazilian opinions on the campaign and to set up a system of communication with them. And in all the controversy over Amazonia since, there have not been many divergences or differences of opinion between the Brazilian and US environmental organisations.

It was one of the ironies of that meeting that it took place when many environmentalists believed that their anti-whaling campaign was nearing success. One or two were specifically talking of transferring some of their resources and people from whales to tropical forests. 'Getting out of whales,' as one of them said, 'and into trees.' And so, two or three days later, when I was having a drink with Craig van Note of Monitor, I said that I doubted that the tropical forest campaign could ever be as successful as the one on whaling. 'Tropical forests may be more important to the world,' I said, 'but they're less emotive, less cuddly than whales,' Craig is an ex-*Time* reporter and his organisation specialises in environmental news and publicity. 'Just wait a few years,' he said, 'and we'll make the whales seem nothing.'

At the time, their public campaign was still more than a year away, and tropical forests were rarely discussed in the media or politics. But after years of plodding around a disintegrating forest, it was a truly heady time. I felt like a deprived alcoholic watching a whisky factory go up. I could have got drunk on brick dust.

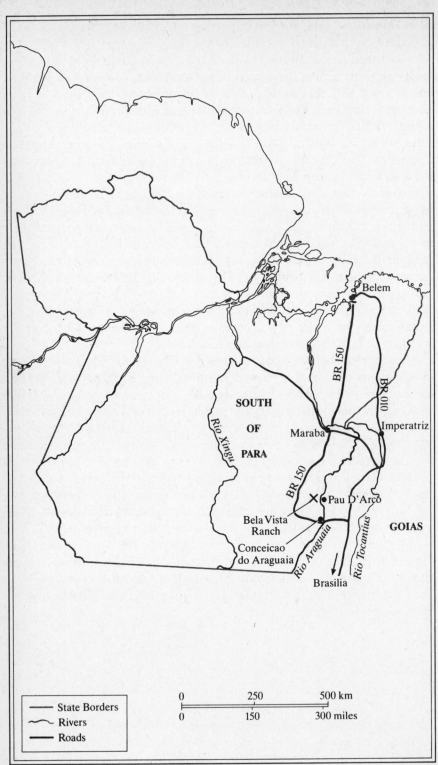

SOUTH OF PARA

four

HUNGER *for* LAND

THE SOUTH OF PARA
1987

It is not easy to understand the stampede for land in Amazonia without some impression of what drives the migrants away from their homes. In the south of Brazil, it is largely the capitalisation and mechanisation of agriculture primarily for export, and in some of the rural municipalities 40 percent of the population has been drained away in not much more than a decade. But in other parts of Brazil, the cause is usually that landowners are holding idle or under-utilised land for speculation. This is why the rural trades unions have often criticised INCRA, the Land Agency, for giving free land to migrants in Amazonia. They argue that the landless should receive plots taken from these idle ranches in their own states in the developed part of Brazil, where there is an infrastructure of roads and warehouses, and where the farmer is closer to his markets.

In 1985, when the civilian government came to power, it created a new Ministry for Agrarian Reform and Development, MIRAD, which announced an ambitious programme of land reform. Though most of this was never carried out, INCRA did identify 281 million hectares of idle land and counted 10.6 million rural workers without land. Or put another way, nearly half Brazil's arable land was owned by less than one percent of its landowners. What was worse, this concentration in a few, very rich, hands was increasing, not decreasing.

Such an unjust system is bound to create enormous pressures. So desperate are the Sem Terra – the Brazilian word for the landless – that they migrate all over the country – not just Amazonia – invading any empty patch which may seem unclaimed. One of the only ways that the big landowners can hold onto what they have is through assassination and fear of assassination, deliberately propagated by professional gunmen using threats, beatings and intimidation. Since 1980, there have been well over 1000 land killings in Brazil, and *the area of greatest violence is the south of Para. This is the part of Eastern Amazonia which was opened up by the first development road, the Belem-Brasilia, and as it is on the rim of the Amazon basin, it received waves of migrants from the neighbouring, very impoverished, north-east of Brazil.*

It was also one of the principal areas to be developed by the government's tax incentive scheme which encouraged big companies to turn large blocks of forest into massive ranches. This was administered by SUDAM (the Superintendancy for the Development of Amazonia) which invested $700 million in a total of 631 projects. Some of these run into hundreds of thousands of hectares, and were the single most important cause of deforestation in this area. This is why the south of Para, one of the first parts of Amazonia to be settled, has the land and feudal problems of the more developed part of Brazil. In 1986, 71 rural workers were assassinated in the state, most of them in the south. In the towns of Maraba and Imperatriz, gunmen could be hired almost openly and the police and courts were so dominated by the landowners, that not one gunman had been convicted for the 411 land murders in the south of Para committed between 1978 and 1988.

ONE

The man in front of me took two rechargeable brass cartridges out of a little cloth bag by his side and pushed them into the barrels of a sawn off shotgun. Then we moved out of the dark of the forest and crossed the road. 'That's the way to the ranch,' he whispered.

Through an opaque haze of dust and smoke, the sky was white with heat. In the dessicated pasture around us, it was unlikely that anyone could be near enough to hear, and yet, as we approached the charred remains of two burnt out houses, the man in front of me whispered again. 'Those are two of the houses the rancher's gunmen burnt.'

Two men with guns then went ahead to check a trail through pasture high with ungrazed grass. As we waited, two other men told me about their ambush in retaliation for the burnt houses. 'There were a hundred of us squatters, and two of the gunmen were riding on the road near here. We only managed to hit one, Adao Barbosa, and he got to this house before he fell off his horse.' He waved at the blackened corner posts which were all that were left. 'The owner of the house tried to protect him. But we pulled him out and each of us stabbed him so that we would all be responsible.' (We later heard that only one man had stabbed him repeatedly and that this version was for his protection.) 'But the police only arrested Oity and Antonio Sabino. And that was for watching over the body, hoping to kill the other gunmen when they came for the corpse.'

When the two scouts returned, our group of about a dozen men marched quietly but quickly through the pasture until we came to another junction of the trails. There we found more men with shabby clothes and battered shotguns; they reminded me of a messianic sect we once met in Burma just after they had leapt out of ambush to stab 20 soldiers to death. Both groups had the same sort of disoriented, demented look, as if they had gone fey. Some of the men carried the antique type of shotgun which does not break at the barrel, but has a ramrod clipped to its underside. Gunpowder, shot, and wax plugs are rammed down the barrel with the rod.

Oity, their leader, was passing round a bottle of cane spirit mixed with gunpowder. He was a small, sparrow-like man with very bright eyes. 'Have a swallow. The powder will give you courage.' He passed the bottle from man to man, and as he did so, I could see his whole body shivering with almost imperceptible, very fine tremors of tension. He was only a few days out of jail.

The date was August the 21st, 1987, the ranch was called Bela Vista and they were all squatters – though the word 'posseiro' in Portuguese implies a greater sense of legality than our 'squatter'. (By the constitution, the *posseiro* has the legal right to any land he has cultivated and lived on for more than five years, whether he has a title deed or not.)

When several other parties arrived to increase our group to about 60 or 70, two men picked up a coffin tied to two wooden poles and we all moved off. Though we walked on a good road bordered by a wire fence, the pasture was very degraded – shoulder high and mixed with scrub and saplings. We walked for half an hour in the battering heat until the men in front started to move very slowly with their shotguns pointed at the low forest to our left. A barbed wire fence and then an awkward ten yard dip separated the path from the forest. 'If they shoot from there,' someone said, 'we could never get at them.' After 50 yards, the low forest closed up onto the path and everyone moved even more slowly, searching the trees with their guns. With every step, there was an increasing smell of decay. Suddenly, there was a fusillade of gunfire. I dived to the right, but then saw through the cloud of gunsmoke that the men in front of our line were standing and reloading their guns. 'It's safe,' Oity called back to the coffin bearers. 'After our shots, there could be no one behind the body.'

The brother and another relative of the dead man started to roll the corpse onto a strip of cloth. It was black with decay, blistered with heat, and holed where the vultures had removed the intestines. Each movement of the body released waves of foul, putrid gas.

'They waited in ambush there,' Oity pointed at the forest behind, 'sitting over the body to shoot whoever came to bury him. But the smell must have been too much.'

'Who was he?'

'Raimundo Piaui, our comrade here in the jungle for six years. He'd gone to buy things at the next ranch. Look, there's his tin of kerosene, and here's the sack of salt his donkey was carrying when they surrounded him.'

'Who killed him?'

'It was Bulhoes, the head gunman of the Bela Vista ranch.' Oity turned to look up the road towards the ranch. 'They came on horses and surrounded him. With the greatest cowardice they killed him, a man who never quarrelled with anyone. He was a Protestant. He didn't even carry a knife.' (In Brazil, many Protestant sects refuse to have, or touch, a gun.)

His brother had now got the corpse into the coffin and they were tying down the lid.

'Why did they kill him?'

'Because he was a squatter, and Bulhoes is paid by the rancher.'

'Why didn't you call the police?'

'We did. It's seven days that the body has been here. We went seven days ago to the judge in Conceicao de Araguaia, and to the police station. But the sherrif said that he hadn't enough police to come here, he didn't have a car or petrol to recover a body being watched over by gunmen, and he told us to look after it ourselves. The police don't help squatters,' Oity said to the crowd around, 'just rich ranchers. They come to get a gunman's body, but not a squatter's.'

As soon as the coffin was ready, we marched away rapidly. 'If they heard the shots,' Oity said, 'they will be after us in the pick-up.'

One of the men at the end of the line was firing the pasture as we walked, so that fire and smoke followed us, leaping in gusts of flame from one side of the road to the other. Between the claustrophobic heat of the dust haze and the searing waves of burning grass, the whole ranch seemed to be turning into a pyre. Perhaps a not unfitting way for a squatter to go.

After half an hour, we diverted off the jeep road onto a narrow trail. And when we crossed a stream, Oity said, 'We will bury him at the other side. If the gunmen come, they will have to leave the jeep at the juncture and come on foot.'

Several men dug the grave for the dead man whose full name was Raimundo Perreira de Nascimento, while the others sat in little groups around tins of gunpowder and lead shot, recharging the brass cartridges they had just fired. They used lethal pea sized shot and plugged the cartridge with black wads of beeswax.

The coffin was lowered into the grave. Everyone threw handfuls of earth onto it and stood around quietly. But the dead man's widow and brother had unexpectedly phlegmatic expressions and showed no visible sign of sorrow. It seemed as if they had been dried out by the grind of labour under such bitter conditions.

'My parents didn't want me to come here,' Dona Maria said wearily. 'And I didn't want to come. But he was crazy that we should. We've been here six years.'

'Did he have trouble with the rancher? Was he armed?'

'No. Nothing. He never had a gun. A man came to tell us he had seen him fallen by the road, and that he was dead. But when we went to get him and got near, we heard someone walking in the forest, coming close to surround us. Then the others said we can't get him now because we are unarmed. Not one shotgun. And I got very nervous. "Oh, my God. We have come all this way and we won't even reach my husband." Then we heard a loud noise. It was only one person, but certainly there were others there. So we left, almost running, looking back with fear.'

Gazing across the dusty, blistered earth for which Raimundo had lost his life, I wondered how men could give their lives for anything so barren. And yet, the 60 to 70 men who had fetched the body were now sitting in a circle around Oity working out plans to do just that. Most of the guns had been stacked in an organised line against a log. But otherwise the squatters looked indisciplined and shabby. Most had shirts in shreds, or shirts that had lost the sleeves. And many wore large uncared-for beards that gave them a ruffian look. The sun was already a ball of red glaring through the haze. And in every direction pillars of smoke were moving with the wind to and fro across the burning ranch.

'No one's going to help us,' said Oity from one side of a wide circle. 'Not the police. Not the courts. The gunmen are supported by the judge, Dr Eronides, and Major Gibson, the head of the police. The gunmen have already learnt how to kill us. We've got to confront them or give up and become slaves for the rancher. Die, who has to die. But we've got to get them, or they will eat us up, one by one. We must set ambushes,' and then he added as an after-thought, 'It's no use ambushing the main road. Waldir says he saw them in a lorry armoured with sheets of steel.'

The group then started discussing details of where the ambushes should be set and who would be in which. Afterwards, the squatters broke up into smaller groups, all marching back to the areas of their own farms. 'We don't want to fight with the police,' one of them said. 'But we will confront the gunmen. There are 400 of us, and we won't leave our farms until the last one of us is dead. And I'm encouraged because even the Protestants – they were the weakest at first – are also fighting. This one's given up his religion,' he said pointing to his companion, 'and gave two cows to buy a .20 bore.'

Over the next few days we travelled from ambush to ambush.

Most were beside a trail into the forest which gave access to a smallish valley where a group of squatters had cut their clearings. Of the 13,000 hectares that the ranch owned, about 5000 had been cleared for pasture in the centre facing out on the Araguaia river. All the surrounding land had been left as forest, and it was here that the squatters had invaded, pushing up along the streams, establishing a dozen or a score of farms in each little valley. It was the trails into these valleys that were now being guarded.

After years with guerrillas in Asia, I was surprised to see the ambush sites in such dense undergrowth, only two or three yards from the trail. The aim was to catch the gunmen as they came to burn the squatters' houses. At such close range, the heavy lead shot would certainly be lethal. But in heavy undergrowth, with a poor view of the trail, it would also be easy to shoot the wrong man or to be outflanked. Many of the ambushers still had the demented look of the funeral party, tensed for a courage that would drip away with the days of waiting.

'What are you waiting for?' I asked one particularly anxious looking man behind a breastwork of logs. 'We're waiting for the bandits,' he said. 'We've been here seven years, and now the rancher wants to throw us out. All our food and belongings are here. Our families will starve.'

'So, if they come, you will kill them?'

'We'll open fire.'

Later we moved on to visit a group that was watching, far away in the distance, the ranch house. This stood beside the Araguaia river, facing the small town of Pau D'Arco on the other bank. On this side of the river, there were half a dozen ranchworker's houses painted white and a large ranch house surrounded by trees. Through the trees we could just make out an occasional distant moving figure. But as the house had the river on one side and open pasture on the other, it was very difficult to get close. This was why no one could be sure whether the police were there.

'Is the ferry moving?' Oity asked.

'Yes. But it is on the other side, and only taking things for the rancher.'

'Have you been close to the ranch?' I asked.

'Last night, we crept through the barbed wire and up close to the generator,' a large, blond man said. 'Six of us got to about 50 metres from the house.'

'Did you see any people?'

'Three.'

'Police?'

'We couldn't see if they had uniforms. They shone a torch, so we lay in the grass, and then they shot six bullets, in the wrong direction.'

'On the other side of the ranchhouse,' said Oity, 'there is a cross by the river. That's where they tied me and beat me after the police had caught us. They broke Antonio Sabino's rib, and left him in the sun all day, making him drink salt water.'

'The manager hit me twice with his revolver,' said Antonio Branco. 'Then a policeman kicked me in the leg and beat me with the butt of his rifle on my chest and then with the barrel on the forehead. All the time they were threatening to shoot me. Or would I prefer to die swimming in the river? But I said, if I had to die, I would prefer to be shot, so at least my blood would be left on the earth.'

'How many of you did they seize?'

'Fourteen. The poor man they got last, they abused to excess. They made him drink the blood of six chickens. Then they forced him to eat a lot of raw peppers and drink salt water. They fired at his feet and close to his ear.'

On the next day, we went to visit the house of Joao Moreira, who had been murdered two days before Raimundo Piaui. We avoided the road and used trails that went from one squatter's house to another. Most were poor constructions with mud walls and thatch rooves that would burn well. And many had been burnt down – about 20.

'Look,' said one squatter, called Gregorio, pointing at the blackened ruins of his house. 'I had tables, chairs, a side board and three beds. It was well furnished. They are the springs of the bed, and look here is my wife's sewing machine – the little thing is all burnt up. And there,' pointing at a particularly thick pile of ash, 'that was my shed with 60 sacks of rice.'

'Did the proprietor give you any warning?'

'Yes. When I was at the ranch one day, he said, "I will only warn you once, and if you try anything, I am going to end up setting fire to the houses and finishing everything."'

'He gave us a deadline of 30 days to take everything out.'

'The police kept capturing us,' said another squatter, Joao, 'and taking us to the ranch house to sign a document giving up our holdings. But we can't leave the holdings, because we can't live without land.'

We found Joao Moreira's house dangerously close to the road which crosses the ranch. Waldir, one of the murdered man's sons, was watching it.

'The gunmen came here three times looking for him,' Waldir said, as he sorted some of his father's tools and belongings. 'They said many insolent things to my mother, saying that my father had to account for himself, that they knew he was hiding somewhere in the bushes around.'

'But they didn't kill him here?'

'No they went hunting after him, sent by the rancher Jurandy, and they found him at the *colonia* Bernardo Sayao in Goias. He left the house to go to a small town to meet a friend, and they killed him coming back from the bar on the road.'

'Did they shoot him?'

'No. They killed him with clubs. Two of them, with the greatest cowardice, beating him.' And he showed us a photograph of his father in his coffin. Joao Moreira's face was swollen and distorted from the brutal battering it had received.

But Joao Moreira had obviously established quite a successful farm in the five years that he had been there. The adobe house was well built, there were a number of large fields of pasture and about 60 cattle. And Waldir said that he and his six brothers had also built houses and established farms close by.

'Now that your father's been killed,' I asked Waldir, 'will you and your brothers leave?'

'I, at least, won't leave,' he said looking up with a bitter gleam in his eye. 'He died fighting for us, so we're not going to leave his sweat for others. We have to profit from his work, to fight on here and see what happens.' There was a grim tenacity on his face which was something I seldom saw in Brazil – except in a land feud.

For outsiders, it's hard to appreciate the bitterness and the ruthlessness of the battle for land. In another feud we filmed, we saw the corpse of a three year old boy riddled with shot, and his father with the top of his head blown off by a sawn off shotgun. The rancher's gunmen even killed a stranger who had nothing to do with the land quarrel, firing both barrels into his mouth so that his teeth spattered over people nearby. Random, meaningless killing increases terror. And it is only terror that can hold onto empty land in the face of an army of landless poor living close to starvation.

On the same day as we visited Joao Moreira's house, we talked to about 30 men from the surrounding area seated, in the shade of a grove of banana trees, around Oity and Orlavo Lau. Orlavo was their representative to the rural worker's union in the nearby town of Conceicao de Araguaia. Most of the men had come from neighbouring states in north-eastern or central Brazil – Goias, Minas Gerais, Maranhao and Espirito Santo. None of them had owned land, but some of their fathers had – until some landowners drove them out or bought them off. With their home state over-crowded by landless poor competing against each other for any sort of labouring job, and fighting for any patch of cultivable land, they had moved over the lip of the Amazon basin into the south of Para where the scrub savannahs of central Brazil gradually merge into low forest. Now that they had found a patch of ground to cultivate, they were quite willing to die for it. 'They want to push us further into Amazonia,' said one, 'amongst the malaria and the Indians where we will die more quickly. It's better to die here.'

'I came from Minas Gerais in 1981,' Oity said. 'There was no work and I had no land. There the ranchers only allowed sharecropping and took half of what you planted. Half the tillage, even half the pumpkins. Half of everything.'

'I arrived from Minas too,' said Orlavo, 'and I thought that here there would be a chance to support my family. We came into Bela Vista because it was unclaimed land. People were just entering and possessing the land.'

'No rancher ever walked round here,' added Oity, 'telling us that this land was his. No farm worker either. It was abandoned. No fences. No marker posts. There were no cattle even on their pasture. Just a sort of watchman-manager in the house by the river. So people came into the forest around the ranch's pasture and took, each one, a plot of 40 to 50 hectares. Sometimes bigger, when the water was far away. But there are very few plots bigger than 100 hectares.'

'Why didn't you take bigger plots?'

'Because these are enough to live on,' said Orlavo 'to grow rice and beans and have a cow. No one's here to get rich, just to eat. Some people here told us that this ranch was a project financed by SUDAM (the Superintendancy for the Development of Amazonia),' said Orlavo. 'But it was only in 1986 that the rancher came here saying he owned the land, and that's when all the trouble started.'

'For fear,' Oity interjected, 'of land reform.'

From what we learned from our subsequent research, the ranch appeared to have been adequately run during the 1970s. But sometime in 1980, its previous owners, the huge construction company Bardella, had given up control of the ranch and Jurandy Goncalves Siqueira had taken over. During this transition period, the ranch's 2500 cattle, 30 buffaloes and 80 horses had been sold off, and the ranch had been left virtually abandoned – until Jurandy returned in 1986.

Why he did provides an insight into the whole business of ranching and land speculation in Amazonia.

In 1986, the government had opened a case against the Bela Vista ranch to abolish its registration as a rural enterprise. This entitled it to tax incentives and subsidies, but it was also the basis of the ranch's legal claim to its land. The new civilian government of 1985 had also promised agrarian reform and to enforce the right of 'usu capiao' – the squatter's right to own land he had worked for over five years. These two events meant that if Jurandy could not drive the squatters out before his rural enterprise registration was abolished, many of the squatters could claim Land Agency titles to their plots.

Jurandy's first step had not been particularly aggressive. He had started to build a fence around his cleared land, and it was when this reached some squatters' farms – and they refused to allow the fence to go on – that the trouble began. The rancher brought in professional gunmen under Julio Cesar Bulhoes, who had experience in using terror to drive out squatters on other ranches. His technique was to arrive unexpectedly at a farm, beat the owner, and steal his pigs, chickens and anything else that took his fancy. The most aggressive of his gunmen was Adao Barbosa, who often drank in the bars of Pau D'Arco, where he would talk of who he had beaten and repeat the names of the squatters on his death list. When he was ambushed and killed, the local judge, Dr Eronides, got an order from the State Secretary of Security to station police at the ranch. It was with the support of these police that the gunmen started penetrating deeper into the squatter areas, burning a score of houses and giving the squatters a deadline of June the 30th to get out.

On their side, the squatters – advised by the rural workers' union in the nearby town – knew that if they could hold out, time was on their side. The Land Agency had publicly opened the Bela Vista case in April, when Jurandy, the owner, had refused to allow it to inspect his ranch. So most of the squatters had decided to hang on in armed groups – each group trying to protect its own area. When Jurandy had started to bulldoze a road into one of the squatters' areas, they had stopped it by destroying the bridge and gathering such a large force that the police refused to go on providing protection.

Gradually, as the legalities unravelled, the case of the ranch of Bela Vista began to expose the very dubious practices behind the policy of establishing ranches in the forest.

The records of the Bela Vista ranch showed that it was held through two companies: Juruparana Pastoril SA, which acquired in 1969 what the Land Agency listed as Lottes 42 and 45, and Companhia Melhoramento de Pau D'Arco SA, which soon after had bought Lottes 37 and 43. Both companies had been set up for this purpose by the multi-million dollar construction group, Bardella SA, based in Sao Paulo, and in the 1970s, their principal directors were drawn from this group. SUDAM, the Superintendancy for the Development of Amazonia, had approved the project as an Amazonian rural enterprise that would be gradually built up to a herd of 6000 cattle, run by 34 employees and selling 1000 head per year. It was this approval which enabled the project to receive more than a million dollars of government money through the Bank of Amazonia. Under Brazil's fairly complex tax incentive scheme, 25 percent of a company's taxes could be given back to it if they were invested in an Amazonian project that was approved by SUDAM.

During the 1970s, the ranch was built up to 2500 head of cattle and accounts were regularly published. But, in 1980, when the Bardellas ceased to control the board, Jurandy Goncalves Siqueira took over as President, left the ranch apparently abandoned, and stopped publishing accounts. The ranch was subsequently inspected by Clando Yokomizo and Jose Garcia Gasques in 1985 for the government's Institute for Economic and Social Planning. They found that instead of 6000 head, it had only 500. (The squatters claimed that these cattle had been borrowed for the inspection from the neighbouring ranches of Sao Luis and Tapava.) Instead of 34 employees, it had 6, and instead of an annual sale of 1000 head, it had never really sold any – except when it was stripped. But the most damning conclusion of all, from the point of view of the government, was that after a million dollars had been invested, Juruparana could only show to the inspectors 2 percent of the cattle projected in the original SUDAM agreement, and the Companhia Melhoramento de Pau D'Arco only 11 percent. Presumably, the revelation of these facts in a government report, began the process of deregistration which induced Jurandy to improve his position by driving out the squatters.

Ronaldo Barata is head of the Land Agency in Para. 'The Bela Vista ranch is no longer registered as a rural enterprise,' he said after a meeting with the squatters. 'It has already been declassified from the register and is now considered as a large estate.' (The Brazilian word 'latifundio' carries the implication of an excessively large and feudal estate.) 'Just the existence of so many squatters on it shows that the proprietor was not working the ranch properly. The process of disappropriation,' he concluded, 'is now in its final stage.'

Not long after, – presumably when Jurandy felt that his case was untenable – he withdrew his gunmen. After months of holding out besieged in the farm house, Bulhoes and his associates got into a boat and, under cover of darkness, slipped away downstream.

A few days later, when the squatters began to realise that the ranch might be deserted, over 100 of them grouped together and invaded the main house. They blocked the airstrip and smashed the SUDAM notices. But they decided to leave the ranch otherwise untouched until it was legally disappropriated. 'Before it was the Melhoramento of SUDAM,' said Oity, making a pun on the company name Cia. Melhoramento de Pau D'Arco. (Melhoramento means improvement.) 'Now it's the Melhoramento of the Squatters. Now we will organise our union and squatters association and rebuild the school and union house which were burnt. And if this ranch house is disappropriated, we will look after it in the name of the community so that everyone can enjoy it.'

'After five months of battle,' said Caju, 'ready at any time to kill or be killed, we have won. Now we will have a more tranquil life.'

In the case of the ranch of Bela Vista, the squatters had won. But this is not typical of the hundreds of land battles every year in Brazil which are usually won by the landowners. So some people may wonder why I have depicted this case and not one of the other feuds we filmed. The reason is the same as the reason for the squatters' victory. The ranch had so misappropriated government money that its position was ultimately indefensible, and this provides an illustration of how a large part of Amazonia has been developed. Recently, as other investigations into Amazonian tax incentive schemes have pressed uncomfortably home, the SUDAM office in Belem was set on fire by persons unknown, destroying much of the evidence.

After I left Bela Vista, I visited Jose Garcia Gasques at the Planning Ministry in Brasilia. 'Well over half a billion dollars has been invested through tax incentives in Amazonia,' said Garcia who inspected the Bela Vista ranch in 1985. 'But the ranches we studied were only selling 15.7 percent of what they should have been . . . and only three demonstrated anything approaching a profit. In fact, a large number of the projects were abandoned, and a large number were also cancelled for misappropriation of funds.'

'The tax incentives were primarily a means to guarantee the possession of land,' Garcia went on. 'The average size of the ranches we studied was over 21,000 hectares, and some were as large as 200,000 hectares. So a great part of the area was not occupied, and could easily be invaded by squatters. Registration for tax incentives, therefore, was a [legal] method to guarantee possession of the land.'

It was, in fact, primarily a device for land speculation, and as SUDAM supported ranches covered 8.4 million hectares, it was speculation on a massive scale. 'Only one of the projects we studied had never been sold,' Garcia added. 'The rest had all been resold several times. The businessmen took the tax incentives as a speculation, and once the project was established and approved, they would sell it.'

I then went back to Ronaldo Barata, the head of the Land Agency in the State of Para. The ranch of Bela Vista had been disappropriated in the interval and he confirmed that the squatters would eventually be given title deeds. Then I asked if it was common in Para for ranches to misuse government money invested in them.

'I believe so,' he said. 'Tax incentives were for a time very prejudicial to the region. When Para was isolated from the rest of Brazil, our land had no value. The occupants of the land didn't even bother with title deeds. But with the opening of the Trans-Amazonica and Belem-Brasilia highways, and with the military government's plan of national integration, Para began to have land feuds. First, because the big businessmen of the south moved to Amazonia attracted by incentives. Second, because the roads made access possible for the waves of migrants forced out by the land situation in the north-east and south. Third, because the Federal Government created an image that Amazonia was a huge, empty space that should be occupied to relieve the land crisis in other states. And since there was no government policy to help the waves of migrants, huge problems began to break out. The great companies found their areas already occupied by early squatters, some of whom had been there for centuries. The squatters were expelled. But after the areas were cleaned out, they were often reinvaded by people from other states who thought them unoccupied because no work was being done. Here, conflict has become institutionalised. Only since the Agrarian Reform programme in 1985,' he concluded, 'has the government tried to do any-thing to resolve this desperate problem.'

Even in the eyes of government officials, the ranch programme – which had destroyed millions of hectares of forest – had been a disaster. And this is also true of the Polonoroeste and Trans-Amazon colonisation schemes. All three together involved a direct investment of over $3 billion, not counting subsidies and indirect investment such as agricultural credit. In 1985, when the Ministry of Agrarian Reform and Development announced its pro-gramme of land reform, an independent research institute, IBASE, calcu-lated the cost at roughly $3000 per rural family settled in the developed part of Brazil. (The Workers' Party election platform in 1989 put it at around $7000.) The $3 billion wasted on projects that deforested Amazonia could, therefore, have settled – on IBASE's calculations – roughly one million families outside the forest and would have certainly gone a long way to defusing the rural tension in Brazil. Perhaps, the aspect of the 1980s that proved to be the most depressing of all was not so much that it was a decade of destruction, but that it was a decade of very expensive, pointless destruction.

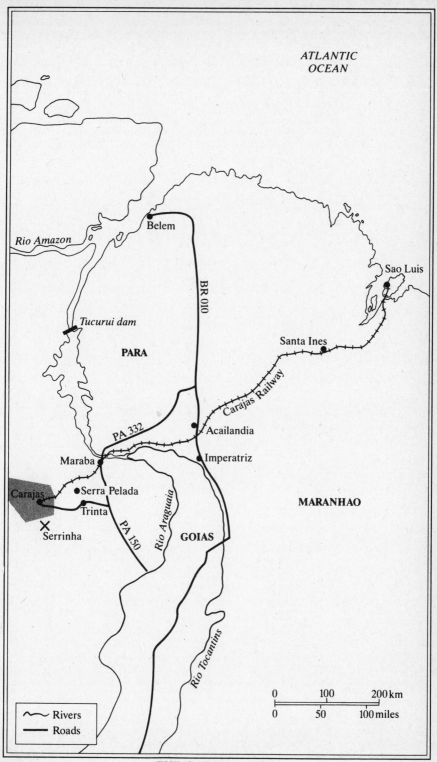

THE CARAJAS AREA

five

THE MEANING *of* EL DORADO

CARAJAS
1985–1987

When Orellana sailed down the River Amazon in 1541 – slaughtering hundreds of Indians on the way – he was searching for El Dorado. And ever since, the Portuguese crown, African slaves, Jesuit missions, bandeirantes from Sao Paulo, garimpeiros and multi-nationals have ransacked the forest for its mineral wealth. Gold was what led the first European to take his first destructive step into the forest of Amazonia, and dreams of fortune have inspired much of the destruction ever since.

In 1980, gold was discovered at Serra Pelada in southern Para, which developed into what is probably the richest manually excavated gold strike the world has ever seen. For the first half of the decade, Serra Pelada produced a dozen tons a year in comparison to Brazil's largest industrial mine, Morro Velho, which was only producing half of that. During the 1980s, the annual production of Brazil rose to between 60 and 70 tons (worth, roughly, $1 billion), and 70 percent of this was from freelance prospectors or garimpeiros. The poor and the adventurous from all over the country flocked to the garimpos – the manually operated mines – and during most of the decade there were a quarter of a million garimpeiros around the Serra Pelada area in the South of Para, with an estimated half million spread across Amazonia – a vast, volatile population, motivated by aims and a view of life very different from the rest of Brazil.

When gold was first discovered at Serra Pelada, it was inside the concession of the Companhia Vale do Rio Doce, the mining company of the Brazilian government. This company's Serra dos Carajas contains not only the world's richest iron ore, but also manganese, copper, bauxite, tin, nickel, wolfram, zinc, lead and, of course, gold. On the foundation of this immense mineral wealth, the government planned to construct an entire industrial region, and to stimulate the agricultural development of eastern Amazonia as well. Their Grande Carajas project was budgeted at $60 billion, and when the Tucurui dam – providing energy – was inaugurated in 1984, and the Carajas railway – providing transport – started to function in 1985, the vortex of Amazonian development moved from Rondonia to the corridor along the Carajas railway. The government hoped that exports from the Carajas project alone would be enough to pay off Brazil's international debt.

One statistic that is sometimes quoted in Brazil is that to earn a million dollars a year in Amazonia, you would need 100 square kilometres for cattle, 14 for cocoa, 2.5 for timber and only 0.017 square kilometres for minerals. In short, the economic activity that should be least destructive to the forest is mining. Of all mines this particularly applies to Carajas. It is the richest mineral province on earth. And the reason that we started filming in the Carajas area was to see whether the mining company, or the garimpeiros, could provide some sort of alternative for Amazonia – a way of profiting from the forest without demolishing it.

ONE

'The explosion was like a bomb,' Vicente said, 'and when I crept with my revolver to the door, a voice on the other side was groaning, "I am dying, I am dying," and blood was seeping under the door. That was my first night in the town. The first day that I started the *garimpeiro* research.'

To prepare for our film about the minerals of the eastern Amazon, Vicente Rios, our Brazilian cameraman, had gone to the satellite town of Serra Pelada. He had been filming with us in Amazonia since 1980, and he has the quickness and shrewdness of a converted Mafioso. At the time, $200 million dollars worth of gold was coming annually out of Serra Pelada's enormous hole, and as alcohol and women were forbidden at the site of the mine, most *garimpeiros* would travel out once a week to the nearest town. This was located at kilometre 30 on the road, and so it had the practical, but less than inspiring, name of Thirty.

'I was astonished at such a frenzy of prostitution,' Vicente said. 'It was just bars and brothels with streets full of prostitutes and drunks. It was a town without a red light district. The whole town was it.'

'When I went to eat, I was in a place which serves really terrible steak, when a man comes up and says, "I can see you are not from here, so I hope you don't mind if I warn you. Most nights at least three people are killed in Thirty, and early in the morning you often find one or two bodies just left in the street. My advice, if you are on foot and alone, is to be very careful."'

'I couldn't be sure that it wasn't someone checking to see if I would be easy to rob,' Vicente said. So I replied, "Thank you, I am being careful," and showed him the .38 in my shoulder bag. Then I went back to the hotel and to sleep.'

'Bang. That enormous explosion wakes me. The revolver is in my hand pointing at the door, and someone is groaning just the other side: "I'm dying, I'm dying." But I wait until I hear voices in the corridor, and then I open the door – carefully. Right in front of my door, there is a man in a great pool of blood, with glass spattered all around him. And the guard is saying to the owner of the hotel, "He's a thief. I saw him creeping in the window. I shot him." "I'm dying" the man is groaning, "I'm dying." But he can't have been dying too fast because when the owner asks why he was trying to get in, he said, "I mistook this for a church. I wanted to pray." *Garimpeiros* may be crazy,' Vicente shook his head, 'but they're not uninspired.'

A few days later, Vicente travelled to one of the new gold strikes at a place called Serrinha, about 200 kilometres from Serra Pelada. It was at the height of the rainy season, and the pick-ups going there left with roughly 25 people packed on board. Twenty-five was enough to push most pick-ups out of most mud holes. 'We carried the car more than it carried us. And despite all the rain, we got through everything until we arrived at a river which had risen so much that 50 trucks were stuck – waiting for the water to go down. They were carrying rice, prostitutes, tinned food, and cane spirit to the gold strike. But mostly prostitutes. Or so it seemed. People had their hammocks slung under the trucks, or between trees under small bits of plastic. The prostitutes were making love in the cabs of the trucks, or in the jungle, and everyone was drunk. One of the trucks was loaded with spirit for Serrinha and the driver was selling it to everyone. There was a lot of confusion, many fights. One very drunk man was singing and people kept applauding and pushing and pushing him until they steered him on top of an ant's nest. He stayed there singing, so drunk that the ants were all over him before he noticed.'

Vicente waded through the river and on the other side found a line of trucks waiting to get out. But one pick-up had decided to give up and turn back to the gold strike and so Vicente piled in with another 20 to 30 people and they pushed and pulled it down the road until they were stopped by a man with a large .45 stuck in his belt. It was Eduardo, the Sherrif of Thirty, with two policemen.

Eduardo simply opened the cab door and told the three women inside to get into the back. He was broad and with a belly. Very authoritarianly, he just took possession of the cab. There were already too many people packed in the back, but his two policemen climbed in and started to humiliate the people – brutally. One, a huge mulatto two metres tall, sat on the shoulders of a *garimpeiro*. "Bear up" he said. "You are the best seat, even softer than the bench in front." Those *garimpeiros*,' Vicente said grimly, 'were really humble people, and they made room without a complaint.'

The pick-up travelled on until about ten o'clock at night when it got itself finally and irretrievably stuck. There was a bright moon and Eduardo, the sheriff, decided to go on to find somewhere to sleep. 'I stuck close to him in case any bandit thought, "ah-ha, here is an easy dish, someone who doesn't look like a *garimpeiro*.' With a lot of gold coming out, there would obviously be a lot of robbing. And if you have to face a bandit, it's always better to have a bandit by your side.'

'Gradually I began to sense that Eduardo was very nervous. It wasn't far to the next strike, but Eduardo stopped at every house, with dogs snarling and biting at him, and shouted to the owner to let us in to sleep. "The house is full up," the people always shouted back, and I could tell that these colonists were fed up with *garimpeiros*. So we went on, and the two or three prostitutes walking with us made a lot of noise. I could see Eduardo getting more and more nervous, worried that someone might shoot him from the dark. Every now and again he would make everyone be quiet. "I heard a shot," he would say, or "I heard someone moving," and he would listen for ten minutes. The moon was very beautiful and clear and it was then that I noticed Eduardo was full of nervous tics. His right hand suddenly twitches up past his revolver, compulsively, as though he was about to draw it and then changed his mind. And at other times he would bang his forehead with his open palm three or four times.' Vicente thumped his forehead with the heel of his hand very hard.

At the first roadside bar, Eduardo asked for food. But there was only a pan of cold rice and spaghetti left over from dinner. So Vicente bought four tins of sardines and they sat together by the light of a candle at the counter of the shop. 'Eduardo was eating and talking about Vietnam. I think the reason he speaks a lot about Vietnam,' said Vicente reflectively, 'was because he, himself, was a man at war. "What a people of character and persistence," Eduardo said. "See what they have done." And I was saying, "Quite so, my brother," and "Yes. They really are like that." Eduardo never looked at me when he was talking, but there was so much tension in his voice that I felt he might explode at any moment.'

'So Eduardo was eating and talking when a rat started to run along the counter. I don't know what was wrong with it to come so close. Maybe it was drunk. Eduardo didn't look at it. He didn't stop eating. But suddenly he smashed his fist right onto it, exploding the rat. Blood spattered onto his clothes and hand. He then just flicked it onto the floor, and went on eating and talking about Vietnam, without even wiping the blood from his hand.'

That night, Eduardo and Vicente slept at the newest strike, called Fofoca, which was several kilometres before Serrinha. It consisted of several hundred huts covered with thick black plastic and lit by dim oil lamps. As they arrived, the owner of the first bar called, 'Ah, Dr Eduardo, are you well?' and several other people received him with great ceremony. But Eduardo's face remained very hard and closed.

'There was music and the usual drunks and prostitutes,' Vicente said. And one man with his back to us was laughing a lot and didn't notice Eduardo, and went on drinking. Eduardo went up, snatched his cup, and smelt it. "You son of a bitch! Haven't I prohibited spirit here?" he said very quietly and coldly. And threw the glass on the ground. Suddenly everything was very quiet. You could sense that everyone was very frightened. "Come. Come. Dr Eduardo," the owner said. "This man has only just come in and brought the spirit with him. It wasn't sold here." But somehow you could tell that all this had happened before, and that next day the owner would go to Eduardo and pay so he could go on selling spirit. I later heard that Eduardo also permitted gambling for a percentage, and I even saw him and his men,' Vicente's voice was caustic, 'take nuggets out of the *garimpeiros*' machines.'

After two or three days, Vicente had made arrangements for our filming at Fofoca and Serrinha and wanted to get back to Thirty. But as no trucks had got through for nearly a week, he was stuck until one day a motor bike arrived. It was one of the travelling gold buyers who stop at all the diggings buying gold from the *garimpeiros*. They carry little portable scales consisting of two small plates hanging from a pendulum of string and wood and they buy gold until their money is exhausted.

'When I saw he was a gold buyer, I went over and said, "Look, my friend. You probably know that someone wounded a gold buyer here last night – shooting at him in the dark. Well, I have a revolver and a licence to carry it, and am desperate to get out. You are travelling just on your own. Wouldn't you like to take me on the back of your bike. We'll both be safer." "Agreed," the buyer replied immediately. "How can I draw a revolver, driving in all this mud. All they have to do is wait by a mud patch where I have to push the bike, then just shoot me from the jungle."'

And so they set out at about two o'clock, with Vicente on the back holding his revolver, and the gold in a sack under the carrier. After some time, another gold buyer with a more powerful motorbike passed them with a man on the back. 'He had a 9mm automatic and fired three times, bang, bang, bang, in the air, as they passed. It was a party. I fired once as they went ahead. The road was like washing soap. There was so much mud that we fell more than 20 times. We would drive slowly, but, zup, we would skid into the mud. Then slower, and zuuup, again. In places the mud was a metre deep and we had to carry the machine across. Not even a truck could have got through. We were literally basted in mud, even inside the ears.'

It was completely dark by the time they got onto the tarmac of the main road. '"The worst is past," I said, but I could sense the buyer was frightened. "They could have decided not to ambush us where we might expect it," he said. "Sometimes they intercept on the tarmac where they can get away fast." And then we saw a car, lighted, ahead by the side of the road, and a man signalling for us to stop. The buyer was literally trembling, and we went past, very fast, with me waving the revolver. Nothing happened, and again I thought the worst was past, until I noticed that the buyer was looking behind, glancing all the time at me. Now it was me he was nervous of, and I realised that he was frightened that I would wait until the end of the journey and then kill him for his gold. It was tragic. How could I say, "Don't worry about me. I'm not going to kill you." That would make him even more nervous.'

When they got to Thirty, the first thing the buyer did was deliver the gold.

And he was so relieved that they immediately had a drink in the nearest bar. 'When I offered to pay for the ride, the buyer said, "For the love of God. You're joking. Who should be paying is me." And he embraced me saying, "I will be in your debt for the rest of my life."'

A few weeks later we arrived to film in the *garimpo* of Serrinha. Several thousand *garimpeiros* had poured in in the intervening weeks, and now a street of shanty bars and shops ran up a steep hillside. On the left, the valley at the foot of the hill had been dug into a patchwork of yellow holes in the mud. An area about a kilometre long was covered by groups of men, each working in a hole about ten yards square. It looked like a cheese which the rats had been at. To the right, the hill-face above was rapidly disappearing – under another horde of rats. And the whole place juddered to the roar of pumps, winches, grinders and generators.

In the valley to the left, alluvial gold was being washed out of the ground. With a powerful jet of water driven by a pump, a *garimpeiro* would carve blocks of mud out of the bank like slices of cake. These would dissolve into the water, and another pump would suck and pour the mud and water over a ridged washing board. The mercury in the grooves of the board caught and held the heavier grains of gold.

To the right, the gold ran in rock veins deep into the hillside. The *garimpeiros* showed us places where the rocks were a vivid green from the oxidised copper ore which was mixed with the gold. With pick-axes and shovels they pounded away at the hill-face. Winches and grinders hauled the rock out and crushed it to release the gold within.

The whole place had the feverish activity of rush hour in the underground – men, in incessant files, climbing up and down ladders with sacks on their heads; trucks constantly unloading food, hammocks, shirts, shovels, pumps. A man running in the street somehow gave the impression that he was dawdling. Even the queues outside the brothel moved at a frenetic pace.

Sometimes, as the mercury-covered gold was scraped into a bowl; or as water, in a prospector's pan, swirled round the cleansed and yellow grains; or as scales pivoted delicately while someone paid for his shopping in gold dust; I would ask if Serrinha was a profitable strike. 'It gives a nice little bit of gold,' the *garimpeiros* would admit. 'Enough to pay expenses and to take home to the family,' they would add. 'But real gold,' they concluded thoughtfully. 'No!'

'If this isn't real gold,' I would ask, 'then what is?'

'Real gold?' No *garimpeiro* could resist the question. He would straighten up from his washing board, glance up from his pan, put down his drink. 'Real gold,' he would say with a sort of withdrawn reflectiveness, 'is like you get over there.' And he would point to another hill, about the same size as Serrinha's across the dividing river that separated them. It was in the prospecting concession of the Companhia Vale do Rio Doce, Brazil's largest mining company.

And so we learnt that most of the people at Serrinha and Fofoca were wet season diggers and dry season 'researchers' – devoted questors after the prospectors' grail – an unbelievable fortune. In *garimpeiro* slang, the word is 'bamburrar'. 'There's gold and many other minerals over there,' they said. 'It is the *serra* of unbelievable wealth. And the company tries to stop us taking the little bit of gold that lies on the surface.'

Eduardo, the sherrif, said that the Company had boat patrols on the river, helicopter patrols in the air, and jungle teams chasing the prospectors in the forest. The *garimpeiros* who were caught were not jailed, but usually sent out stripped of their gold, food, tools and sometimes, clothes. It was questionable whether the Company had a legal right to do this.

The minerals in the Serra dos Carajas had first been discovered by Breno Augusto dos Santos, a geologist working for Union Carbide whose helicopter had landed on the bare summit of the forest covered range. When he bent down to examine a piece of brownish gravel, he had discovered the world's richest and largest deposit of iron ore, and later prospecting revealed deposits of another dozen minerals. If Amazonia ever had an El Dorado, this was it.

In 1977, the right to exploit the find was bought out by the Companhia Vale do Rio Doce from its previous associate, US Steel, which in turn had acquired it from Union Carbide. This would eventually make the Companhia Vale do Rio Doce the biggest iron exporter in the world, dominating the international market. In December, 1986, the Brazilian Congress confirmed that the Company had a concession of 411,946 hectares and the Congress was asked to extend this to another 200,000 hectares where the Company already had prospecting rights. But these were not titles of landownership, and it was debateable – at least for the local *garimpeiro* and rural workers' unions – whether this gave the Company the right to arrest *garimpeiros* panning for alluvial gold.

The mountains of that very beautiful range are covered in dense forest which rolls away like the waves of a jungle sea. Cloud and mist swirl about, making them look secretive and alluring. And this was the reason that we came back several times to Serrinha to make friends with the *garimpeiros* who used it as their base. The most famous of them was Jova who would disappear into the ranges for two or three months with his partner Luis. They would then emerge, buy supplies, collect 50 men, and go back to exploit their find. The famous strikes of the Gruta de Cotia and Gruta de Jova had been found by them. Once Jova and three other men, working with a spade and pan, took out nearly two kilos (worth $30,000) in 20 days.

On our last night in Serrinha, we drank with Jova and Luis. Where Luis always looked stolid and reliable, Jova had a quizzical expression and was a beguiling talker. He was one of the few *garimpeiros* we met who preferred not to carry a revolver and to talk himself out of trouble. That night, he drank so much that he slept on a pile of beer cans outside the bar. A man was shot in the street just outside Jova's house where we were sleeping. And, 100 yards away, another killed his partner in a quarrel over gold.

Next morning, Jova agreed that we could film his next prospecting trip. As the *serra* was a National Security area, he suggested that I, as a foreigner, should not go. But otherwise he would have everything ready when Vicente and Vanderlei – the sound recordist – arrived.

'When we got to Thirty, nothing had been arranged. Nothing.' Vicente said grimly. 'So we went to the bar and had a drink. And it was in that bar that Jova fixed everything. When *garimpeiros* see another drinking in a bar, they come in because they know he must have money. And a *garimpeiro* with money buys drinks for the others. Of course, that day, it was me who was paying. "Let's go on a prospecting trip," Jova would say. "Let's go," the *garimpeiros* would reply and have another drink. By one o'clock in the afternoon we had 15 men. But to get these 15 men, we had had to drink a lot. So we started with everybody drunk.'

At one o'clock, Jova went to buy supplies. Sacks of rice, beans and mandioca flour. Spades, prospecting pans, machetes. 'Some of the *garimpeiros* had literally nothing. All they had was their profession of *garimpeiro*. They would come and say, "Lend me the money for a pair of tennis shoes," and I would give them the money. How could they travel in the forest without shoes? But, of course, what they did was to buy bottles of spirit and hide them in their haversacks.'

'When we were loading the pick-up, they were so drunk it was like getting pigs into a truck. It was already six o'clock, and I wondered, "what am I going to do with 15 drunks in the night?" Jova's speech no longer even sounded like Portuguese. But then I thought, "well at least the car journey will get them sober." Hmmm! They had brought bottles with them and continued drinking all through the journey.'

'And so we travelled during the night, and when we came to the stream where we had to cross into the forest, what an agony it was getting that pile of drunks moving. Sambica asked for a cigarette, and when I gave it to him together with a haversack, bang. He fell over. Then I pulled him up and put the haversack on his back, and he took two paces and, bang, he fell like a sack of pumpkins. He got up again, and I said, "Man, do you know why you're falling?" "No." "Don't you think your cigarette is weighing you down in front?" "You're right," he said, and threw away the cigarette and didn't fall again.'

The security patrols of the company regularly watched that river, so Jova's party crossed at dawn and set off into the forest. The *garimpeiros* were carrying haversacks of food and supplies, but some were still so drunk that they only discovered where they were two days later – when the spirit was finished. Then they woke and asked, "Where are we going? What am I doing here?" Jova, for instance, had bought cartridges for hunting, but was so drunk that he forgot to bring the shotgun.

They walked, cutting a trace through dense forest. Some of the hills were so steep that they had to climb up without their packs, and then make a line so the sacks could be passed from one to another. And many of the streams were in such steep ravines that the only way to cross was along a fallen tree trunk. 'The worst,' Vicente said, 'was where there was nothing on either side to hold for balance. Once we had to sit on a log, with our haversacks on, and pull ourselves along on our bottoms. The trouble was there was an ants' nest in the middle. The first who passed got bitten by a few ants. But everyone else got covered with ants biting them like crazy. My legs and bottom were covered with bites. One *garimpeiro*, Moroinho, stupidly stopped, to try to knock them off. And so many swarmed all over him, that when he arrived at the other side he was almost hysterical.'

At night, they would stop by a stream to cook. 'Every night, if you let them get close enough, every *garimpeiro* would tell you his life story. And since we kept finding parts of deer eaten by jaguars, also tortoise shells scraped out with their claws, we all slept very close to the fire. So night was the time for confession. Everyone telling all his adventures.'

'The one who worked hardest was "Dismantled". That was what everyone called him. If you asked him what his name was, what he answered was "Dismantled". His story was that one day he had been carrying such a heavy sack on his head that his neck disjointed. Certainly, it still twitched suddenly and swivelled uncontrollably. But he was the best trail cutter, and the best fisherman and the most reliable.'

'Manoelzinho, on the other hand, was a little crook always making trouble. He traded marijuana and also sold confiscated revolvers for the police. He said that once he had been carrying a sack of marijuana across a river which got deeper and deeper. At the next step he knew he would be swept away and so he swore to God that if he survived he would never sell marijuana again. The next step got shallower and he came out safely – and he has been selling marijuana ever since.'

'There was also an Indian from the Urubu tribe who carried the heaviest load. He was always humming, and every time he fell over, he laughed. He always looked a happy man, and when I asked him one night how he had become a *garimpeiro*, he said, "My profession before was gigolo. All I had to do was make love and put on the records – because my woman was the owner of the brothel. I worked at this profession for one year, until I found out that she made love with another man. So I made love with another girl. Fwhah! That woman became a tigress. She tried to cut off my penis. The knife missed, but she sliced my stomach right across and I nearly died. So, today my profession is *garimpeiro* because," he laughed, "it is much safer."'

After ten days cutting through trail-less forest, they arrived at a high and beautiful mountain with a rockface which gave a magnificent view over the ranges. At its bottom on the other side, they found a stream red with earth. The Company was washing minerals or earth somewhere upstream, and they knew they were getting close.

'We started to walk on the company's trails and through their abandoned camps,' Vicente said. 'In one camp the fires were still warm, and another night we slept in a very big hut beside a plantation of sugar cane. Once, on a very quiet night, we heard the machines of the mine, and when we walked on the Company's roads, we had to dive for the jungle when we heard a car coming. Once someone shouted at us from ahead, and while we hid, I heard one of the searchers say, "Well, if they're *garimpeiros* they'll be kilometres away by now."'

On the Serra dos Carajas, the Company's town, processing plant and railway terminal are located close to their main mine. But in the mountains around, there are so many additional deposits of iron that they will last at least 500 years. All the deposits have a camp and guards and Jova had to by-pass them carefully, sometimes watching what they were doing for a few hours before moving on.

But the main danger came from the patrols sent out from security headquarters. These would consist of half a dozen men armed with revolvers and shotguns and they would creep up to a group of *garimpeiros* and try to surround them before they could flee with their gold. This was why the scores of *garimpeiro* teams working in the Company area ran off through the jungle as soon as they heard Jova's party approaching. They left their spades and other tools in the diggings. But each had his food and gold and hammock hidden somewhere else in the forest. When Jova called, 'I am Jova, don't you know me? Come out,' they very slowly came back.

The third group of *garimpeiros* they met said that their excavation was yielding a lot of gold, but that 15 days before, a security patrol had crept up. They heard a shout, and when they looked round, they were all covered. They were kicked and hit and their equipment broken. Then they were taken to the Company's security base to be registered. Finally, they were threatened and deported to the nearest town. It had taken them eight days to get back, and they now worked with watchers looking out for patrols.

Jova and his party worked near them for five days. But though the area they worked was close to the other *garimpeiros*, it did not yield the third of a kilo that the others had already produced.

For the last week, the only food had been tortoises, fish and palm hearts. And so Jova decided to move on. Half the party would go out to get more food, and as his film stock was finished, Vicente decided – very luckily – that he and Vanderlei would go too. For though the next place yielded a lot of gold, Jova was caught by a security patrol, and deported penniless.

Vicente eventually made several trips with Jova, but the first was the most gruelling. 'As we were coming out,' he said, 'we were all emaciated, starved. Each mountain seemed to be steeper, and I kept saying, "it just can't be as steep as this. This can't be true." But, finally, at the place where we emerged from the jungle, you could see the house from a long way away. It was like paradise. There were thousands of fruit trees – guava, mango, orange, pineapple, sugar cane, and we ate as we walked. It was the house of one of the squatters who had been there for many years. He received us very well and made a dinner of three chickens, and we ate till we burst.'

Carola, the squatter, told them that the company had tried to force him out many times. They would arrive and insist that he sign papers. By law, they said he had to sell his land to them. But he always refused to sign saying he was there long before them and just what he had planted was worth much more than what they were offering. Sometimes they descended by helicopter and threatened him saying he mustn't give hospitality to *garimpeiros*. 'It's my house,' was his reply, 'and anyone I invite is welcome.'

'The next day we arrived at a ranch,' Vicente went on, 'where, of course, one of the *garimpeiros* managed to arrange some cane spirit. Everyone got drunk. We were all weak and unaccustomed to spirits. There was no one who wasn't drunk.'

'One *garimpeiro* called Rich Mouth – because he had a lot of gold on his teeth – was so drunk that we had to carry him to his hammock. But Boca Rica kept shouting, "I have just struck gold. I have a fortune. So I refuse to leave my apartment. I want to have my bath here. In my own bathroom. Peasant," he called to one of the other *garimpeiros*, "bring water here because I am going to pay you three grams of gold to give me a bath." And the other *garimpeiro* was drunk enough to do it. With Boca Rica all the time laughing and shouting, he got water and poured it over him by his hammock. "Don't you want a bath too?" Boca Rica shouted at me. "Just leave it to me. I will pay this peasant to give you a bath as well."'

'Being a *garimpeiro*,' said Vicente reflectively, 'is like being a drug addict. You have no money and everything you do and everything you think about is finding gold. But when you do find gold, then your search is over. There is no more addiction. You are no longer a *garimpeiro*, but could be a rancher, shop-keeper, businessman. That's why I think,' Vicente concluded, 'that *garimpeiros* unconsciously waste all the money they make – to go back to being a *garimpeiro*.'

The *garimpeiros* of Amazonia are the poor, the dispossessed and perhaps the ignorant of Brazil. But they are open, generous and enterprising. Of all the dreams of the forest, theirs is the grandest. The worse life is, the more they hope. 'There is a song,' Vicente said, 'which says that God makes it cold according to the size of your blanket. The more the *garimpeiro* falls in the shit, the more he dreams. They live in dreams.'

In Amazonia, waves of *garimpeiro* money have built countless towns like Itaituba and Peixoto de Azevedo, and spurred the economies of Rondonia, Roraima and Para. At the least, the *garimpos* provided a minimum living for half a million unemployed with the dignity that comes from hope and self-reliance. But there is something obviously transitory in the *garimpeiro* character and business. And of all the travellers in the forest, they are the most abandoned. They construct nothing, and they will leave nothing for the future beyond a number of inexplicable holes and hundreds of tons of poisonous mercury, dispersed, with total irresponsibility, into the rivers. One report estimates that as much as 1800 tons of mercury were dumped in Amazonia's rivers during the 1980s.

So though mineral extraction should be one of the least harmful ways of using the Amazon forest, it was obvious that the *garimpeiro* alternative was less than a planner's dream. It was strange, therefore, that the *garimpeiros* should share the same *serra* with the Companhia Vale do Rio Doce. For, by contrast, their mining operation was highly rational, organised and far-sighted. The first time we visited the Carajas mine was for the inauguration of its railway in February 1985. It was a single track, 900 kilometre line that would take the ore out to the coast. Together with the mine, it had cost the government $3 billion dollars, and when the President inaugurated the railway, he said it would be the axis of development for the whole of eastern Amazonia. 'This enterprise will bring inestimable benefits,' Joao Figueiredo said through a microphone to assembled mineworkers and press. 'Thousands of small agriculturalists will manage for the first time to get their crops to the city. Industries will develop. New businesses will be created. Commerce will expand. The resulting creation of wealth will give a new impulse to the towns of Belem and Sao Luis. Along the railway the population, and also the spirit of enterprise, will multiply, contributing to the accelerated occupation of the vast spaces of Amazonia.'

At the time, the mine was going through its trial phase and was processing the ore through a pilot plant. First enormous mechanical excavators on caterpillar tracks dug huge spadefuls of red ore out of an open face quarry and dumped it into gigantic 170 ton trucks. These poured their load into the first of a series of washing and grading plants laid out one beneath the other on a hillside so that the iron was crushed and washed as it travelled downwards to the rail loading yard at the bottom. There, a train of 160 wagons, each carrying 98 tons, waited to make a round trip to the coast where, without being uncoupled, each wagon was turned over, pouring its contents onto a conveyor belt. This funnelled 16,000 tons of ore an hour into the holds of the huge 250,000 to 350,000 ton ore carriers which transported the iron to Japan and Europe.

'The iron ore alone should earn $700 million a year at today's prices,' said Eliezer Batista, the President of the Company. 'And our profit is calculated on the lowest prices. This is the beauty of the project. It is economic from the beginning. It can't go into the red.'

By 1987, the iron mine was already exporting 22 million tons per year, the manganese mine was coming out of its trial stage into its first phase of full production, whilst at the copper pilot processing plant, engineers were analysing the amount of copper, silver, and gold extracted from each ton of rock and, therefore, the economic viability of their extraction. Simultaneously, the Company's prospecting sections were gradually drilling and testing all the surrounding deposits of iron, copper, manganese and bauxite so that their exact composition and economic viability were precisely known – ready to be developed when time and changes in the international market called upon them.

Each time a mine or prospecting area was deforested it was afterwards carefully replanted with Amazonian tree species specially bred in the Company's nursery, and all the roads inside the concession were lined with beautiful forests protected by notices like 'Air, Water, Forest, Soil are the heritage of all.' In 1987, the mine's 1600 permanent staff started to move into its specially built, neat company town and all along the railway, terminals for cargo and passengers were being built so that the line could become the springboard for the development of the surrounding region. In

1988, the north-south branch line started to be driven 1000 kilometres into the cerrado or scrub area of the north of Goias, and the final plan was for the railway to reach across almost the whole of eastern Amazonia. It was an immense, thoroughly planned, and logical programme of development.

Then, in 1988, the industrial phase began. The first of 22 factories producing pig iron and various types of steel began to export the raw ore in a partly processed form, and the plan for the year 2010 was to produce a total of 16 million tons of pig iron and metal products. The project also envisaged that a whole series of secondary industries would start to use this iron and steel, turning the corridor along the Carajas railway into one of the great manufacturing regions of the world. It would be hard to imagine a more studied and organised use of the *serra's* ore, or one that was a greater contrast to the haphazard frenzy of the *garimpeiros*.

From the first discovery of iron ore in 1967, to the inauguration of the railway in 1985, to the huge industrial expansion of the twenty-first century, this measured development project was a planner's dream. Here was greater treasure than any Amazonian adventurer had ever imagined – the El Dorado beyond all hallucinations of wealth. But like all the conquistador visions before it, it was completely unconscious of the forest. For the production of its pig iron could only be profitable if it was based on the piecemeal incineration of the Amazonian forest.

'No one will intimidate the present State Government not to use this forest,' the Governor of Para, Helio Gueiros, said when he inaugurated the first blast furnace in January, 1988. 'It's very convenient for those who have already achieved development, like the people of Sao Paulo, to support ecologists. The people who created Cubatao, now that they are developed, try to give lessons to Amazonia: "Look," they say, "don't touch the forest."' Everyone on the platform with him laughed. For Cubatao was the world's most polluted industrial complex. 'People from other planets – because,' the Governor said in an aside, 'the rest of the world is another planet for us in Maraba – people from other planets send telegrams telling the Governor to leave the forest untouched. Well, the Governor is going to touch the forest, has to touch the forest – but rationally, with lucidity, with competence. We want the forest to serve the people, and not the people the forest.' The Governor is a florid, graying man with the gestures of a Shakespearian actor. 'We can't waste time with poetic movements of lyrical dilettantes who say that Amazonia mustn't be touched because it will be a catastrophe for the world. The forest is for us to use. The mines are for us to use. The hydroelectric energy is for us to use. When God created the world, He said, "Of all this, you may eat", though he did make one little exception.' One of the impresarios on the platform chipped in smiling, 'the apple'. 'The apple was the only exception He made,' the Governor smiled back. 'And Adam, our father,' the platform started to giggle in anticipation, 'even in this, didn't obey God.' Besides the 60 to 70 people invited, there was no one else to hear the Governor except for the work force sitting laconically on the ground. The police had allowed no one else to get past the security gate.

Later, when the Governor was being shown the blast furnace, a local TV reporter asked about his plans for reaforestation of the areas cleared for charcoal. These were to be outside the mining concession of the Companhia Vale do Rio Doce, but along the railway line. In answer, Helio Gueiros remade his point of using the forest with 'lucidity and competence'. But the only specific example he could cite of reaforestation was that he knew of various experiments by other organisations, and that the Government of Para had just founded its own forestry institute. Considering the dozen years of prospecting, tests, pilot plants and trial production before the Company began to export its ore, the scanty preparation for reaforestation was startling.

In fact, not one of the pig iron companies, at that time, had started any form of tree plantation or reaforestation. And if you just asked what species of tree they hoped to plant, none could give a definite reply. The reason was that every major experiment with tree plantations in Amazonia had, to that date, been a disaster. Not far from the Governor's State capital, Belem, Henry Ford's Fordlandia and Daniel Ludwig's huge forests of planted gmelina at Jari had been decimated by disease and were massive, constant reminders that monocultures had, to that date, never succeeded in Amazonia. There were also a number of experiments under the care of the State's Faculty of Agrarian Science in Belem. Its Professor of Forest Management was Juris Jankauskis.

'Success with planted forest is difficult, very difficult,' he said, showing me a plantation of stunted, sickly trees. 'It's difficult because in Amazonia the environment is completely different for the foreign species brought here. The species tried by the Companhia Vale do Rio Doce and Jari, eucalyptus and pines, demonstrate clearly the unsuitability of using this type of species in Amazonian conditions. Also planting monocultures always produces problems of pest and disease. It would be better to try four or five Amazonian species together like Brazil nut, Para-Para and Morototo.'

'So, it's still a question of "try",' I suggested. 'No one, as yet, knows whether planted forests will do well, or which is the best combination of trees to plant?'

'At present there are two main risks.' Juris was now showing us the Brazil nut and Para-Para plantations which he thought might do well. 'The first is the lack of knowledge of the biology of the Amazonian species. The cycle of insects and bacteria which inhabit or interrelate with the species. With a change in environment, that insect or bacteria can start a sickness that is practically uncontrollable. The second risk is forest fires. COSIPAR (the blast furnace the Governor inaugurated) alone requires 50,000 hectares to supply its yearly demand whilst all 22 companies approved so far will require between 600,000 and 700,000 hectares – these huge areas will mainly be in a region which sometimes lacks rain for eight months.' (The charcoal area is the frontier between the semi-humid forest and the dry north-east of Brazil.) 'The risk of fire, therefore is fantastic.'

'But the most serious problem is the nutrients. This is very, very serious. In the short and medium term, it could make the whole blast furnace operation unviable. 80 percent of the nutrients in the Amazon forest are in the biomass, in the leaves and principally in the trunk. Plants need these nutrients to grow. So when we transform a tree into charcoal, we are withdrawing those nutrients from the environment. No one in Para is even thinking about how to replace them. Or even who is going to replace them. Without mineral salts, plants can't grow. So as the nutrients are exported (when the wood is taken away), the productivity of the soil will fall violently. In our estimate, each crop will have a decreasing production with a maximum of three crops. This means that within 40 to 50 years, we will finish the nutrients. Clearly what they will do then is to cut even more natural forest.'

And so, from the beginning, it was more or less obvious that all the talk of reforestation of the areas cut down for charcoal was lip service – to deflect environmental criticism. Even if they did discover in the future how to grow tree plantations for charcoal, this would double the cost of the charcoal and make the pig iron too expensive to export. It was a fact clearly stated in a memo for the Companhia Vale do Rio Doce by its own Superintendent of the Environment. The following are excerpts from Francisco de Assis Fonseca's analysis of a plan for pig iron production.

The rise in the price of charcoal, which represents 68 percent of the cost of pig iron, is inexorable. The report estimates that the charcoal from natural forests costs US $45 per ton and that the charcoal from planted forests costs US $56. In reality, the cost of charcoal from planted forests is much higher. In Minas Gerais (the home state of the Company and most pig iron production in Brazil), the cost is double that of natural forests. Even the KTS report admits that in current conditions the cost would be US $75 per ton . . . To implant the industry and only afterwards worry about the charcoal is an inversion of values which will lead to 'predatory mining' of the native forest. The native forest is not 'a renewable resource'. On the contrary, it is a fragile resource whose principal value is in its biological diversity. It is a genetic reserve of incalculable value. The way it is being treated, it will be exhausted long before the mineral deposits of the region.

We know that the companies which are building pig iron factories are not taking any steps for reforestation, and even if they have this intention, there still does not exist sufficient agro-forestry knowledge to start large reforestation projects in the short term.

The responsibility of the Company is greatly increased by the fact that it has the monopoly of the mineral and of the rail transport . . . It will be difficult for the Company to defend itself from accusations of being the principal organization responsible for the devastation of the equatorial forests in its area of influence in the north. To preserve the forests only within the areas under its direct control will not be sufficient to mitigate its responsibility.

When you drive into the Company's mining concession, up into the beautiful Serra dos Carajas, you are constantly delighted by the rich forest on either side. Views are provided with parking places where cars can stop so that passengers can look across the ranges at the primaeval *hilaea* sweeping unblemished into the distance. Company officials will tell you with pride how, yesterday, a deer leapt across their bonnet, or how last week a jaguar glared into their headlights. And yet, from the beginning, the same people who planned this beautiful environment for their mines planned an industrial expansion that depends on stripping the forest outside the concession. For a transitory and relatively small profit, which they did not need, they planned to convert El Dorado into the pig iron jungle – reminding us that, ever since the first conquistador, the meaning of El Dorado has been slaughter and destruction. Even before the first blast furnaces were inaugurated, charcoal ovens were smoking all along the course of the railway – stock-piling charcoal for the huge demand that would come. Towns like Acailandia which, a few years before, had been a village of a few hundred houses, were lurid with industrial smog – smoke belching out into the surrounding forest from sawmills, charcoal ovens, and the first of its six pig iron complexes. And satellite photographs show the forest decimated all around.

'Amazonia today is the lungs of the world,' said the Mayor of Maraba. 'Setting up blast furnaces could bring about what we all fear . . . transform Amazonia into a desert.'

'In ten years we won't have any forest left,' said the sub-Mayor of Parauapebas, a small town just outside the Company's mining concession. 'The only forest left will be in the concession of the Companhia Vale do Rio Doce where deforestation is forbidden . . . We're worried about the pollution from the manufacture of charcoal and pig iron and that the rainfall will probably decrease.'

Today, a lawsuit brought by nearly a score of Brazilian citizens organisations, alleging that the pig iron plants are damaging the environment, is running through the Brazilian legal system. The sub-procurator general of the Republic, Claudio Lemos Fonteles, found that the granting of licences to the plants without an environmental impact statement was illegal, and this decision is now being contested by the companies in a variety of courts. In 1989, the government environmental agency, IBAMA, fined a number of pig iron factories for burning charcoal produced without a deforestation permit. These fines are also being disputed in the courts. Therefore, it is possible that one day the pig iron plants may be forced to use alternative sources of power – charcoal produced as a bi-product of processing babacu oil; gas from the new wells being discovered at Marajo or elsewhere; electricity using the arc furnace process; or coke imported to factories on the coast at the end of the railway. But we had come to Carajas looking for people with a sustainable way of using Amazonia's wealth, and what both the *garimpeiros* and the mining company had shown us was that they were predators, not guardians, of the forest.

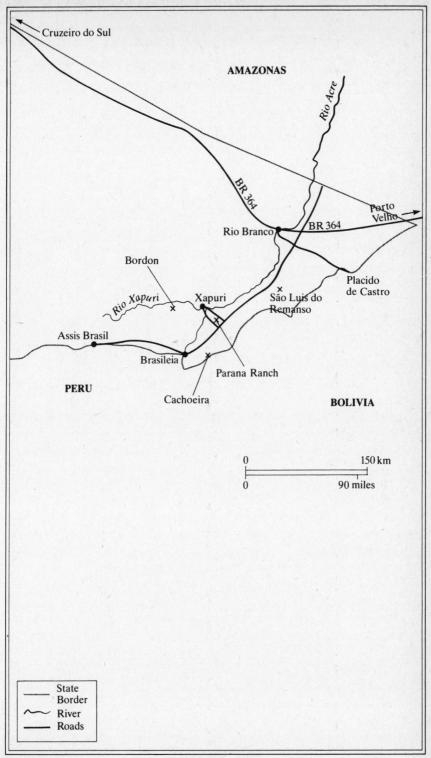

EASTERN ACRE

six

CHICO MENDES *and the* SERINGUEIRO ALTERNATIVE

ACRE
1986–1990

Acre is the most isolated state of Brazil on the borders of Bolivia and Peru in the south-western corner of Amazonia. In the early 1970s, the military government built a road from the State capital of Rio Branco through Xapuri to Brasileia and Assis Brasil on the frontier of Bolivia – partly to control left-wing penetration across this frontier. (It is close to where Che Guevara launched his Bolivian insurrection.) The Governor of Acre then used the access provided by this road to encourage wealthy companies to buy up the old rubber estates, which had been decaying since the price of rubber dropped in the 1950s. Scores of companies, many with tax incentives from SUDAM, set up cattle ranches and thousands of rubber tappers were expelled. The Catholic church and the Brazilian labour organisation, CON-TAG, the Confederation of Agricultural Workers, then started to help the seringueiros resist by setting up rural trades unions. The first was the rural workers' union of Brasileia created in 1975 with Chico Mendes as its secretary. Later Chico became the president of the neighbouring union of Xapuri, and over the next ten years these two unions developed an increasingly effective opposition to the ranchers.

It was only in 1985, however, that they broadened their local struggle into a national campaign. In October, 1985, Mary Allegretti, an anthropologist who worked with seringueiros, organised the first conference in Brasilia which brought together rubber tappers from all over Amazonia. They published their first manifesto and set up the National Council of Seringueiros, with Mary creating the Institute for Amazonian Studies as a support organisation. In September 1986, Jose Lutzenberger, with Ailton Krenak of the Indian organisation, UNI, made the first public announcement of the Amazonian Alliance of the Peoples of the Forest. And thus, after years of unchecked deforestation, the Indians, rubber tappers, caboclos and fishermen of Amazonia had at last acquired the political machinery to defend their forest. In 1987, their movement was espoused by the Green Party in Rio de Janeiro and environmental organisations all over the world, and Chico Mendes received awards from the United Nations Environment Programme and the Better World Society in the United States. Finally, in 1988, the seringueiros achieved their primary demand. Flaviano Melo, the Governor of Acre announced that his state would set up the first extractive reserve at Sao Luis de Remanso and that was soon followed by the Federal Government with announcements of extractive projects in other Amazonian States.

During this time, the locomotive force behind the seringueiro movement was the union of Xapuri under its president, Francisco Mendes Filho – Chico Mendes.

ONE

Our three years of filming with Chico Mendes started with the death of my son, Xingu. And though this occurred thousands of miles from Acre, it's impossible for me to think of Chico except in the light of how I started to work with him.

July the 1st, 1986, was the day before I was to fly from London to Acre to begin our programme with the *seringueiros*. On that day, Xingu who was 18 years old, was training in his kayak in the rapids of the alpine River Inn hoping to compete in the Irish slalom trials. Xingu had started life during that golden summer Pilly and I spent in the Parque do Xingu. And as a boy he paddled his first *seringueiro* canoe on the placid Rio Sao Miguel, and grew into an athlete testing his strength and skill in white water. At 18, he was a man from whom I cannot remember an angry word and few without some underlying current of amusement.

At midday on July the 1st, Xingu's kayak touched a submerged rock in the River Inn and was then swept onto another. (The Indian Agency expedition on the River Jamari lost three boats like this in 1980.) Held broadside between the two rocks against the full force of the current, there was nothing anyone could do to get Xingu off. A helicopter arrived nearly an hour later, but trapped for that time in the glacial water, he was clinically dead when he reached hospital. And though they revived him, I could hear the Austrian doctor crying at the other end of the phone when I rang her that evening. During the night there were no commercial flights to Innsbruck, so Pilly, Katia (Xingu's girl friend) and I took off at three o'clock in the morning, in a small plane that we managed to charter after it had delivered the night mail. At seven o'clock on July the 2nd, we dropped down out of the dawn into the grim gorge of Innsbruck – to hear that Xingu had died two hours earlier.

After two or three weeks in Ireland, I felt that the only way I could avoid sliding – like Pilly and Katia – into the black hole in the core of my being was to go back to work. And that is how I started to film Chico Mendes at the worst period of my life, and why I can only think of him as a very nice man who was particularly kind to me.

It was a doubly vicious twist of fate that Chico's wife, Ilza, soon after gave birth to twins, and that when we arrived with Chico at the house where she was staying, we heard that one of the twins, a son, had died. It was the unhappiest of common bonds and the unlikeliest beginning of a friendship.

It is also impossible for me to write about Chico except in the light of his political proposition. For, long before I met him, that proposition had seemed the answer to everything that had concerned me over the previous 30 years.

In the great, and apparently limitless, forest of Amazonia, every mile and every inch is divided among the species. No territory is without its owner fighting off his plant, insect and animal rivals. And, of course, the same is true of man. Title deeds, even government reserves, are meaningless against the pressures of speculation and migration – unless there is some man with the strength and ability to use the legal and political system to keep the invaders out. Forest or ecological reserves had proved nothing more than government-created vacuums during the 1980s, sucking the hungry inwards from their borders. And that is why, as soon as I heard that the first national *seringueiro* meeting was to be held in Brasilia in October 1980, I resolved to go. Just as the Camponatus species of ants defend the trees which they feed upon, so the survival of the Amazon forest depends on its defending human species – the *seringueiros*, the river fishermen, the *caboclos* and the Indians. Before their entry into politics, all the environmental protests of the early 1980s had been nothing more than unanswered prayers.

At that first national meeting, there turned out to be over 100 *seringueiros* with many different positions and a multiplicity of demands. Some of them didn't seem to know what they really wanted, and others didn't appear to be even sure of what they were trying to say. But on the second day, the meeting was chaired by Chico Mendes, who with a calm, almost avuncular manner somehow got everyone to agree on a common position. And that, more or less, was to become the cornerstone of the *seringueiro* movement – Mary Allegretti organising and finding the money, Chico binding the *seringueiros* together. Of all Chico's qualities, perhaps the most useful to the *seringueiros* was the ability to produce agreed resolutions out of mental confusion and political rivalry.

At the end of the week, the *seringueiros* voted on their manifesto, and its principal demand proved to be 'extractive reserves'. Until that time, whenever the Land Agency, INCRA, moved into a rubber tapping area, each *seringueiro* usually received a plot of 50 hectares. But as a *seringueiro* needs perhaps about 500 trees to make a living, most *seringueiro* holdings are normally between 300 and 500 hectares – depending on the density of the rubber trees. Fifty hectare plots from the Land Agency were, thus, not viable for extracting rubber, and most *seringueiros* 'regularised' by INCRA sold their land and eventually ended up in the slums of Manaus, Porto Velho or Rio Branco.

What the manifesto demanded was that each *seringueiro* should be confirmed in the actual area of forest he used, but, even more important, that he should not receive a saleable title of ownership. Instead, the government should set up reserves for extractivists – like reserves for Indians – and that these should be for all the extractivists of Amazonia, including river people and the gatherers of fruits, medicines, oils and Brazil nuts. When a family abandoned or misused its holding, it should go back to the reserve for another applicant.

It was a proposition that was to become the cornerstone of most alternative plans for the development of Amazonia. And, immediately after the meeting, I asked Chico if we could film with him during the next deforestation season in Acre. I wanted to discover how he and the *seringueiros* would develop their proposition, but, at the time, I had no idea of the even more remarkable voyage that Chico was about to embark on. 'We started fighting for the rubber tree and Brazil nut tree and the good little life we had in the forest,' he was to say not long before his death. 'And then we discovered that we were defending the whole of Amazonia. And now I have come to realise that what we are fighting for is all of humanity.'

TWO

'In this area there were a thousand rubber trees,' said Chico as he walked across a barren stretch of cattle pasture. 'But they're all dead and I don't know how many Brazil nut trees and how much commercial timber as well. All the game has been destroyed,' he concluded grimly, 'and it was so rich here.'

It was 1986, and Chico was with a small group of *seringueiros* crossing an outlying part of the Bordon ranch. It totalled 46,000 hectares and was owned by the giant Sao Paulo meat packing company Frigorifico Bordon SA. Their exports alone amount to more than 140 million dollars per year, and their ranch in Xapuri was the largest of the municipality. 'Bordon has always been the centre of things,' Chico said. 'Amongst the ranches, they are the most powerful and the most reactionary. They have always made the most pressure to drive *seringueiros* out. We have been fighting them for ten years.'

During the 1950s and 1960s, as the rubber price had dropped and the *seringais* of Acre had fallen into decay, many rubber barons had gone off to the cities. The *seringueiros* left behind in the forest had fended for themselves and developed a more independent way of life. Thus it was that when a rubber 'estate' was bought by a company like Bordon, there was almost always a dispute about what this purchase covered. For in the past, when the government had granted an area of forest to a rubber baron, what he was given was the right to extract rubber and Brazil nuts. He did not receive the right of land ownership. And under modern law, the Land Agency, INCRA, was obliged to respect a squatter's right to the land he occupied. This meant that when a rancher bought a rubber estate, he could only deforest after he had either driven out the *seringueiros* or bought up their squatters' rights.

It was now the beginning of the dry season and the Bordon ranch had started its annual deforestation. Chico was on his way to an 'empate' – the *seringueiro's* remarkable non-violent technique for preventing deforestation. ('Empate' literally means a draw or deadlock.)

The party of *seringueiros* left the pasture and walked down a trail that led into the forest. 'In the early days,' Chico said, 'in 1978 and 1979, Raimundo and I travelled this whole region together. But there were threats from all sides. So one day we sat down to talk. "Look, Raimundo," I said, "If they set an ambush, they will get us both. So you chose an area to operate, and I will chose another, and every one or two months we will visit each other."' Raimundo was Chico's cousin and the union representative for the area in which the *empate* was to occur.

'We were born and brought up in this Amazonia living off the rubber tree and the Brazil nut tree and from all this wealth and beauty around us,' Raimundo began grandly, addressing a small gathering of *seringueiros*. 'But today this is threatened by the big landlord putting the cow in our place. So we must unite and make them respect us.' The little group of about 40 to 50 *seringueiros* didn't look as if it would command much respect. There were several women and children, and the unarmed men did not seem particularly threatening. In comparison to ranch *vacqueiro* – who are usually bronzed and burly – *seringueiros* often seem puny and pallid from the shade of the forest.

But soon the whole party was marching down a broad rubber trail, singing a typical song of the left.

'Enough to such suffering. Enough to such waiting. The fight is going to be so difficult. But by law or struggle we will win.'

The scene was like a Russian film. Poor but noble looking peasants marching resolutely through the forest. And I soon came to regard this as a characteristic of unionism in Xapuri. For the techniques and language of international trades unionism had become essential tools for the *seringueiro* defence of the forest – though sometimes the two seemed an improbable match.

After a few hours, they arrived at a poor house of thatch and logs belonging to Antonio Candido, the *seringueiro* whose holding was threatened. And he took the party down a narrow, badly cleared trail, until the sound of a motor saw got close. Chico then called everyone to gather round. 'I am sure that there will only be a few of them and that they won't react against us,' Chico looked round mildly at everyone, a little like an uncle at a childrens' party.

'But we must show that we're peaceful. I ask you not to make them nervous, not to say anything aggressive.'

Then Raimundo, who is very tall, and his wife Mariazinha, who is decidedly small, moved forward, pushing aside the undergrowth. I later learnt that it was Mariazinha who first insisted that women take part in *empates*. She moved close behind Raimundo's tall, daunting figure, like a torpedo boat in the wake of a battleship.

Almost immediately, the motor saw stopped, and when Raimundo heard someone moving about on the other side of a wall of undergrowth, he called out, 'Comrade, come here. We want to talk.' And then as he got close to a startled man in a torn shirt, 'Don't be alarmed.'

'No, man,' the cutter replied, looking round uneasily, 'I'm not frightened.'

'Of course, not,' Raimundo replied firmly, as Mariazinha and some of the others joined him. 'You're a worker like us. But where are the rest of you?'

'I work alone,' the cutter replied. 'Every 700 metres, there's a trail with people cutting.' And then he changed his tone looking abruptly at the scrub he had cut down. 'But you don't believe I'm to blame for this?'

'The ranchers are so intelligent that they never cut down a tree themselves.' Raimundo launched into what sounded like a much repeated speech. 'Even the manager, Sr Tomas, doesn't cut one single stick of tomato. But they put a comrade, a worker cast down by the precariousness of life, to do the job. And their objective is to remain with all this in their hands,' Raimundo waved round the forest. 'For once you have finished off all this richness, which is yours, which is ours, which is the *seringueiros*' and workers', it is wonderful for them. Because they will have fenced it with wire and filled it with cattle. And then what will we live on? So comrade,' Raimundo concluded, 'you must be conscious of this. Today, you have forest to cut. But in ten years, there won't be any left.'

'Like Mato Grosso,' the cutter suggested.

'Then what will you deforest?'

'Nothing at all.' The cutter was getting into the spirit of the thing. And yet – amongst so many people – there was little else he could do. *Seringueiros* are as at home in the forest as Indians. To a cattleman, the group must have seemed as frightening as an Indian war party.

'You're workers like us, not ranch gunmen,' Chico wound up the discussion amicably. 'Now we will go and talk to your companions. I hope that one day we will all work together.'

'God willing,' the cutter said devoutly, and then – as he shook hands – formally added his name, 'Horacio Serafim de Lima.'

The *empate* did not appear particularly dramatic, and I later came to regard this low key approach as characteristic of both Chico and the *seringueiros*. But deforestation did stop that day, though whether because the cutting teams had been convinced, or whether because they told the rancher they wouldn't go on without police protection, it's hard to tell. The Bordon company immediately went to court, and the ranch manager, Tomas Coelho, explained their position to Vicente.

'The ranch has 3782 head of cattle and there are 4000 hectares cleared – 500 badly.' The ranch house is a white building close to the River Xapuri, and its corral and fences are lovingly painted and maintained. 'We have an average of 1600 breeding cows, so from now on we have to increase our pasture at least 500 hectares per year. This year, if the *seringueiros* don't succeed in stopping us, we will clear 700 hectares to try and provide for all our cattle.' Tomas has a broad, bluff face and an impressive Stetson hat, but he spoke wearily. 'We now have 808 head on land rented from the Fazenda Boa Vista, because in other years we have been prevented from clearing. And though we never cut forest where a *seringueiro* is living, and always pay indemnity, and often have a document at hand showing that we have already bought that particular holding, the *seringueiros* still block the deforestation. They just want to keep the forest,' Tomas said in exasperation, 'to live their little lives in.'

'They want to go on living in the forest collecting a little rubber. Then take that to the town, have their little fair, sell it, and buy some goods to bring back. Some get so drunk that they return without any goods. I think they suffer a lot in the forest. We have offered to put them on a piece of cleared land with a house and school. We have also offered three times the minimum salary. But they won't accept it. I don't know whether it's them or the union that won't allow it.' Tomas clearly felt that he had exhausted all reason. 'But we made this proposal through the State Government, and they would not accept.'

Tomas then took our team to film some pasture at a distance from the ranch house. 'I got a licence from IBDF, the Forestry Institute, to clear this pasture. And there wasn't a single *seringueiro* holding on it. But when we were half way through cutting, a group of 40 *seringueiros* appeared – some from other *seringais* – and said we must stop. So I obeyed and agreed to go to court. Then the court confirmed that my licence was legal and that I had authority to deforest. So the judge sent police to protect us, and during the cutting the *seringueiros* did not come back. But, what was much worse,' Tomas said indignantly, 'they set fire to the deforested area before it had had time to dry. And we couldn't put the fire out. So it burnt badly, and is badly cleared. I am having to spend 300,000 to 400,000 cruzados per hectare to replant these 500 hectares.'

Tomas Coelho was beginning to sound weary of the struggle.

Up to this time, I had been preparing one of our films for transmission in England, and the description of the *empate* comes from Vicente and our recordings. But I joined them in July 1986 in time to witness the climax. The Bordon lawsuit ended with the judge sending police to protect the cutters. And the deforestation was then finished, though most of Antonio's holding was left standing. But – as in the previous year – the deciding factor would be how well the cut timber and undergrowth would burn at the end of the dry season.

At the beginning of September, we were in Rio Branco, the capital of Acre, when we received the news that Tomas had decided to burn that day. We immediately chartered a plane and set off in the direction of Xapuri. The haze was so profound that we could see no further than a few hundred yards, and fires were all around us, pushing dark plumes of smoke up into the lighter smog. But following the road, we managed to find Xapuri, and following the river, we located the Bordon ranch. Then turning in from the river, we perceived, through the haze, a cloud of billowing smoke. A huge deforested area was pouring columns of smoke into the sky. But we confirmed what Chico had suspected. The cut forest was burning very badly and, as in the previous year, it would cost Bordon a lot more money to clear.

Soon after we began to hear a rumour that Bordon was putting up their ranch for sale. A company as rich as theirs had no need to make money confronting *seringueiros* – with all the bad publicity that that involved. And within a year, Chico's oldest enemy did, in fact, sell up. It was thus that we witnessed what was probably Chico's greatest victory. But since it threatened all the other ranchers in the area, it was also – probably – the deciding factor in his assassination.

THREE

'This year we have had a victory against Bordon.' Chico said, standing, mild and plump, under a jaguar skin nailed to the hut wall. 'We have defended the holding of a comrade who stood firm, and if every comrade followed Antonio Candido's example, no rancher would deforest again. It just needs courage, love for your children and the solidarity of your comrades to keep the forest safe from the ranchers.' Chico was speaking at the beginning of his campaign for election to the State Assembly of Acre.

'Now we must think about politics.' Chico looked round his small audience of about 30 *seringueiros* in a holding on the edge of the Bordon ranch. 'Worried by our resistance, Bordon and the ranchers have created an organisation called the UDR, the Uniao Democratica Ruralista. [This is, in effect, the ranchers' party of Brazil.] They are auctioning cattle to raise money for their candidates in the election. Here, in Acre, according to our information, the PMDB candidate for Governor, Flaviano Melo, has already received 800 million cruzados from ranchers. And if he is elected, deforestation will continue. The police are obviously going to defend Bordon's interests while it fills their pockets. They earn 720 cruzados per day from Bordon (when they protect its cutting teams.) So, comrades, what's the point of blocking Bordon's deforestation and on election day voting for Flaviano Melo who will command the police to do Bordon's bidding?'

Chico then threw the meeting open, and though none of the speakers disagreed, the implications behind his question made me think.

Seringal Cachoeira was the next *seringal* we visited during the campaign and the *seringal* for which Chico was later to be killed. In a large airy school house, built by the local *seringueiros*, Gomercindo Rodrigues, Chico's political lieutenant, started the meeting.

'We all need to vote for Chico. But he has nothing to give you.' Gomercindo spoke directly, almost gruffly. 'He doesn't have any money or shirts to give away. And I ask you,' he looked round the 40 people packed into the tight-fitting desks of the schoolroom, 'is that the sort of thing that will solve the workers' problems?' No one responded, and soon after Chico began.

'Comrades, once again I am a candidate for State Deputy.' (He had run and lost in 1982.) 'Everyone knows I don't have any money. I have no salary. I have no house to live in because I haven't the means to buy one. My aim is that the fight should go on. But it's apparant that the worker cannot organise himself politically. The worker fights and fights with Chico Mendes. But on election day, he doesn't vote for Chico Mendes because he is poor.' Chico's placid, friendly manner, which made him a good negotiator, didn't help his speeches. It tended to make them uninspiring and prosaic. 'Have you ever thought that if we had one or two deputies committed to fight Bordon on behalf of our class, that we would be more successful. We manage to defend the holding of a comrade, but we don't stop deforestation. And that's because there are 24 deputies elected by you to the State Assembly who don't want to hear the workers, only to criticise them.'

Thus from the start of the electoral campaign, Chico's speeches implied that most *seringueiros* had not voted for him in the past, and would not now. 'Brazilian politics are always won with money,' Vicente explained, 'and people don't vote for candidates who can't win. If they do, it's called wasting your vote. Chico is a patron saint who can't do miracles. Most *seringueiros* won't believe he can succeed in politics.' It was this that started me talking to Chico about where he thought he was going and what it was that motivated him.

'I was always a *seringueiro*. My father was a *seringueiro* and I started cutting when I was nine years old. For 20 years I cut rubber, and it was only in 1975 when the ranchers began to arrive, that I joined the union and cut less.'

We were sitting on the top step of Chico's home looking across a field of grass towards a dark border of forest. The moon was so bright that if you looked across the little valley to the right, you could see the holding of Chico's brother, Zuza. He is a slightly plumper and an even more affable Chico.

The canvassing had been put on hold for several days and Chico had come back to see his wife and family. Without a salary, he was too poor to rent a house, and Ilza, his wife, lived with her father Moacir on his holding half an hour's walk off the main road between Xapuri and Brasileia.

'There were no schools in the 1960s,' Chico was smoking an after dinner cigarette, 'and none of us could read and write except for one *seringueiro* who wasn't really a *seringueiro*. Whenever, this man passed our house, he would come in and read out the news from the papers. I don't know where he got the papers,' Chico puffed the cigarette reflectively. 'which were very old. But I was 18, and I always listened and one day Euclides asked if I would like to learn to read for myself. And that's how I started, to go every weekend to his house, two or three hour's walk from ours.'

At that time, Chico's family had lived on a holding called Pote Seco, close to the Bolivian border. The house is in a small clearing, with many flowering trees and bushes, and nearby is a very beautiful grove of old Brazil nut trees. One of them is several hundred years old and yielded the remarkable quantity of 240 kilos of nuts when we visited the holding.

'Was Euclides really working as a *seringueiro*?' I asked.

'He had been taught to cut rubber,' Chico replied. 'But he must have been hiding from something, because he was very clever. He taught me all weekend, and we also read the papers and he would explain the news and tell me about the workers' struggle all over the world. Then when the revolution came, (the Brazilian military coup d'état of 1964), Euclides showed me how to listen to the radio for the Voice of America, the BBC of London and Radio Moscow, so we could hear news different from the government's about what was happening. Euclides said the military take-over had been to prevent land reform and that the workers of Brazil were now in chains and their leaders had been killed or jailed. But he said this had happened many times before in the world, and the capitalists had never been able to crush the seed. The seed would stay in the hearts of the workers and, one day, maybe many years ahead, it would flower again. And so,' Chico said gravely, 'Euclides told me to wait, and to study, and when I heard that a trades union was being set up, to join it.'

I was fascinated by this story of a revolutionary passing on the seed deep in the jungle, and I asked who his teacher really was. Chico said that he had seen his picture amongst a group of officers in a book about the long march – the Brazilian long march of 1922 to 1924 led by the Communist leader, Luis Carlos Prestes. At the time, Chico did not mention his full name. But several of his union colleagues have since confirmed that he was Euclides Fernando Tavora, who had been very young when he was captured after the long march. As his relatives were influential, he was released from jail and exiled to Bolivia. For many years he had worked there for the Bolivian Communist Party and various workers' movements, until – presumably – a right wing government forced him to flee across the border into Brazil. There he had lived on his holding until he became increasingly ill in 1965. He went out to find a doctor, and was never heard of again.

'Without him,' Chico said, 'I was half lost. But I started to teach other *seringueiros* how to read and write. They all wanted to learn, because when you could read you saw how much the store was cheating when it bought your rubber and sold you food.'

'That was the time, I met Che Guevara,' Chico beamed. It was obvious that he enjoyed retelling this part. 'In a bar one day, someone introduced me to this man who said he wanted to travel about the region. He was looking for a guide, and we talked for a bit, and I offered to help. But I never saw him again, and it was only after his photo was published, that I knew it was Che.'

The story which is told in Acre, and which I have never been able to confirm, was that when Che was setting out to start his Bolivian insurrection, he travelled to Porto Velho with the intention of crossing from Rondonia into Bolivia at Guajara-Mirim. But as he was leaving Porto Velho, he heard that the Federal Police had swooped on Guajara and were searching everyone for cocaine. So Che had changed his plan and branched right to Acre. There, the present road from Xapuri to Brasileia and Assis Brasil is seldom more than 20 kilometres from the border, and many frontier holdings, like Chico's father's, had trails running into Bolivia. Someone like Chico must have taken Che across.

That night, as I lay in my hammock listening to distant calls in the forest, I thought that no revolutionary could have had a more prophetic start. It was the stuff of legend, like the boy Arthur pulling the sword, Excalibur, from its stone. And though, of course, his meeting with Euclides had just been luck, Chico's frequent telling of this story, and Che's, did imply that that was how he saw himself – as part of the great, international army of the left, fighting to liberate the working class from capitalism.

Accordingly, when CONTAG, the Confederation of Agricultural Workers, moved into the region to defend the *seringueiros* against the ranchers, Chico took a short course as a union leader. He was then elected secretary of the first *seringueiro* union in Brasileia in 1975, and in 1980 founded and became president of the union in Xapuri. And though those early years were the most hard pressed for the *seringueiros*, I felt it was significant that Chico now looked back on them almost with envy. 'All the *seringueiros* were frightened of the ranchers,' Chico said, 'and so there was a massive participation in the union.'

During the 1980s, however, the *empates* became increasingly successful, and with their holdings less under threat, many *seringueiros* began to drift away from the union.

Canvassing with Chico, travelling from holding to holding, it was easy to see why. Most of Xapuri's *seringueiros* lived in a fairly large clearing with up to a dozen cattle and horses. Many had big airy houses made of logs and thatch, with a number of subsidiary huts that sheltered chickens, a mandioca oven and a store for corn. Invariably there were chickens wandering about, usually with guinea fowl, ducks and pigs. For after gaining independence from the rubber barons, the *seringueiros* of Xapuri had become small holders first and rubber tappers only second. Most grew rice, beans, corn and mandioca, and had bushes or trees of coffee, pepper, oranges, limes and cashew. It was seldom that we visited a house that didn't have some sort of meat – usually a deer, pig or armadillo killed in the forest. And so, though many *seringueiros* were poor in their lack of ready money, Chico's electorate was – quite visibly – not made up of the hungry and the desperate.

Most of the places where Chico campaigned were holdings where there was to be a festival – a forro dance, typical of the north-east, or a football match between one *seringal* and another. Usually Chico would watch the match or dance, and then use the gathering to make a speech. And it was very noticeable that though everyone seemed to like him, less than half would come to his speech. And sometimes I would catch Chico talking to a small group of more active union members and looking sadly at a much larger group laughing and talking about something else outside.

From time to time, I would discuss our impressions with Elson Martins in Rio Branco. He was a journalist who had covered the *seringueiro* movement from its beginning in the 1970s, and a particular friend of Chico's. 'The *seringueiro* is not a socialist, a leftist,' he said. 'He is a person who has the same ambitions as the *seringalista*. Often he possesses nothing, is a person without heritage. But he is a conservative and a moralist. He may seem a revolutionary because of his difficult life, his love of nature, because he wants a civilisation different to what the rest of the country wants to impose on Amazonia. But the *seringueiro* is not a revolutionary in the marxist-communist line that the left wants to impose on him.' That was the problem of Chico's campaign.

In himself, Chico combined both trends. From his upbringing, he had the practical, conservative nature of the *seringueiro*, but the seed of Euclides had flowered in his heart and mind. As a union leader, Chico seemed capable of synthesising both forces. But the problem came when the two were launched into politics, the *seringueiros* pulling in one direction and party extremists in another. 'Chico is in a cross-fire,' Vicente said. 'Everyone dragging him in a different direction. The Church inside the Workers' Party attacks him as a Trotskyite. The left says he is not a real revolutionary. And the *seringueiros* don't know who Trotsky is and don't want to hear about revolution.'

I suspect that it was this need to reconcile differing forces that turned Chico – a practical and, apparantly, plodding man – into a political innovator.

It was the day of the first campaign rally of the Workers' Party in Xapuri. A platform with loudspeakers and lights had been set up in the square that faces the church and union office. And all day Gomercindo, Chico's political agent, had been driving round the town on his motor bike. 'Chico Mendes for State Deputy,' he shouted into a loudhailer in his left hand, wobbling a little on the cobbles. 'Chico Mendes, a candidate in defence of the workers. Chico Mendes for extractive reserves. In defence of the Amazon forest. Against devastation. Against the expulsion of men for cows.'

The meeting was warmed up by a singer from Rio Branco and consisted of short speeches from many candidates, representing different interests, including an Indian and a leper. It was to conclude with a speech from the candidate for Governor of Acre on behalf of the Workers' Party.

But when Chico was called to the microphone – to cheers from friends, neighbours and union members – his first sentence was: 'Comrades, I would like to ask everyone to pay attention first to the words written in large letters.' He then turned to a red banner stretched behind him and pointed to four words painted in white: IN DEFENCE OF AMAZONIA. Chico then repeated the theme into the microphone. 'In Defence of Amazonia'. That comrades, is the centre of the question and the centre of my commitment to the workers of Acre.'

It is my guess that that was the first time ever that 'the Defence of Amazonia' became the central plank of a political platform. Previously, few politicians had even mentioned such a vote-losing issue during their speeches. But now, here was a man from within the forest, on behalf of voters who lived within the forest, raising the political banner of its defence. It was the beginning of a great change.

A few days later, I left to fly to Washington to cover the opening of the tropical forest campaign. I flew with Lutz and Ailton Krenak of the Indian organisation, UNI, and we left Jaime da Silva, the then president of the National *Seringueiro* Council, a dejected little figure in Manaus airport. His passport and visa were in a plane that had been delayed and would only arrive after our departure.

In Washington, the tropical forest campaign was launched by a conference of non-governmental organisations, and Lutz presented to it the Amazonian Alliance of the Peoples of the Forest – with Ailton representing both the Indians and the *seringueiros*. And this was not unfitting. 'I don't really understand it,' was what Chico had said when I had discussed the alliance with him. 'Why don't we leave it to Ailton?' But when I enquired from Ailton about how he saw UNI's relations with the *seringueiros*, he had put both his fists dramatically at opposite ends of the table and said, 'Sometimes we are like this – apart.' And then he joined both his fists in the middle. 'And sometimes we are like this – together. And then,' he pushed both fists to the opposite ends of the table, 'we are apart again.'

That was the reason it was called an alliance and not a federation, and from the start, it was Ailton who saw with the greatest clarity, both its limitations and great possibilities: that on the scale of national politics, an alliance of all the forest peoples would be the most effective voice to advocate alternatives to the destruction of the forest.

When I got back to Xapuri, Chico's campaign was not going well. Chico said that many voters were being given presents, like pressure cookers, and that large families with influence and a number of votes had even received motor saws from the richer candidates.

'Many of us still only believe in those who speak fair,' I heard Raimundo saying to a group of *seringueiros*. 'In those who live in the city and appear only at election time with a jacket and good shoes and a brief case in their hand, clapping us on the shoulder and giving us a few crumbs. But our *empates*, our day-to-day struggles, are no use unless we vote at election time for those comrades, like Chico, identified with our struggle.'

On election day, as the various parties trucked their voters into Xapuri, the streets, outside the voting centres, were feverish with people obliquely, or directly, trying to negotiate their votes. The Workers' Party had given Chico luncheon vouchers for voters who had a long way to come, and also a little money to buy such people coffee or soft drinks. As Raimundo, Gomercindo and other union activists watched the voting booths to see there was no cheating, Chico walked the streets encouraging his *seringueiros* to vote, and giving out the vouchers to people who asked for them.

It was surprising how many approached him directly for money.

'Give me 40,000,' a woman said quite openly. And another, 'Give me the money for some drinks.' But the most inspired approach was from an eleven year old boy who walked up and said, 'For 1000, you could at least be sure of my mother's vote.'

As the day went on, we interviewed Chico several times, and I tried to give him the opportunity to discount defeat. 'With so much money and organisation on the government side,' I asked, 'do you really think you can win?'

'I am very optimistic,' Chico replied. 'I am perceiving an advance in the conscience of the workers and this time it seems as if neither the economic power of Bordon, nor the government, can twist that conscience.'

It was one of the few occasions I saw him really elated. 'So you really hope to come out well?' I pressed him again.

'Since my first election campaign, this is the first time I have felt optimistic before seeing the result,' Chico said decisively. 'After years of organising the workers, the fruits are beginning to appear – the workers are beginning to show conscience, to be committed to the struggle, to vote for their candidate.'

On the next day the votes were counted in Xapuri's court-house – the scene two years later of Darci and Darli's murder trial – and every hour brought further news of a government landslide.

That night, as he was having dinner with us, Chico looked really depressed. The votes across the whole state had still not been counted. But Chico had won only ten percent of the vote in Xapuri – less than when he ran for prefect in the previous year. Since Chico's union had over 2000 members, many *seringueiros* must have voted for other candidates.

'They have been dominated by the *patrao* for generations,' Chico defended his fickle union members. 'This land has been moulded by slavery, ever since it was opened up. So we can't expect the people to change from one moment to another.'

All in all, Chico won three times as many votes across the State as any other Workers' Party candidate for State Deputy. And because of Brazil's proportional representation, he could not have been given a seat, even if he had won more votes, because his party only won three percent of the vote in Acre. But Chico's depression seemed to stem from his failure to convince more of his union members – and also from his financial desperation. For years, he had been working as an unsalaried union official in the hope that he would be elected one day as prefect or state deputy. He would then, as a member of the Workers' Party, have to give a third of his salary to the party, but the rest would have been enough to pay his debts and rent a house for his wife. Now, his last hope had been dashed. Since we were filming his political campaign, there was no way we could give him money without compromising both him and us. And the only time I broke that rule was when Ilza was very ill after giving birth to the twins. The afterbirth had not been treated properly, and we paid for her to go to a better doctor and hospital. From months of living and travelling together we knew, only too well, how poor Chico was.

'What will you do?' I asked that night.

'The fight must go on,' Chico said doggedly. 'It's almost the Brazil nut season. I can make some money collecting nuts.' Chico looked so easy-going that it was often hard to remember that stamina was the hallmark of his long career.

And that was the situation which led me to ring Steve Schwartzman of the Environmental Defence Fund to ask if he could use Chico's help at the annual meeting of the Inter-American Development Bank.

A few days before, in the town of Placido de Castro, Mary Allegretti, Raimundo, Chico and I had had a drink in a bar while Vicente was setting up the lights for one of the last night rallies. (The town's generator was so weak that every time Vicente switched on the lights, the loudspeakers went off.) We discussed Chico's speeches criticising the Inter-American Development Bank and its loan for the BR364 road. This was the extension of the road to Porto Velho which had been paved with World Bank money and which caused massive deforestation in Rondonia. Now a sister multi-national development bank in Washington, the IDB, was financing its extension into Acre. As I had just come back from Washington, I said that I thought that the US environmental organisations would support Chico's criticism of the IDB. But that they could only do this if formally requested by the *seringueiros*. Mary, Raimundo and Chico had then talked about writing a public letter or sending a *seringueiro* to the United States. Now, after the election, that idea seemed to have the additional advantage of taking Chico away from his defeat. The 'internationalisation of Chico Mendes' was as unpremeditated as that.

FOUR

'Cattle ranching has brought nothing to the region. The only thing it has been good for is the concentration of landholdings and the expulsion of thousands of *seringueiros*.' Chico was wearing a jacket lent him by Steve Schwartzman, and was sitting in the lobby of the large and very noisy Inter-continental Hotel. At the end of his first day in Miami, at a cocktail party for 2000 people, he had looked what he was – a man from the jungle lost at a bankers' meeting. His eyes had seemed cross-eyed from all the babble and foreign chaos.

But by his second day, he was adapting quickly. 'Another very serious result,' he said to Bo Jerlstrom, the Swedish Executive Director of the Inter-American Development Bank, 'is that there seems to be a climate change taking place in the region. The rivers are drying up.'

Steve was taking Chico to meet as many directors of the IDB as possible, and Chico was arguing – in the light of what had happened in Rondonia – that the road into Acre should not be paved until there were adequate measures to protect the environment, the *seringueiros* and the Indians. Hundreds of bankers and government officials were hurrying to and fro between the lobby and the main auditorium where the annual meeting was in session. But Chico was definitely making an impact. It can't be often that someone as exotic as a jungle rubber tapper attends the IDB annual meeting.

'We may consider to take some action to get the loan on the right track.' Bo Jerlstrom said to me later. 'I should tell you that I was invited to come down to the area by this Brazilian rubber tapper, and I might consider that.'

The US Executive Director was even more positive. 'There are countries that are very strong on opposing the introduction, in the lending, of environmental concerns – because they have cost implications. Of course, the US Government doesn't view it that way. We feel that one of the mechanisms is to stop funding when it's justified.' Which was exactly what Steve was recommending – suspension of payments under the loan, until the environmental problems were sorted out.

On the next day Steve took Chico to Washington where he met Alec Echols, Senator Kasten's enviromental aide. And a few days later, a strong letter signed by Senators Inouye and Kasten was sent to the IDB. Its key sentences were: *We cannot allow a repeat of the devastation which occurred in Rondonia . . . For this reason, we insist that further work extending the BR364 be terminated, until the Bank can certify that the necessary environmental components of the loan have been implemented.*

'What we're seeing today, unfortunately, is the Inter-American Development Bank not living up to its basic responsibilities,' said Senator Kasten with feeling, 'expressed in a contract, I might add. And I think you can look at this as a shot over the bow if you will. If they continue not to heed the basic environmental components of this agreement on the Acre project, I think that the entire funding of the Inter-American Bank, the funding from the United States of America, could be in jeopardy.'

While we were in Washington, news came that Jaime da Silva, the president of the National Council of Seringueiros, had gone into hiding from gunmen sent to kill him – allegedly – by the prefect of his home town of Aripuana. So on Chico's return to Brazil, we all waited anxiously to hear what would happen. Before he had left, we had discussed very thoroughly whether Chico's trip would increase his risk of assassination, and Gomercindo had summed up the position as follows: 'We're at risk all the time. So going abroad can't increase it very much – and it could help.'

Now Mary phoned, to say that Chico had been denounced in the Senate in Brasilia and in the State Assembly in Rio Branco. The idea that a humble rubber tapper should ask foreign banks to cut off a loan to the Government had infuriated the elite of Acre. But fortunately no-one threatened his life. And soon after the fruits of his visit began to appear.

At first, the Inter-American Development Bank had dismissed Senators Inouye's and Kasten's letter. 'We cannot enter into an individual negotiation with an individual committee or sub-committee of either the United States Senate or a European Parliament,' said Jerome Levinson, the IDB chief counsel. And this had not pleased Senators Kasten and Inouye. After Hearings in which Steve Schwartzman for the Environmental Defence Fund – supported by Barbara Bramble for the National Wildlife Federation Club – recommended cutting the US contribution to the IDB, the Senate Appropriations Committee slashed 200 million dollars from the US contribution to the IDB in December 1987. 'We made a major differentiation between the Inter-American Development Bank and all the other banks today,' said Senator Kasten. 'This Sub-committee (the Foreign Operations Sub-committee) on a unanimous vote, without any discussion or without any objection, has taken 200 million dollars away from the IDB request. And I think that clearly is going to send a message to them – that if they're not willing to meet with basic environmental reforms and standards, they're not going to get money from the Senate Sub-committee.'

A few weeks later, the IDB gave way and suspended payments under its Acre loan. And almost overnight the ranchers in Acre were shocked into an awareness of the efficacy of Chico's contacts abroad. 'The ranchers in the hotel in Xapuri,' Vicente said, 'kept looking at Chico. And you could see that they just couldn't believe that he had done it.' In the past, they had always regarded the *seringueiros* as a nuisance, but never as a challenge. Now their vital interests were under threat. The paving of the road had led to soaring land prices, and one real estate company had even advertised Acre as the filet mignon of Amazonia. With suspension of the paving, speculation and land prices paused.

It was more or less at this time, that Chico won his two international awards. A few months before, Robert Lamb – who works for both the United Nations Environment Programme and the Television Trust for the

Environment – had asked me to suggest some South American names for the UNEP Global 500 award. And I could think of no one more deserving – after five assassination attempts and a dozen years of struggle – than Chico. Robert had met Chico when he had joined us for two weeks in Brazil. He strongly agreed, and also suggested that I write up a second nomination to the Better World Society. Chico won both awards, and this brought him a wave of publicity and recognition inside and outside Brazil.

Chico was elected to the national directorate of CUT, Brazil's trades union federation. The Green Party of Brazil – which campaigned with the Workers' Party in 1986 – made him an honourary citizen of Rio de Janeiro. And all the publicity helped Mary Allegretti raise money abroad. The Gaia Foundation gave Chico a few hundred dollars a month to cover his expenses and living costs, and then the Ashoka Foundation took over from them. This made it possible for Chico to rent a simple wooden house in Xapuri and to bring Ilza and the children to live with him. Later when Chico's landlady wanted to terminate the lease in order to sell the house, Mary Allegretti suggested that she, Steve and we should put together $500 to buy Chico's little house, as a sort of Christmas present. 'Adriano, you have no idea,' Chico said several times that year, 'how much things have improved.'

These improvements were largely the result of Chico's success in projecting the *seringueiro* case not just abroad, but in a completely different ethos, that of the environmentalists. And I suspect that it was because Chico was so convincing at this that some foreign journalists described him as charismatic.

'Charismatic,' Vicente snorted, when I read out an article. 'Chico's so comfortable that he can't get in our car without falling asleep. Five minutes and you hear the first snore.'

'Chico's placid and diplomatic, not ambitious or incisive,' I said to Elson Martins. 'So how is it that he is so innovative? He has worked out how to adapt trades unionism to the needs of forest people. Then he took over the environmentalists. And now he's learnt how to make use of foreign politics. Within just a few days, you could see he already knew the difference between a Senator, his aide and a lobbyist – and how to deal with each of them.'

'I think it's because he's a listener,' Elson said. 'He doesn't talk much because he's genuinely humble and wants to learn. He listens and thinks and thinks about what he has heard.'

I believe Elson was right. But if so, then why did Chico, during the next year, go beyond his basic task of defending rubber tapper interests and begin to campaign for 'the whole of Amazonia and humanity' – to try to put an end to all deforestation and thus confront Darli Alves and the UDR?

In the ensuing events, what many non-Brazilians find hard to understand is why Darli did not just shoot Chico at once – why he preceded his killing with an almost operatic prelude of threats and menace. But this is common in the assassination of Brazil's rural leaders. And the reason is linked to the fact that less than one percent of the landowners own nearly half Brazil's agricultural land. For such a small minority to retain such a disproportionate amount of land, it is not enough just to eliminate the leaders of the landless. It is essential to do it in such a way as to terrorise the masses. Joao Branco, the leader of the ranchers' UDR party in Acre, later denied planning Chico's murder. But what is undeniable is that the 'Rio Branco' newspaper, part-owned by him, sent a reporting team to Xapuri to cover Chico's death – in advance. (Their claim to have been telephoned the news and to have achieved a racing miracle driving over 150 kilometres on a potholed road in the rainy season in an hour and a half is believed by no one – especially by those who touched the cold bonnet of their car that night.) Their photograph of Chico in the morgue, his bare chest riddled with pellets, his mouth bound up with a handkerchief, was spread across the front page of the 'Rio Branco' next morning. Thus the guillotining was broadcast and it's terror disseminated to the masses. To understand the elaborate ritual of Chico's murder, it's necessary to think of it in the terms of a public execution.

FIVE

'For eight years, we, the *seringueiros* at Cachoeira, did not let them deforest,' said Duda, Chico's cousin. 'The rancher brought people from the land agency, to give everyone either a plot or to receive an indemnity in money. But the *seringueiros* of Cachoeira, some 80 families, never agreed. And it was then, when the owner saw that the *seringueiros* would never give way, that he sold an area to that ruffian, Darli.'

'When did you know that Darli had bought?'

'When he arrived we still weren't sure that he had already bought,' said Chico's uncle, Joachim. 'People always regarded Darli as the wild beast of Acre, and so we thought he was being sent in by the rancher.'

Seringal Cachoeira was legally titled under the name of Seringal Mucuripe Cajazeiros and totalled 24,973 hectares, with 68 holdings and 353 people. Of this total area, three blocks of roughly 6000 hectares each were sold to other buyers, and one of 6874 hectares went to Darli Alves, owner of the Parana ranch. Significantly, it was at the far end of the *seringal*, so that anyone using it had to pass through most of the other holdings. And the rumour was that it had been donated to Darli by a group of landowners in order to provoke a confrontation with Chico Mendes. Cachoeira was where Chico had grown up; half its *seringueiros* were his relatives. Its deforestation was bound to lead to a confrontation.

'Darli's reputation was that when he had a property no-one stepped close, or he would order them killed. So what we told Darli was that no-one would sell him a holding, that the *seringueiros* here had always agreed never to sell to the rancher. And when this character, Jose Brito, quarrelled with another *seringueiro* and offered to sell his holding to Darli, we fought to stop him, all combining together to buy the holding for the same money that Darli would give. But Jose Brito did not accept. He sold and fled.' (Jose Brito's mother and brother had equal rights in the holding and had refused to sell.)

'Then Darli said that he knew we were very Catholic and that he would build a little church for us to pray in. He said for us to sit quietly and that the help he wanted from us was only to let him enter. That he would just put a store on the holding to buy rubber and Brazil nuts and sell goods. He was a little saint on that day.'

'Did he threaten you?'

'Not to us. But when he stopped at the store, he spoke to old Walber, the rubber buyer, saying that he would come in slowly and start to knock down the leaders, kill the most experienced. The rest would run and he would take over the whole of Cachoeira.

'Then, on the 18th of March,' Chico's uncle wound up grimly, 'when we started the strike, (the sit in at Cachoeira), Darli called Jose, our son, who is in the civil police in Xapuri and said, "Tell your brothers to get out, because I am going in there and will run over everyone." And Jose called us and advised: "It's better to leave in peace," he said. "For if you stay, that man will create an enormous confusion and everyone will die."'

Thus began the struggle that was to be Chico's last.

At the time, the *seringueiros* had had a decade of experience in scores of similar campaigns, and obviously no one forsaw that this *empate* would be Chico's nemesis. So I have used some of the explanations given later by Chico, or other people involved, earlier in the narrative, in order to make what follows easier to understand. Otherwise, it's difficult to comprehend what made Chico hang on grimly during a period of ever increasing intimidation.

The opening events were like those of any other *empate*. On March the 18th, 1988, the *seringueiros* blocked the trail into Jose Brito's holding in Seringal Cachoeira, and when two of Darli's men arrived, they were prevented from taking possession of Jose Brito's holding. Then Darli went to court, and was given police protection. But the *seringueiros* never let him take possession or cut a single tree.

Soon after they all stopped the deforestation in the neighbouring Seringal Ecuador. There, the rancher had marked out 300 hectares to be cut down, but the *seringueiros* had discovered that his licence from the Forestry Institute, the IBDF, was only for 50 hectares. So the union launched an *empate* against the cutting teams and staged a sit-in at the IBDF building. And this was where the normal pattern of an *empate* began to change. One night, two of Darli's gunmen emptied their revolvers into the building, where, fortunately, all the *seringueiros* were lying down, asleep. Two boys were wounded, one with seven bullets in him, the other with two.

'We are living at a time of violence when the gunmen of the Parana ranch shoot ruthlessly at our defenceless comrades in the IBDF building.' Chico said in a speech to about 30 rubber tappers at a nearby *seringal*. 'We are living in immediate danger. We see bodies falling, with the possibility of many more. Today, dozens of our comrades are on their black-list of death, and we must avoid this. After death, we are nothing.' Chico repeated one of his more constant themes at the time. 'What's important is people alive. Live men achieve things. Corpses nothing.'

And that was the prelude to the strange almost operatic contest that has more or less come to symbolise the twentieth century argument between developers and environmentalists.

The position of Darli Alves is all too easy to understand. 'Bordon sold their land cheap, very cheap.' Darli spoke fluently and plausibly. But I was very conscious of a strange, almost manic glint in the eyes behind his spectacles. 'They didn't sell. They gave it away. They didn't even receive half of what it had cost to set up. Twenty million for 3000 alqueires cleared. (In fact it was about 12,000 acres). They had I don't know how much rubber and mango planted, with the ranch buildings and airstrip. They lost it all. Sold for nothing. Helio (another rancher) has also lost. Aldao lost. And Rubi as well.'

'What you're saying,' I suggested, 'is that the UDR, [the rancher's party], opposes Chico because he will finish off the ranchers?'

'I know nothing of this business of the UDR,' Darli replied. 'I don't like societies. I like,' he added piously, 'to pray alone. Not in association with anyone.'

And yet there is no question that Darli's house was frequently visited by Joao Branco, head of the UDR in Acre. And witnesses would eventually emerge who would tell of rancher's meetings to collect money for Chico's murder. For after Chico had stopped all deforestation in Xapuri, and threatened to do the same for the whole of Acre and Amazonia, Darli became the natural champion not just of the local ranchers, but of all the landed interests in Amazonia.

On the other side, Chico was getting more and more national and international support. In Vicente's terms, Chico had become a patron saint who had shown that he could, now, do miracles. A brand new blue jeep had turned up for the Xapuri union – donated by the Canadian government. The Ford Foundation was funding the travel and administrative expenses of the National Council of Seringueiros. And above all, the BR364 road was paralysed – apparently at Chico's bidding. In the practical, down to earth vision of the *seringueiros*, Chico had become a politician who could pull the levers of power.

'Chico has been greatly strengthened,' said Elson Martins, the journalist. 'In the past, he had suffered a process of demoralisation from groups of the left and from the press. This help from abroad has given him a new stimulus, placed him as a leader of capacity, with his voice respected again. And people haven't understood Chico's advance in formulating a political strategy. In the last two years I have, on various occasions, heard a certain satisfaction in him, a joy that he has been acclaimed and that he could leave politics and become once again a trades unionist with his proposal of the preservation of nature. At one time in the past, he had reached a moment when he even thought that he might be exposing himself to death because of some sort of mental sickness. Chico's so happy to have discovered an ideal form for his battle. Despite the fact that he's being threatened with death, he's so happy with this strength, this stimulus, that he could confront anyone.'

And so it was that – supported by the environmentalists on one side, financed by the ranchers, on the other – Chico Mendes and Darli Alves began to face each other in an increasing tournament of nerves.

The field of play was Xapuri, and more specifically, the two blocks and church square that contain Chico's house, the union office, the CTA, (the Workers' Centre of Amazonia where Gomercindo lives and works) and the municipal police station and the state police barracks. Most of the people involved lived in this small area and daily watched as Darli's gunmen walked round and round this circuit.

'They never have the courage to look directly at me or Chico,' said Raimundo, Chico's cousin. 'They never threaten us to our faces. But they talk to other people so that they will pass on the information. One meets them every day, and we see from the way they pass us their will to offend. They pull at their shirts, or put their hands beneath their shirts as if to say "I am going to shoot you now," to see if they can intimidate us. Darli and Alvarinho pass the whole day sitting on that bench, in the bus station, in front of the union, watching all the movement in the square. They spend the day there, doing nothing, watching.'

'At the time of the strike at Cachoeira,' Ilza, Chico's wife added, 'Chico had just arrived and was walking from the union office with six companions. There was Raimundo, there was Zuza, his brother, and four others from Cachoeira. And when I looked out the front, I saw Darli and Alvarinho walking towards them and thought, "Puxa", and went out the front and stood watching. Chico even greeted Darli, "Oi". But when they passed him, they put their hands in their bags, and I saw Alvarinho pull out his revolver, and look at Chico and then at Darli, with the revolver in his hand as if to ask, "do I shoot?" I wanted to scream. But I think they decided that it was not the moment to kill Chico. He had six people with him. But if Chico had been alone at the time . . .' Ilza didn't finish the sentence and her dark eyes widened.

Darli and his brother Alvarinho were the sons of Sebastiao Alves who had a score of children. Darli himself had four wives and in his own words 'thirty-odd children'. It was thus a large clan with some living in Xapuri, but many living on Darli's ranch a dozen kilometres out of town. Amongst these was Genesio Barbosa da Silva, who was 14 years old, and who had been brought up by Darli since his father had died. He has sombre, experienced eyes. 'Soon after they quarrelled over Seringal Cachoeira, Darli said that Chico did not have a year of life left,' Genesio explained. 'That he would kill Chico because no man had ever ridden over him before.'

'How many people have they killed?' Vicente asked.

'I think nine,' Genesio said grimly. 'There were two Bolivians who went by the house of Mineirinho and they asked for water. They had some baggage with them so Mineirinho came to the ranch and said that they should take a look at what they were carrying. And so Darci and Oloci went with him, and they found marijuana in the baggage and they killed them. Darci and Oloci smoke marijuana, and so do the two Mineirinhos.'

'Then they also killed Raimundo Ferreira whose daughter they asked for in marriage. But he refused and thwarted Oloci. I saw Raimundo dead with his ear, nose and lips cut off in the cattle pasture. At the ranch they hit me, and put a knife to my stomach, and said that if I told anyone I would die.'

'What sort of a person was Darli?'

'He was very bad. He just talked about killing others. He didn't talk about anything else. They practised shooting every weekend with a .765, with a 9mm, with a .38 and with a shotgun.'

At this time, Gomercindo was also given a strange warning.

'A woman came up to me in front of the union office,' Gomercindo said, 'young and attractive and said that she wanted to talk to me. But that it couldn't be in the street. So I said, "let's go to the CTA office," and she asked, "Is it safe?" So I said, "I will put on the radio loud and you can speak low and no one will hear." Then when we got there she said she was in the Federal Police and had got to know the sons of Darli. She had visited the ranch several times, where they had a store of arms and practised shooting. They spent days practising, shooting at moving targets and from different positions. And she had practised with them. Then they offered to pay whatever she wanted if she got to know me and took me to Rio Branco to an agreed place where they could finish me.'

'So I looked at her,' Gomercindo said, 'and asked, "why are you telling me this?"'

'"You're too handsome to die," was the excuse she used – so as not to say why. "I didn't accept," she said, "but another woman might. Take care. They are even practising to shoot from a motorbike, one driving and one shooting from the pillion, to get you while you are on your motorbike."'

The next victim, however, was not Gomercindo but Ivair Higino de Almeida. He was a leader of the Church's base community in Xapuri, an ally of Chico's and a candidate for town councillor on behalf of the Workers' Party. On June the 18th, he was shot down, after milking his cows, beside the BR117 road into Xapuri. Chico believed that it was a rival candidate for the government party that paid for him to be killed.

'Comrade Ivair,' Chico said in a speech not long after, 'should be speaking here today as a candidate for town councillor. But he has been killed in an ambush. And once more this murder has gone unpunished. In fact, the candidature of the person who planned Ivair's murder, [Chico did not mention his name] has not even been cancelled. Why? Because the PMDB party commands the government and is protecting the assassins who are spilling the blood of the workers . . . You know very well that the group of the Parana ranch is terrorising the population of Xapuri to defeat the lesser workers' leaders so as to get at me, at Gomercindo, at Raimundo Barros, in short to strike at all the directorate of the workers' movement in Xapuri. We are on the black-list.'

'It was Oloci and Darci who killed Ivair,' said Genesio, the boy who lived on the ranch. 'They left the house in the car and picked up the two Minheirim armed with shotguns and a .38 revolver. When they came back, they said they had gone up a bank and shot at him and that there had been a five litre kerosene tin beside him.'

Soon after, on the 20th of June, Jader Barbalho, the Minister of Agrarian reform, flew to Rio Branco to sign decrees setting up three extractive reserves, and Chico took the relatives of Ivair Higino to meet him. Chico then asked for Seringal Cachoeira to be disappropriated and declared an extractive reserve.

'I hardly ever go out,' Ilza said. 'We live in a climate of terror. It's so terrible that I don't let the children out in the street. For they've said that if they don't get Chico, they will get a child of Chico's or his wife. And so we stay in the house, with shutters closed. Chico goes out. But at four in the afternoon he is in the house, and I won't let him take a shower at night.' (The bath-house was in their backyard.)

'They pass right in front of the house, circulating, 10, 20, – even 25 I counted one day. Passing in front and lifting up their shirts to show the handle of a revolver (sticking out of their trouser belt). One day, Chico wasn't here and they were whispering and pointing at the house, and I was so frightened that when one raised his shirt and grasped the handle of his revolver, I closed the shutters and went to the kitchen and locked the door. I was dying of fear, trembling, without being able to speak.'

'One night, a man arrived at one in the morning calling, "Chico, come help me. They're trying to kill me." And when Chico was getting up, I said, "Don't go. It's a trick. This man is going to get you in the doorway." And I caught his arm and said, "You mustn't go because he will get you." and Chico said, "No. He's calling for help." But there was a seringueiro in the house with a shotgun, and he said, "Let me go in front." So he went, with me beside him, into the kitchen and Chico behind. It was dark, so no-one outside could see inside. But as the lamp of the bath house was lit, I could see the man through a crack in the door, with his hand held behind him, peering about to see if he could see anyone in the house. Then the seringueiro cocked his gun and Chico said, "Don't shoot." And the man outside said, "For the love of God don't shoot," and ran away, jumping over the fence.'

Chico's attitude to all this was more controlled, a leader's calculated calm. During most of the year of 1988, we were very occupied in the south of Para filming land feuds. But at a 'Decade of Destruction' conference in Goiania organised by our co-producers, the Catholic University of Goias, I had dinner with Chico. He talked calmly about the confrontation in Cachoeira, very much as though it was just another empate. And the only thing that revealed something more was his almost morbid interest in the details of the killings we were filming. He asked to see the photographs, and on the next day I brought them and showed him a little boy riddled with shot, the top of his father's skull blown off with a sawn-off .12 bore shotgun, and the blasted body of another man shattered beside an adobe wall. (For lack of space, that feud has not been described in this book.) Chico studied the photographs carefully, lifting one off deliberately to gaze at another beneath. Then he handed them back without a word, and without explaining why he had wanted to see them. He seemed heavier and less placid than before.

On September the 15th, I phoned Chico from London while he was with Mary Allegretti at a conference in Curitiba, in the State of Parana. (It was the occasion when they searched for evidence of Darli's past murders in Parana.) But when I got through to Chico, he told me calmly that he had just received the news that Jose Ribeiro had been murdered and that he was immediately flying back to Xapuri.

At the time, Vicente and the unit were in Rondonia and so they were able to join Chico quickly. The first thing that Chico showed Vicente was his new licence to carry a revolver.

'Chico said a *delegado* from the Federal Police came to Xapuri and said, "here's your licence to carry a revolver," and put it in Chico's hands. It's rare to get a licence to carry a revolver outside your house,' Vicente said, 'but very rare for a policeman to actually bring it to you. It shows that they knew Chico had a serious problem.'

Vicente said that a doctor had forced Chico to stop smoking – during the campaign he had smoked about 60 a day – and Vicente wondered whether this was the reason that much of the spark had gone out of him.

Next day, Chico took Vicente to meet the mother of the murdered Jose Ribeiro, Dona Lucinda. 'He was 27 years old with four sons and about to have a fifth,' his mother said. 'Jose was someone who offended no-one. He was persecuted by the lechers. They attacked him on the 11th of September at two thirty in the morning, with three bullets.'

'Who?'

'The gunmen of the Parana ranch.'

'Jose asked a girl to dance,' explained his wife, Maria de Socorro. She has a beautiful face like a sad Mona Lisa. 'But this thug said she had to dance with him and hit Jose in the face. So he returned the blow, and the man said, "Grab him. It's the worse for him for hitting me." There were many of them, and they beat him and he fell. Afterwards, I and his sister and the police got him out, pouring blood, and we put him in the car. But they invaded the car and said, "you may escape the bite of a cobra, but, shameless swine, you won't escape me." And later, when Jose was going out of our house and I was crying, he said, "Whether I am in the house or the street, my body won't escape becoming bait for his revolver." And at two in the morning they killed him.'

'One Saturday,' Ilza said, 'the police arrested some gunmen of theirs washing naked in the river. And when they were bringing them to the station, Oloci arrived with Darli and Alvarinho and soon the city was full of gunmen. We locked everything and they kept walking around – up our road, then right along beside the CTA (Gomercindo's office) and down the road of the union.' This was the two block rectangle of their confrontation with Chico.

'There were 28 of them in front of the police station' Gomercindo added.

'Then Darli went in and the sherrif released the four they had arrested. But, afterwards, they just kept circulating around the town.'

'Why?' I asked.

'Intimidation. To show they had 28 and that they would kill.'

'Did Darli have the money for all this?'

'No.' Gomercindo said grimly. 'Asking where the money came from, brings you to the head of the snake. There are very important people involved. For a long time they have been trying to get Darli into these disputes, and I think he entered in exchange for that 6000 hectares in Cachoeira.'

Some time after this, the news arrived that Chico's meeting with the Minister of Agrarian Reform had born fruit. Seringal Cachoeira had been disappropriated, on the 22nd of July, 1988, and declared an extractive reserve. Darli was to be compensated by the government. On the face of it, the situation had changed.

'I never had had the opportunity to talk to Chico,' Darli said to me, 'except when we were summoned to the police station. And I said, "Chico, it's all over. My land has already been negotiated with INCRA [the Land Agency], and from the time I was promised indemnity, my heart has been clear and I have slept tranquilly. I went home and said to my boys, "We're all going to be tranquil because the disputed land is no longer ours. Now we have money with the government earning interest." So what I said to Chico was that everything was well and the only thing he should do was to stop defaming me in the papers.'

That was Darli's public position. But what he actually got for over 6000 hectares (15,000 acres) was not much more than US $5000 in the form of Land Reform titles payable over 20 years. And when Vicente asked Genesio, the boy who lived on the ranch, what people visited the ranch, he said, 'Gaston Motta, Joao Daguabi, Joao Branco, Benedito Rosa, and Delegado Enoch. They asked Darli if he would let the business of Seringal Cachoeira stay like that. And Darli said "they can take the *seringal* from me, but he won't remain alive." Then Darli asked them what they would think if he killed Chico. And Joao Branco said that if he killed him like he killed the others, then he could kill with tranquillity.'

On October 8th, Seringal Cachoeira was inaugurated as an extractive reserve and the celebration was at Fazendinha, the large and prosperous holding of Chico's uncle. *Seringueiros* from all the forests of Xapuri arrived by truck, horse and on foot.

'We're celebrating the victory of the *seringueiros* of Cachoeira,' said Chico, with a glass of cane spirit in his hand. 'But it doesn't resolve one percent of the problems. All the *seringueiros* of Cachoeira and the neighbouring communities will now fight for other extractive reserves. This victory is going to stimulate many others in defence of the forest.'

But Chico seemed unusually thoughtful, even preoccupied – as if he knew that he would have to pay for this victory.

At a mass celebrated under a large mango tree, the parish priest of Xapuri,

Father Luis Ceppi, spoke the following prophetic words. 'I would like to reflect on the path that has led us here. This has not been a bloodless journey. Some have already fallen defending extractive reserves. No-one likes to die, but if it has to happen, then it should be to create more life.' Chico was listening with a sombre expression on his face, as if he knew what his death might do for the *seringueiro* movement. 'Christ was crucified. He gave his last drop of blood. But since that day millions of communities have been born that believe and fight for brotherhood. And so it should be for us. The blood spilt in these recent days must be the seed of a new liberty, a new life.'

On the 26th of September, the federal police in Rio Branco received a warrant for the arrest of Darli and his brother, Alvarinho. This was for a murder in the State of Parana, more than 15 years before, and the old case had been reopened by lawyers working for Mary Allegretti's Institute for Amazonian Studies. On the next day, the 27th, Chico phoned the Federal Police in Rio Branco telling them that he had just seen Darli outside their office. Nothing happened.

More than two weeks later, on the 13th of October, the warrant was forwarded to Xapuri, where Darli's brother was the clerk of the police station. So when the police finally went, on the 19th of October, to arrest Darli and Alvarinho at the Parana ranch, it was hardly a surprise that they were not there.

After that, Chico wrote to the Judge of Xapuri, on the 17th of November, telling him that Darli and Alvarinho were planning his assassination, and followed that with letters to the State Government, the Secretary of Security in Acre, and the Superintendent of Federal Police. The letter to the Superintendent, dated 30th of November, contained the following outspoken passage: *To the surprise of the State Police, when they surrounded the house of the gunmen, they found that they had been warned in advance and had already fled. At the time, there was much speculation as to who had warned the gunmen. To my surprise, and that of my companions, we have learnt now that it was you who provided all the information to keep them free.*

This revelation comes from the gunmen themselves and their sons who take pride in saying that their fathers have many friends, including friends in the Federal Police, that keep them aware of everything.

You know that I am obliged to live today with two bodyguards because Darli and Alvarinho have said that they will only give themselves up after they see my corpse. Their gunmen walk about at will, spreading intimidation, and when the State Police in Xapuri arrest them, the town police release them immediately on orders of the sheriff and the mayor.

Chico also gave many interviews to the press predicting his own murder. 'If a messenger from heaven descended to guarantee that my death would strengthen our cause, it would even be worth it.' Chico said in what was to become one of his most quoted passages. 'But experience teaches us the contrary. So I want to live. Public manifestations and numerous funerals have not saved anyone in Amazonia. I want to live.'

'The last time they were in front of our house,' Ilza said, 'Chico was playing dominos in the house of a neighbour when Oloci came in a car. He stopped in front of the house and pointed behind at the bath house. There were three others with him and they looked and went away. When I told Chico he said, "I will return to the house, and if they stop, I will shoot." By good luck they didn't come again, and that was the last time. For Chico went to Feijo, the last journey he made. When he got back, the gunmen vanished for 18 days. And I, who saw them everyday, kept thinking, "where are they now."'

'I noticed that they had gone too,' said Gomercindo. 'And I said to Chico, "when I don't see them, I wonder what they are doing."'

And thus, as ponderous as a death sentence at the Old Bailey, as widely heralded as a royal guillotining, the day for Chico's murder had arrived.

'Many people were commenting that Chico was a great man,' said Ilza. 'I think they wanted to kill Chico because they thought that he might in the future, who knows, become king.'

Certainly, if Chico's friend, Lula, had been elected President of Brazil in 1989 – as he nearly was – Chico was planning to run for Governor of Acre in 1990. And then the threat to the ranchers would have been very real.

'Who was sent to kill Chico Mendes was Darci and the Mineirinho,' said Genesio, the boy on the ranch. 'But Darli said that Darci was not to shoot, to go only as company.'

Darci and Minheirim crept along a narrow gulley surrounded by trees into the backyard of Chico's house. They waited in the dark for the chance to fire, cool and ruthless.

'At the time that I served dinner,' Ilza said, 'Chico told the two bodyguards to start eating while he took a shower. But when he got to the door, he said, "It's so dark out there, they could get me." So he went and got a torch.'

And thus it was, that after months of threat and intimidation, and actually speaking of his waiting killers, Chico put his hand on the door. And the obvious question that troubles so many of his friends is why did he not act with more caution.

Chico could have insisted that the two bodyguards, who were eating only two yards away, go out first. There was also no real reason why he could not wait till morning for his shower. But what is easy to forget is that Chico knew that if the gunmen did not get him this time, they would the next, or the time after next. As Jose Ribeiro had put it, 'Outside or inside the house, it won't stop my body becoming bait for their revolvers.'

Over the three years that we filmed Chico, we recorded many expressions on his face. But it was during the last month or two that I had noticed that, when he did not think he was being observed, his expression was often charged, almost overloaded with pressure.

And so by December the 22nd, I believe that Chico had been completely worn down by Darli's long drawn out campaign and that – exactly as Darci must have planned – he was just too tired to insist the guards go out first. 'I want to live,' he had said. But, in that manner, I suspect he could not have gone on much longer. He opened the door, and that much forseen, so often discussed, shot must – in many ways – have been a relief.

SIX

Shortly after Chico's body was brought back from the morgue, Gomercindo phoned Vicente – at three o'clock in the morning. Vicente thus got me at seven London time, and not long after I rang Mary Allegretti in New York and Barbara Bramble of the National Wildlife Federation in Washington. By the time I reached Steve Schwartzman of the Environmental Defence Fund, he had already heard from the Ford Foundation in Rio de Janeiro. So the next call I made was to Charles Clover of the Daily Telegraph who had interviewed Chico in London and Acre. I caught him going out of the door on his Christmas holiday. He immediately cancelled his trip and started covering the story. Then, as I was picking up the phone to ring the Independent, John McGrath of Oxfam came on the line to check the news with me. Since he is Oxfam's media officer, I suggested that I leave the press to him so that I could concentrate on getting our team into Xapuri. (We had one camera in customs and one being serviced in London.) And thus it must have been with dozens of other people, inside and outside Brazil, all responding with grief and outrage. Jan Rocha who reports for the BBC in Brazil said that at first BBC radio news did not appreciate the importance of what had happened. But within a few hours, they certainly made up for it. Jan and the BBC World Service covered the story in some form or other every day for six days – to the embarrassment of Brazilian embassies all over the world.

Like Chico, I would not describe myself as an environmentalist. I do not belong to the Friends of the Earth or the Worldwide Fund for Nature. There are no animals and few ecological scenes in my films. But a movement is strong precisely when people who don't formally belong to it recognise its truths and act according to its ethic. At the end of 1988, environmental consciousness must have been approaching one of its summits. Like the accumulated electricity of a storm, its discharge was instant and its effect on Xapuri was as shattering as a bolt of lightening.

As hordes of strangers and foreigners poured into Xapuri, Vicente said that the local population looked on transfixed. 'It was if they were thinking, "Who is it that we have killed? Could it have been Jesus Christ?"'

The wave of worldwide revulsion – channelled by Brazilian embassies back to their government – combined with a similar wave inside Brazil, swept away the political cover of the murderers like a tidal wave. The government sent Romeu Tuma, the Director General of the Federal Police, to Xapuri with orders to arrest the killers as soon as possible, and Tuma arrived with roughly 60 police armed with submachineguns. He immediately transferred the Superintendant of Federal Police in Acre – accused by Chico of being in league with Darli – and teams of policemen started pounding round the countryside hauling in all Darli's gunmen and associates. In similar circumstances in the past, it was not uncommon for the accused to be mown down by a hail of bullets, 'while resisting arrest'. One of Darli's gunmen, Zezao, was found riddled with bullets on a road near Xapuri. And so it was that Darci gave himself up and confessed to the police, and shortly afterwards, to Vicente.

'Chico Mendes knew that my father had bought a *seringal* by the name of Cachoeira and made an *empate*,' Darci explained. 'So my father talked to the people who deal with land [INCRA], and they asked my father to sell it to the government. But he [Chico] then went on messing with my father. And it was the same in [the State of] Parana. He got a warrant for my father's arrest, and it was this which made me kill him.' Darci looked like a contrite, frightened, student after a university brawl.

'So your father had to flee?' Vicente suggested.

'Yes. He had to flee because they were sending police constantly to the ranch, 50 police, without proper orders. And when we came out, there were too many police everywhere. And that was how it was. It was anger that made me commit the crime . . . I had nothing against him before. It was after he persecuted my father that I decided to commit the crime.' Darci's lawyer persuaded him to retract this confession soon after the interview.

'What happened to your brother [Oloci]?'

'He saw a car racing behind him, and he raced away thinking that it was people trying to kill him. It was the Federal Police and they shot at him. They broke his arm.'

'And why did you hand yourself in?'

'Because everyone was saying they would attack our family . . . We heard a lot of talk that they would kill my whole family.'

'Did you think Chico's death would cause such a reaction?'

'I never imagined it. No.'

A few weeks later, the State Police paid another visit to the ranch and – possibly because she had been forced to betray Darli – one of his wives slashed her wrists and committed suicide. It has also been alleged that the State Police murdered her. Shortly afterwards Darli gave himself up.

Darli's lawyer used all the tactics of delay, and after the Brazilian equivalent of our inquest, he appealed that there was insufficient evidence for a trial right up to the Supreme Court. But in March 1990, the prosecution case was finally sent to Judge Adair Longhini of Xapuri with instructions to hold a trial by jury. And in December 1990, Darci and Darli were both convicted of the murder of Chico Mendes and sentenced to 19 years in prison. Darli's conviction was the first time that the planner, or mentor, of a rural murder in Brazil had ever been convicted.

The *seringueiros* are also beginning to recover. At first, traumatised by Chico's death and overwhelmed by the tidal wave of unknowing sympathy and support, they entered a period of stunned disorientation. Probably the national and international support was more confusing for people locked in an internecine small-town struggle than if the world had approved of Chico's killing and rewarded his assassins. The gale of horror and revolt swept Chico's family, friends and colleagues from side to side and when it cheapened into a Hollywood auction for the rights to make his film, it blew family and colleagues apart in bitter rivalry and divided interests. Chico may not have been a particularly effective public speaker, but he was a born negotiator who helped put together a complex pattern of human relationships called a movement. He was a true father of his people. So that when he died, the movement lost the cement of personal alliances that held it together.

Now, more than a year later, those bonds have all been re-established and the movement is stronger than before. For what had been obscured by Chico's slaying was that all the groundwork for the *seringueiro* alternative for Amazonia had already been laid by the last year of Chico's life. All the stages of the evolution which I had been watching for, had come into existence. All that was needed was to apply them.

The essence of what Chico had been working towards was that the realities of the forest, expressed through its peoples, should influence the different levels of government that dictate policy for Amazonia. To begin with, he had found a way of binding *seringueiros* together in trades' unions, so that they could defend their interests at a local level. In 1985, through the National Council of Seringueiros and, later in 1986, through the Alliance of the Peoples of the Forest, the *seringueiros* had acquired the means to project their policies on a national scale. Then, in 1987, cooperation with international environmentalists had extended this into the international sphere. Finally, the *seringueiro* proposal for extractive reserves had been elaborated in great legal and constitutional detail by Mary Allegretti's Institute for Amazonian Studies, so that by 1988 it was a very specific, practical proposition. What Chico's death added to all this was the aura of martyrdom.

Today, all over Amazonia, in Ariquemes and Amapa and Aripuana, *seringueiros*, who never thought of themselves with pride before Chico won universal approval for their cause, are now organising, demonstrating and protecting the forest – with great pride.

A year after Chico's death, the extractive reserve of the Jurua was created with over half a million hectares. And the Institute for Amazonian Studies worked against the clock to produce the detailed survey and legal information for the outgoing Sarnay government to declare three more reserves three days before it left power. The largest was the Chico Mendes reserve. 'It is nearly a million hectares,' Mary said, 'and covers the four municipalities of Xapuri, Brasileia, Rio Branco and Sena Madureira – about six percent of the State of Acre. Virtually every *seringal* Chico ever fought for is in it. The ranchers are stunned, furious and waiting for the new government to get established. Then they will fight back and there will be a lot of trouble.'

Altogether, there are in existence today ten extractive projects (set up by INCRA), and four extractive reserves (set up by IBAMA). And the National Council of Seringueiros will continue campaigning until all the 300,000 extractivist families recorded by census, have been given at least 300 hectares each. This will amount to about a quarter of the remaining forest standing in Amazonia and will represent a major contribution towards solving the region's problems.

The main outstanding threat are the huge plantations being set up all over Sao Paolo to produce rubber at a price half that of the *seringueiros*. In a decade, the extractive reserves will only be able to survive if the scientists working on the issue have discovered other more valuable products that can be extracted from the forest. But between the scientists and the vast hidden wealth of Amazonia, few people doubt that some solution will be found.

Chico's death has, therefore, not shattered his movement – as the ranchers hoped. But for those who knew Chico, that is small compensation for the irreplaceable individual who has been lost.

On the morning that I phoned Mary in New York to tell her the news of Chico's murder, I spent two or three useless minutes trying to prepare her for the shock. But when I eventually came out with it, Mary burst into floods of tears and said something which I did not hear very clearly, like, 'If only I had been there, he might not have gone so far.' And all of us – those who helped, filmed and worked with Chico – all felt very much like that at the time. But afterwards, thinking more carefully about the confrontation with the UDR, I believe that we have to accept that Chico was the leader, and that we were the friends, journalists and assistants. And that the messianic course Chico took was something that he did not develop overnight, but as slowly and as tenaciously as a sapling shaded by the forest.

And why should not the boy, who through a whim of fate found education and a creed in the depths of the forest, why should not he – as a union leader – aspire to become the Lancelot of his people, the knight of Amazonia and humanity? It was because Chico was so placid, practical and unassuming, that his dream was so touching.

seven

THE DECADE *of the* ENVIRONMENT

On the 15th of March, 1990, Fernando Collor de Mello took office as President of Brazil, and amongst the Ministers he presented to the public was Jose Lutzenberger, his National Secretary of the Environment. Lutz is Brazil's best known environmentalist who started campaigning against chemical agriculture in the 1970s, and who began filming with us in Rondonia in 1981.

'I think this is going to be the decade of the environment,' Lutz said as he was setting up his new National Secretariat of the Environment. 'When the President invited me, he said that he doesn't want Brazil to be seen as the pariah of the environment. When the big UN environmental conference meets in Brazil in 1992, he wants to be the Gorbachev of an environmental perestroika.'

Lutz looked very unministerial – coatless, tieless, in an open neck shirt – and some of the staff in his temporary office in IBAMA, the Brazilian Institute for the Environment, were visibly startled by his abrupt movements and gestures. When the phone rang as he was composing a letter, he tore at his hair, and another time he strode through the outer office waving his arms.

'Before you came this morning,' Lutz said, 'I had a meeting with the President to talk about the Yanomami Indians. I thought there would be just a few Ministers there, but they filled a small auditorium and the military then gave an exposition of their Calha Norte plan. [This is a military controlled development scheme for the north of Amazonia.] And though they mentioned the word ecology every now and again, it was just as an afterthought to a type of development which has nothing to do with ecology. And I thought, well, if it's to be like that, within a month or two I'm going to have to resign.'

But then when we were all having coffee, the President took me aside and said, "Lutz, I was not very happy with that. Will you talk to them for a bit?" So I did. I talked for 40 minutes about the forest and the importance of Amazonia to the climate. I even talked about the Gaia hypothesis that the biosphere functions as a single living being, and I was surprised to see that they were all listening, really listening, except for one or two who just kept their heads down. And many came up to me afterwards and said, "Lutz, we are with you."' He turned to me. 'You yourself were there, when the Minister of the Air Force came across the lobby of my hotel to say, "Lutz, I am flying with you to the Yanomami this week-end. And I want you to give a talk to my officers like the one you gave this morning."'

Lutz then introduced some officials of IBAMA which forms part of his secretariat. Six months before, we had filmed their regional inspectors sending out helicopter patrols to fine ranches for deforestation, and I asked if the fines had been paid.

'No,' said Werner Zulauf, the then head of IBAMA, 'they're being fought through the courts.'

'I flew around with the IBAMA patrols in the south of Para,' Vicente said, 'and when I filmed them giving a fine notice to one rancher, he laughed. "Okay, I will turn up at your office next week. But don't you remember? You gave me a fine notice for the same thing last week."'

No one round the table in Lutz's office used the Brazilian phrase 'para Ingles ver': 'for the English to see' – probably because I was English. But the previous year's helicopter operation had largely been a public relations operation designed for the foreign press. What it had proved, however, was that the technology devised by Alberto Setzer of the Brazilian Space Institute worked. At one o'clock every afternoon, the NOAA 11 satellite had passed over Brazil photographing the fires, and within a couple of hours a computer had worked out the latitude and longitude of all the fires and was sending them out in a telex to IBAMA's regional offices. By four, you could literally jump into a helicopter and fine a rancher before his fire had died out. The only problem had been enforcement of the fines.

'In Sao Paulo,' Werner said, 'we cleaned up pollution by making them pay first and letting them go to court afterwards. Let's see if we can do that this summer.'

At the beginning of April, Barbara Bramble and Mary Allegretti came to see Lutz on behalf of a coalition of foreign and Brazilian environmental groups. 'We're not talking about a debt for nature swap,' Barbara said. 'If Brazil can significantly reduce its fires this summer and implement alternatives to deforestation, then our environmental groups, and many others, will lobby for a straight reduction in Brazil's international debt. We already know many Congressman who will support us.'

In fact, a general campaign against all Third World debt was already under way. The Friends of the Earth (UK) were to demonstrate against Third World debt in a hundred British cities on April 21st. They would carry huge cheques to high street banks, or logs symbolising the links between debt and deforestation. On April the 22nd, there were to be similar events during the Earthday celebrations in the United States. And on July the 5th, at the economic summit of the seven richest countries, a large number of non-governmental organisations would press for Third World debt to be reduced by $50 billion dollars a year. ($50 billion dollars is the annual outflow of capital from the Third to First World and represents roughly ten percent of the Group of Seven's military budgets.)

Mary Allegretti suggested that Lutz could launch his campaign against deforestation by inaugurating the Chico Mendes reserve at the beginning of the summer when the cutting season begins. And if there was a significant reduction of fires, Barbara proposed that Lutz should take his case to Europe and America. He would be in a strong moral position to challenge banks and ministries officially, whilst the environmental groups attacked them – so to speak – from the rear.

As I listened to the details of yet another campaign being planned, I reflected that much of what had happened during the decade had started with this Polonoroeste axis – the alliance between Lutz's Rondonia campaign linked to the *seringueiros* and Indians, and the small group in Washington which had set out to reduce damage to the Third World environment by challenging the World Bank. Today, the tropical forest campaign is a world-wide movement with hundreds, maybe thousands, of organisations operating quite independently. But, historically, much of it had developed out of that first Polonoroeste victory.

And so I began to wonder whether a decade of great destruction was not also bound to be a decade of great evolution, whether a bi-product of senseless, wasteful folly is not the inevitability of its own reform. Certainly, many other events had contributed to the growth of environmental consciousness during the 1980s – Chernobyl, the widening of the ozone hole, the US drought of 1988 which concentrated attention on the greenhouse effect. But the annual incineration of Amazonia, the destruction of more biomass across the tropics of the globe than at any previous time in history, seems to have had an effect like the unending flow of casualties during the Vietnam war. The news images just wore politicians and the public down.

The Federal District of Brasilia stands on the lip of the Amazon basin. Its waters drain south to the River Parana and north into the Tocantins and Amazon. The capital was built to symbolise Juscelino Kubitschek's onslaught on Amazonia through his two great development highways, the Belem-Brasilia and the Brasilia-Porto Velho. It is, therefore, ironic, that Brazil will soon be the host to the UN's great 1992 conference. For the main aim of that conference is to sign a climate treaty which could be the major environmental achievement of the century, and perhaps, the saving of Amazonia as well.

Eneas Salati is Brazil's authority on the Amazonian rain system, and we made a film with him in 1982. During the period that Lutz was setting up his Secretariat of the Environment, Salati was in Brasilia, and I asked whether the climate treaty could ever have enough bite. 'When we filmed President

Bush at the Inter-governmental Panel on Climate Change in February,' I said, 'his speech was so restrained as to be almost negative. In particular, the United States did not follow Holland's promise to cut carbon emissions by 20 percent in the 1990s.'

'I think it should not be done by unilateral declarations but by international negotiations based on scientific facts.' Eneas Salati has smiling, but very shrewd eyes. He gives an impression of being much more a manipulator of bureaucracies than, for instance, Lutz. 'I am on the scientific committee of the IPCC, and two weeks ago our meeting in Edinburgh drew up the IPCC's scientific conclusions. Now the other two committees will first have to find a way of putting those conclusions into practice and then the political means of negotiating them into a treaty.'

'Do you think it has a chance?'

'I do.'

During that first month of the new Collor government, there were many setbacks for the environmentalists in Brasilia. 'The new agricultural policy is like "the Green Revolution" 20 years ago,' said Fabio Feldman, the Congressman who steered the environmental clauses of Brazil's constitution through the Congress. 'To save the forests, the new agricultural policy wants to turn the *cerrado* (the scrub country bordering on the Amazon forest) into a vast export plantation for soya beans.' He complained that the Ministry of Agriculture was also trying to take over the departments which controlled rubber and fishing that had previously belonged to IBAMA. And a number of times during the month, Lutz felt under such pressure that he questioned whether he could last as a minister more than a few months or even weeks.

On the other hand, all the people visiting or working with him were making assumptions about what they could fight for which were beyond their wildest dreams only a year or two before. Not they, but the ground under their feet had somehow moved, and though they discussed setbacks potentially even more disastrous than those of the past, the context in which these events were occurring had somehow changed. And thus it was that I gradually came to feel that the Decade of Destruction was now behind us, and the Decade of the Environment had already arrived; and if that should seem an improbable, enormous leap, is it any greater than those already described in this book – the highly unlikely transformation of the isolated and disorganised *seringueiros* and Xinguanos into cohesive political movements.

EPILOGUE

Thirty years ago, during my first journey in Xingu, I went with the Villas Boas brothers on a trip up the Rio Liberdade searching for a nomad band of Txukahamei. After days of hauling our boat along a shallow, rain-starved stream, and after hours of tracking footprints across the sun-battered *cerrado*, we heard – when it had become quite dark – an unexpected cry in the distance. Looking round, I saw many torches bobbing like fishing boats in the black sea of the plain. Soon, with red faces leaping in the flame of their rushes, with wild yelps echoing in the empty night, the Txukahamei were upon us, chests gleaming, savage, frightening, but dressed in the many gorgeous colours of head feathers. As the shrieking mob swept around, each man went up in turn to Bebcuche, our Txukahamei guide, and with one arm leaning on a bow and with his head bent over the other wrist, he shook with convulsions of sobbing; they were mourning for relatives who had died since they last met. And soon after, we were marching again with two boys running ahead carrying bunches of flaring rushes. Leaping to either side of the path, they tore at grass and dry leaves and plunged them into the flames which they fanned in the air and held above their heads. When I looked back, I saw embers glowing for a long way into the distance, where torches had been dropped and were still red on the savannah.

An hour and a half later, the track made a twist in a patch of forest and we could see fires flickering ahead. As we approached, dry rushes and leaves were piled on them to throw a swirling, roaring light over a scene that became so chaotic that it seemed we were in the middle of a forest disco. Tribes-people shouted and whirled about. A score of dogs yapped at our legs. Women and children pawed at our clothes. There was a strange wailing I had no way of understanding. Aggressive faces rattling lip-discs peered into mine, and then whirled away. We had leapt, quite suddenly, from the peaceful night into the glare and chanting of a forest society which until a few years before had killed all *civilizados* on sight. That society had gone berserk at our coming.

Half an hour later, Rauni came up and offered us large chunks of a tapir that had been killed earlier in the day. His new wife, a very young-looking girl, was introduced and Rauni said proudly that she had cooked the pieces on red-hot stones, reserving for us the best lumps attached by two inches of blubber to the hide. This fat was soft, and the thick hide required a great deal of tearing with the teeth to chew. My face was soon smeared all over with grease, and I asked Bebcuche if I could wash.

'Here,' was the reply, 'Txukahamei don't wash,' and he took me with a flaring torch to see the stream. It was dry, except for a hole dug out of the river bed. Seepage had filled the cavity with a sandy concentrate of liquid, and this I drank after most of the dirt had settled to the bottom. At his turn, however, Bebcuche stirred the water round and round so that he could swallow as high a percentage of earth as possible. The Txukahamei were then one of the few peoples in the world that ate earth as a regular part of their diet.

Soon after, the fires started to die, and I tried to rest on a wild-banana leaf on the ground. But the dogs made sleep impossible and I wondered why a people who sometimes ate worse than any dog in London, should keep an enormous canine band to increase starvation and turn their lives into bedlam. Indians have a different sense of discipline, and though they beat dogs with sticks and stones on the crest of annoyance, it is not as a regular instruction to discourage crime. As a result, beating is accepted in the Txukahamei canine mind as an unpredictable hazard of village life; the dogs devote themselves to a career of loitering and burglary. They are seldom fed, and as night comes down, the skinny beasts creep between the bodies, nosing for meat and licking at unwashed lips. Occasionally, a sleeper will wake and strike at a belly passing over him. The animal screams and journeys hastily towards the forest. The other dogs wake, and suspecting he has got away with a haunch of meat, pursue like a collectivisation committee in a pre-war, Russian film. The stampede is on, fast moving shapes hurtling over sleeping bodies, till, in my case, a dog slipped on a banana leaf and put its paw into my eye. I swung out in temper. The animal fled bleating into the dark and the stampede turned and came pouring back in my direction.

Lying awake most of that night, with the bare savannah under my back, with the taste of earth still in my throat, with the scent of tapir's grease rising from my beard, and with the hordes of dogs commuting above my nose, I – as blithe as Fitzcarraldo – wondered whether these nomadic roamers of the wilderness, this human manifestation of the evolving forest, had brought me as close as I would ever get to the pulse of that vast living being, Amazonia.

And for the next 30 years, the way I have tried to understand the forest has been through its reflection in the people that live within it – through the Indians, *seringueiros*, *garimpeiros*. But now, after three decades, I have begun to feel that where their vision has led me is not towards some mystic soul of Amazonia, but simply to a more intense awareness of my individual and social relationship with the forest.

Once when we were in Thailand making a film about Therevada Buddhism, a man about to meditate filled a highly polished, lacquered bowl with water and then concentrated his eyes on the fluctuating reflected image of himself, passing his mind through his image deeper and deeper into himself. In a similar way, I believe that all these years in Amazonia peering at the unknown along the frontier has done little more than to make me conscious that the frontier is a reflecting screen for the people that confront it. Our visions of the forest, all our El Dorados and development schemes, say less about Amazonia than about ourselves and our needs.

That is why I wondered what my ultimate vision with the *garimpeiros* meant: One day when we were travelling with Jova, we came out from a dense thicket of *taquari* onto the rock shoulder of a *serra* and suddenly, there below us, wreathed in mist, criss-crossed by bands of crimson macaws, was the unmoving, but quietly breathing, forest. It rolled away, range after range, towards a limitless horizon.

When you live and travel under its canopy, the forest so confines your mind that it's hard to think of it as a whole. So when you step out of the trees and suddenly gaze down on what has the appearance of that whole, it's even harder to restrain the imagination – not to believe that your own particular El Dorado is bound to be somewhere in those secret valleys. Perhaps we were exhausted from the journey, or perhaps lusting for gold even more than Jova, so that we could film his face as he watched 20 grams emerge from a swirling pan. But, suddenly, standing on that rock, I had a moment of awareness of the immense and multi-splendoured thing that breathed and photosynthesised for a thousand miles before us: a vision which combined the yellow thorn savannahs of Northern Goias with the rubber groves of Acre; the cloud forests of the Andes with the varzea swamps where huge trees, on tripod roots, stand about like oil rigs in the water.

Amazonia is the forest of man's wildest visions very simply because something so vast, so amorphous and so detailed is hard to comprehend except by taking a pattern from your mind and stencilling that image on it. When I first went hunting with Kaluana, I had sometimes asked the name of this bird or that root only to be told, 'It has no name. You cannot eat it.' The mass of vegetable, animal and insect detail pressing in on the hunter's consciousness was so confusing that it was impossible to relate to his environment except from a highly selective viewpoint.

This does not mean that the hunter's view of the forest is untrue or incompatible with the prospector's or the biologist's. But all visions of Amazonia begin with someone's linear and motivated view of the forest's complex and multi-dimensional reality. And so, on that day when I stood with Jova and beheld that great cauldron of life, the earth's greatest engine of photosynthesis, its hothouse of evolution, I wondered what had inspired such a purple vision. For 30 years, my most persistent impression of the forest had been as a vegetable fog obscuring sight. Why, after so much time, should I come to such an operatic mirage.

It is the paradox of Amazonia today, that once the indestructible, all-powerful forest has been publicly conceived as potential farmland waiting to be cleared, even the forest that remains undergoes a subtle transformation. Species, whole eco-systems, enormous valleys can be saved by legislating for them as reserves. But when the fences, guards and aerial patrols are all in place, there has taken place an imperceptible but essential change. The great primaeval forest, the result of naked evolution and unrestrained competition between its species for millions of years, will now continue to exist in certain limited areas because of a man-made protective decision. Competition with one of the species that inhabits the forest has been deliberately restrained. The evolving eco-system will, in fact, be frozen into a museum of itself as it was in the 1980s.

In an evolution which is increasingly influenced by conscious thought, it is man's role to restrain a destruction which means suicide for the whole, and which could waste the earth's billenial investment in its own evolution. And it is because our greatest present need is the preservation of the forest that I think my picture of it has changed. Images are computer programmes of needs, attitudes and policies condensed into a mental picture. They are the way man governs his relationship with things around him. Hence the new El Dorado of Amazonia has, almost unconsciously, shifted away from gold and lost cities. It is now the tourist industry's forest beautiful – a wider, more consumer-oriented image than before. For thousands of years the forest was absolute and therefore without defences. Now its danger is so great, that it requires approval from millions of admirers to preserve it from the thousands who would consume it – who wish to convert trees into charcoal for smelting into pig iron to export to Europe. And so, like the original El Dorado – manufactured by the priest chroniclers of the conquistadors to support their quest for souls and gold – the new El Dorado of today's writers and film makers will only be partly based on fact. What the vision reveals is less the forest, than our current, overwhelming need of it.

And mine has been greater than most. In the days after my son died and during our film with Chico Mendes, I started writing this book, quite compulsively. Some mornings I would wake at five, and in some *seringueiro* hut, with my back against a log wall, my head bent under faintly aromatic tobacco leaves hanging from the beam above, I would scribble manically as Chico and Vicente snored peaceably in their hammocks across the room. At the time, I found the motive behind this compulsion difficult to understand. If asked beforehand, I would have guessed that the death of someone I loved would – if anything – have stopped me writing. But I now have come to think that it was like Aruyave as he paddled his brother's corpse through the rushes. There was nothing else he could do for his brother, and so he sang, and what he sang about was the forest world about him, for there was nothing else he knew.

DATES *in the* DEVELOPMENT *of the* BRAZILIAN AMAZON

BY RIVER

1541   Orellana sails down the Amazon.

1616   The Portuguese found Belem.

1870   The rubber boom begins.

1876   Wickham takes rubber seeds to Kew Gardens where they are developed for plantations.

1911–19   The rubber price slumps under competition from cheap plantation rubber from Malaya.

1926   Henry Ford tries plantation rubber at Fordlandia.

1940s   The rubber trade revives with wartime finance from the United States.

BY LAND

1943   The Fundacao Brasil Central launches the Roncador-Xingu expedition.

1956   Juscelino Kubitschek starts his new capital, Brasilia, on the watershed of the Amazon basin.

1957–60   Juscelino Kubitschek builds two development roads into Amazonia – the northwards Belem-Brasilia and the westwards Brasilia-Porto Velho.

1958   The Roncador-Xingu expedition completes its chain of airstrips across southern Amazonia.

1964   The military government paves the Belem-Brasilia highway.

1966   The military regime launches Operation Amazonia which includes tax incentives for large ranches.

1967   Daniel Ludwig starts his Jari project.

1970   President Medici launches the Trans-Amazon highway and colonisation scheme.

1970   INCRA starts colonisation in Rondonia.

1971   The BRo80 and BR163 roads cut through the Parque do Xingu and Cachimbo en route to Santarem.

1970s   Booms in tin prospecting in western Rondonia and gold prospecting on the River Tapajoz around Itaituba.

1980   Gold dredging starts on the Rio Madeira and gold is discovered at Serra Pelada.

1980   The Indian organisation, the Uniao das Nacoes Indiginas, UNI, is founded.

1981   The World Bank lends nearly half a billion dollars for the Polonoroeste project.

1984   The BR364 road from Cuiaba to Porto Velho is paved.

1984   The Tucurui dam starts generating electricity.

1985   The Carajas railway starts exporting iron ore.

1985   The World Bank suspends payments under its Polonoroeste loan, then resumes them when the Uru Eu Wau Wau reserve is demarcated.

1985   The BR429 road goes through to the Guapore valley.

1985   The National Council of Seringueiros is founded.

1986   The Tropical Forest public campaign is launched and the Amazonian Alliance of the Peoples of the Forest is formed.

1986   Paving starts on the extension of the BR364 road from Porto Velho to Rio Branco.

1987   Barber Conable, the President of the World Bank, admits mistakes connected with the Polonoreste loan.

1988   The Balbina dam starts generating electricity near Manaus.

1988   The first pig iron factories are inaugurated along the Carajas railway.

1988   The first extractive reserve is announced at Sao Luis de Remanso.

1988   Chico Mendes is assassinated.

1989   The Samuel dam starts generating near Porto Velho.

1989   IBAMA attempts to control deforestation, by locating fires with photographs taken by the NOAA 11 satellite.

1989   The Uru Eu Wau Wau reserve is rescinded.

1990   The outgoing government of President Sarnay creates the one million hectare Chico Mendes reserve.

ACKNOWLEDGMENTS

One of the characteristics of a film is that the list of credits at its end often seems as long as the film itself. And the reason is that film-making is a communal process with different people providing specialised skills. Since this book has evolved out of a number of films, and as each was photographed and recorded by several cameramen and recordists, it has been too confusing to name them in the narrative. This is why the book is written by an 'I', though the whole process of documentary film making is a 'we', the director seeing events through the techniques of his team, and taking attitudes that have been moulded by discussion amongst a group that works and lives together.

The main exception in this book has been Vicente Rios because he carried on filming when I was editing in England, and so was often there when I was not. Across eleven years he was my companion through three-quarters of a million feet of film and a like number of bars and bottles of whisky. So were, at different times, Mario Arruda, Vanderlei de Castro, Rafael de Carvalho, Nelio Rios, Auro Luz, Albert Bailey, Godfrey Kirby, Chris Cox, Jimmy Dibling, Terry Twigg, Chris Christophe, Andrew Mason, Kees t'Hooft and Pasco Macfarlane – who died tragically about a year after filming the early part of the Uru Eu Wau Wau expedition. Throughout the decade, we were supported by our co-producers, the Catholic University of Goias which used our films in Brazil's increasingly intense debate over Amazonia. They projected them on television, in the Brazilian Congress and at literally thousands of conferences, seminars and meetings so that at least a small part of the growing change is attributable to them.

One of the secrets of film-making is never to inform your financiers – quite – how deep they're getting into it, and so the 'Decade' project started with a six month budget, though Central Independent Television's Charles Denton, Richard Creasey, Roger James and Andy Allen knew – from long experience – where they were being led. 'Never again will I get caught by a title with "decade" in it,' said Andy Allen. Yet he saw the decade out. As did Michael Kirk, Nelsa Gidney and David Fanning of our American co-producers, WGBH Boston. 'Couldn't you condense it into one programme?' they would sometimes enquire wistfully. In fact, we put out eight during the decade in the UK, and another five at the end.

In the case of the book, the manuscript would never have been finished if Valerie and Thomas Pakenham had not suggested how to restructure it. And it would never have been read if Deborah Bick had not won the last of many skirmishes with the computer. It would also not have gone to publication if Molly Friedrich and Deborah Waight had not found publishers when all other publishers said it was too late, and if Marian Wood and Myra Bennett had not then done the editing when everyone claimed that time was inadequate.

Finally, I would like to remember friends whose deaths are not mentioned in the narrative: Ze Bel, the leader of the Uru Eu Wau Wau expedition whose suicide was attributable, at least in part, to the hopeless task of protecting Indians against overwhelming odds; Baiano-Maia, the head of the Post of Comandante Ari who was shot in the back by a colonist; Ari dal Toe a pilot friend who crashed on a flight for us to Comandante Ari – which is named after him; and Fr Josimo who was working with us on a film, but was assassinated before we could take a single picture of him.

ADDRESSES *for* FURTHER INFORMATION *about the* PEOPLES *of the* FOREST

UNITED KINGDOM

Friends of the Earth, 26–28 Underwood St., London N1 7JQ
The Gaia Foundation, 18 Well Walk, London NW3
Survival International, 310 Edgeware Rd., London W2 1DY
World Wide Fund for Nature, Weyside Park, Catteshall Lane, Godalming,
  Surrey GU7 1XR

UNITED STATES OF AMERICA

The Environmental Defence Fund, 1616 P St., N.W., Washington,
  DC 20036
The National Wildlife Federation, 1400 16th St., N.W., Washington,
  DC 20036
The Rain Forest Action Network, 301 Broadway Suite A, San Francisco,
  CA 94133

BRAZIL

C.E.D.I., Av. Higienopolis 983, Sao Paulo, SP 01238

Conselho Nacional dos Seringueiros, Trav. Thaumaturgo Azevedo 51, Rio Branco. AC 69900

Instituto de Estudos Amazonicas, Rua Monte Castelo 380, Curitiba, PR 82500

U.N.I., Praca Dr Ennio Barbato S/N, Sao Paulo, SP 05517

ADDRESSES FOR CASSETTES OF 'THE DECADE OF DESTRUCTION' SERIES

United Kingdom

Central Independent Television Enterprises, Hesketh House, 43–45 Portman Square, London W1H 9FG

United States of America

Bullfrog Films, Oley, PA19547 Tel: 800-543-3764

Brazil

Verbo Filmes, Rua Verbo Divino 993, Chacara Santo Antonio, Santo Amaro Sao Paulo 04719

ABOUT THE AUTHOR

Born in Tongshan, China, in 1934 and educated at Cambridge, Adrian Cowell has been making prizewinning documentary films since his first trip into Amazonia in 1957. An author, environmental activist, and cofounder of the Television Trust for the Environment, he is known for his epic projects—his award-winning series *Opium* was filmed over an eight-year period (including nine months when he was trapped behind the lines in Burna)—and his total dedication. Working on *The Decade of Destruction* filming, he had the support of the Television Trust for the Environment and the Catholic University of Goias as well as of close friends like Chico Mendes, the outspoken leader of the rubber workers who was murdered during the course of the filming; Jose Lutzenberger, long a lonely voice in opposition inside Brazil to the destruction and now the new regime's designated protector of the region (as Secretary of the Environment); and a local film crew that proved itself to be as skilled and as dedicated as Adrian Cowell himself. Their efforts, combined with those of many others, have given hope that the next decade may be one of respect for the ecosystem that is the rain forest.